(Re)defining Success in Language Learning

Full details of all our publications can be found on http://www.multilingual-matters.com, or by writing to Multilingual Matters, St Nicholas House, 31-34 High Street, Bristol BS1 2AW, UK.

(Re)defining Success in Language Learning

Positioning, Participation and Young Emergent Bilinguals at School

Katie A. Bernstein

MULTILINGUAL MATTERS
Bristol • Blue Ridge Summit

DOI https://doi.org/10.21832/BERNST8991
Library of Congress Cataloging in Publication Data
A catalog record for this book is available from the Library of Congress.
Names: Bernstein, Katie A., 1983 – author.
Title: (Re)defining Success in Language Learning: Positioning,
   Participation and Young Emergent Bilinguals at School/Katie A.
   Bernstein.
Description: Bristol, UK; Blue Ridge Summit: Multilingual Matters, 2020.
   | Includes bibliographical references and index. | Summary: 'This book
   follows four emergent bilingual students in an English-medium
   pre-kindergarten in the US and examines how students' differing social
   positions in the classroom shaped their participation in interaction
   and, thus, their English language learning across a school year' –
   Provided by publisher.
Identifiers: LCCN 2020016665 (print) | LCCN 2020016666 (ebook) | ISBN
   9781788928984 (paperback) | ISBN 9781788928991 (hardback) | ISBN
   9781788929004 (pdf) | ISBN 9781788929011 (epub) | ISBN 9781788929028
   (kindle edition)
Subjects: LCSH: English language – Study and teaching (Preschool) – Foreign
   speakers. | Language arts (Preschool) – United States – Case studies. |
   Education, Bilingual – United States – Case studies.
Classification: LCC PE1128.A2 B47 2020 (print) | LCC PE1128.A2 (ebook) |
   DDC 372.65/21049 – dc23
LC record available at https://lccn.loc.gov/2020016665
LC ebook record available at https://lccn.loc.gov/2020016666

British Library Cataloguing in Publication Data
A catalogue entry for this book is available from the British Library.

ISBN-13: 978-1-78892-899-1 (hbk)
ISBN-13: 978-1-78892-898-4 (pbk)

Multilingual Matters
UK: St Nicholas House, 31-34 High Street, Bristol BS1 2AW, UK.
USA: NBN, Blue Ridge Summit, PA, USA.

Website: www.multilingual-matters.com
Twitter: Multi_Ling_Mat
Facebook: https://www.facebook.com/multilingualmatters
Blog: www.channelviewpublications.wordpress.com

Copyright © 2020 Katie A. Bernstein.

All rights reserved. No part of this work may be reproduced in any form or by any means without permission in writing from the publisher.

The policy of Multilingual Matters/Channel View Publications is to use papers that are natural, renewable and recyclable products, made from wood grown in sustainable forests. In the manufacturing process of our books, and to further support our policy, preference is given to printers that have FSC and PEFC Chain of Custody certification. The FSC and/or PEFC logos will appear on those books where full certification has been granted to the printer concerned.

Typeset by Riverside Publishing Solutions.

Contents

Figures, Tables and Images	ix
Acknowledgements	xi
Transcription Symbols	xiii
Introduction	1
Project Origins	2
Why Study Young Language Learners? Age and Second Language Learning	3
A More Complex Picture of Young Children Learning New Languages in School	4
Aims of the Book	6
Structure of the Book	7
1 Participation in Interaction and Language Learning: A Layered Approach	10
Introduction: Interaction in Language Learning	10
Participation in Interaction is Key to Language Learning	11
But Getting into Interactions Involves Power and Positioning	13
A Layered Approach to Examining Positioning, Participation and Learning	17
2 Language and Language Learning as Social Practice	20
What's in a Context?	20
Learning as Social Activity: A Sociocultural View of Language Acquisition	22
Language – and Human Activity – as Social Practice	23
Practice Theory Continued: Social Fields	27
Positioning in a Theory of Practice	28
Language in a Theory of Practice	29
Linguistic Practice is Social Action	29
Linguistic Practice as Translingual	32
Linguistic Practice as Embodied	35
Linguistic Practice as both Stable and Emergent	37

3 From Bhutan, Uzbekistan and Berkeley to River City:
  Arrival Stories   39
    Welcome to River City   39
    Refugee Resettlement: River City and Beyond   40
    Resettlement in River City   42
    Starting School   43
    The Teachers   44
    The Classroom   46
    The Children   47
    The Focal Students   48
    A Final Arrival Story: The Researcher   50
    Approach to the Project   51
    Ethical Research in Contexts like Classroom Three   54

4 Adults as Context-makers: Parents' and Teachers' Beliefs
  about Language   57
    Language Ideologies   57
    Language Ideologies and Language Policy   58
    Teachers and Parents as Policymakers   58
    Parents' Beliefs about Language: Additive Bilingualism
    and Biculturalism   60
    Ellen's Beliefs about Language: 'English Above All Else'   63
    Lucia's Beliefs about Language: 'You're in America;
    Speak English'   68
    Conclusion   73

5 The Social Field of Classroom Three: Policies and Practices   75
    The Social Field of Classroom Three   75
    Classroom Language Management and the Place of English
    in Learning   81
    Children as Socializers   83

6 Becoming Students, Becoming Speakers: Positioning
  in the Social Field of Classroom Three   86
    Kritika's Story   87
    Padma's Story   93
    Rashmi's Story   96
    Hande's Story   100

7 Who Learned What? Three Perspectives on Success in
  Language Learning   105
    Perspective 1: The Teachers   106
    Perspective 2: Language as Stable System (Use, Vocabulary
    and Syntax)   107

	Perspective 3: Language as Social Action (The Power To Be Heard and Listened To)	110
	Discussion: Speech Acts and Participant Frames	118
8	Beyond English: Multimodal, Multilingual Repertoires at Work	121
	The Linguistic and Social Field of Classroom Three: Conditions Right for Kritika's Repertoire	121
	Repertoires Beyond Words: Kritika as Semiotically Resourceful	123
	Affordances: Kritika's Repertoire and the Classroom Three Field of Practice	129
9	The Edge Has its Advantages: Participation and Learning on the Periphery	132
	Social Network Theory: The Affordances of Centrality and Peripherality	133
	What the Focal Students' Positions Afforded	135
10	Concluding Thoughts: Success Stories	141
	Participation in Language Learning: Quiet Learners and Productive Silence	141
	A Case for Submersion Education?	143
	Double Opportunity, Double Obligation: A Different Explanation – and a Better Question	144
	A Call for Layering – and Another Question	147
	Toward Aligning Linguistic and Social Aims	148
	Supporting Teachers, Preventing Harm	151
	Success in Language Learning	153
	Appendix 1: Details about Conflicts that Brought Classroom Three Families to the United States and their Experiences with Resettlement	155
	Becoming Refugees: What Happened in Bhutan	155
	Becoming Refugees: What Happened in Uzbekistan	158
	Appendix 2: Detailed Methodological Information	160
	Methods Details for Chapters 3 and 4	160
	Methods Details for Chapter 6	161
	Methods Details for Chapter 7	166
	References	169
	Index	183

Figures, Tables and Images

Figures

2.1	Bronfenbrenner's model	21
2.2	The construction of a rope	22
5.1	Classroom Three floorplan	76
6.1	Social network map – Kritika	92
6.2	Social network map – Padma	96
6.3	Social network map – Rashmi	100
6.4	Social network map – Hande	103
7.1	Graphical representation of students' speech act data from Table 7.6	114
A2.1	Building the social network map of the class	163
A2.2	Classroom Three social network map	165

Tables

3.1	Classroom Three at the beginning and end of the year	48
3.2	Shifts in class demographics for Classroom Three	48
4.1	Structural parallels between Ellen's descriptions of the children's language learning and her own	67
4.2	Parallels and differences in Ellen's and Lucia's family language narratives	72
5.1	Schedule according to clock time and classroom time for Classroom Three	77
6.1	Rashmi and Prakesh attempt to evict Hande from the sand table	89
7.1	Students' English use, vocabulary, and complexity in fall and spring	109
7.2	Kritika's request	111
7.3	Hande's request	112

7.4	Rashmi's request	112
7.5	Padma's request (three attempts)	112
7.6	Percentage of students' speech acts that were successful or not in each of the three elements	113
8.1	Kritika as authority figure and dispute settler	124
8.2	Kritika engages in conversational repair	128
9.1	Kritika is upset at being misunderstood	136
9.2	Hande in conversation with herself	138
A2.1	Students whose parents participated in an interview	161
A2.2	Matrix of students' responses to 'Show me who you like to play with'	164

Images

| Image 1 | Hande's close observation | 101 |
| Image 2 | Hande's carefully timed physical action | 101 |

Acknowledgements

It was a long road from Classroom Three to writing this book. There are many people (and one dog) to thank for helping me along the way.

Thank you, first and foremost, to the children, parents, and teachers in Classroom Three for letting me spend a year with you. It was without a doubt the most fun part of this project. I'm also very grateful to Claire Kramsch, Sarah Freedman and Bill Hanks for their help in designing this study and for our many conversations as I analyzed and wrote. Thank you, too, to The International Research Foundation for English Language Education (TIRF) for funding the project.

I'm appreciative of Sona Shilpakar and Olena Tumanova for interpreting during parent interviews, and of Sapana Sharma for transcribing and translating many hours of classroom video in Nepali ... and for again checking those transcriptions and translations five years later! Thanks also to Sue Jones (Laura's mom) for help with transcription of parent interviews, and to Ellie Bernstein (my mom) for all the copyediting – both of my dissertation and again of this book. Mom, you are a woman of many talents and much patience.

I'm also grateful to my colleagues, Matthew Prior, Cindi Sturtz-Sreetharan, and Brendan O'Connor, for their feedback on the book proposal, for moral support as I wrote, and for once saving me from being impaled by a flying umbrella (which would most definitely have kept me from finishing this book). Thanks are due as well to my excellent editor, Anna Roderick, who pushed me when I needed it and who also graciously absolved me of my sin of slow writing. Thank you, too, to the two anonymous reviewers who made this book much stronger.

Finally, thank you to my parents, Ellie and Robert Bernstein, and my favorite thinking/writing partner, Noah Katznelson, for helping me not give up on this process, even when it got very messy. And thanks most of all to my husband, David, for not giving up on me when *I* am very messy.

Oh yeah, and thanks to Fred the Dog, who supervised this whole process (mostly through his eyelids). Thanks for keeping me on task, Freddo.

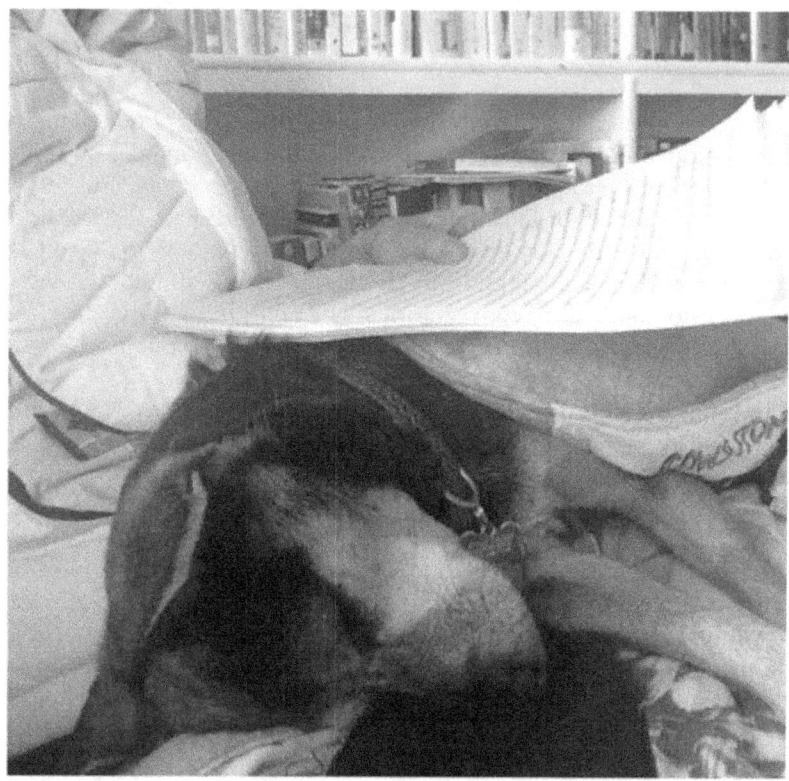

Fred the Dog, 1992–2020

Transcription Symbols

The following table gives a list of transcription symbols used in the text. All other punctuation marks (periods, commas, question marks, exclamation points) are used as in standard writing.

(.)	Brief pause
(1.0)	Pause of 1 second
(5.0)	Pause of 5 seconds
-	Speaker self-repairs or restarts (E.g 'I saw him- saw them driving.')
::::	Elongated sound in middle or end of word
=	Turns before and after are latched together (no pause between)
(*laughs*)	Nonverbal behavior
[the students]	Clarifications added by the researcher
I'm NOT going	Said more loudly than surrounding speech
<u>look</u> at me when I'm talking to you	Said with emphasis
saati	In a language other than English

Introduction

On a bright winter morning, in a former Rust Belt city that prides itself on the word 'former,' 4-year-old Padma[1] walks to school with her grandmother. Her grandmother wears traditional Nepali clothing over her snow boots, and Padma's breath forms a cloud as she talks excitedly in Nepali about the police officer and his helper dog that came to visit her class yesterday. Padma and her grandmother walk from their apartment complex to the school in an early morning parade of other parents and children, many of whom were in the same refugee camps before moving to the United States.

Padma is a student in Head Start, a program funded by the United States government that allows low-income students to go to preschool for free from age three to five, in order to help prepare them for kindergarten. The parents of Head Start students, whether newly arrived refugees or graduate students, all meet the income criterion for their children to attend the six-hour daily program, where students eat two meals, brush their teeth, nap, and learn the routines of school that are intended to help them enter kindergarten just as 'ready' as their higher income peers. Later, I will follow Padma into her classroom and introduce her teachers, parents and classmates, but Padma begins this book for another reason. The things that have brought Padma's family to the city mirror those that have put the 'former' in the city's Rust Belt status. Since the collapse of its steel industry, the city has slowly transformed into a center of both medicine and education, with hospital and university buildings filling the skyline in several city neighborhoods. Many international students have come to the city to earn degrees, to do research, or to train in the hospitals. These changes have also meant steady growth of lower wage jobs, such as hospital cleaning staff. And decades after heavy industry left and prices plummeted, it is still an affordable place to live.

This combination of jobs, affordability and infrastructure has also made River City a particularly good place for refugees to resettle. In fact, many refugee families who have been placed in other American cities have chosen to *re*-relocate to this one. Padma's family was one of these families. Having initially been resettled in a city in the western United States, they made their way to River City after hearing of jobs and a low cost of living, and they are now part of the largest Nepali Bhutanese community in the United States. While local media continue to describe the city as 20 years behind the rest of the country in terms of immigration, the population is changing. And whether their parents have come on student visas, as doctors, as refugees, or by any other path, many children in the city, like Padma, now come to their first year of school speaking languages other than English.

This book is about children learning English, along with everything else there is to learn, in preschool. Through an ethnographic study of Padma's classroom, I look to understand how emergent bilingual students[2] like Padma, who come to school speaking languages different from those of their teachers and schools, begin to make their way in the complex social worlds of their classrooms. I explore how students learn to simultaneously manage both language-learning *and* peer social worlds and ask how participation in each shapes the other.

Project Origins

This work began long before I met Padma – several years before Padma was born in fact – across the Atlantic ocean, in my first year of teaching. My first teaching job was in Belgium, as an assistant teacher at an international school. That year, my 20 three- and four-year-old students spoke 14 different languages between them. Watching them learn English raised many questions for me about social interaction and language learning in young children.

One event in particular shaped my eventual path to writing this book. On a November day, during snack time, one of the very posh British students in the class, Charlotte, called to her friend at the other end of the table: 'Please pass the biscuits!' An Italian student, Sofia, who was learning English, observed the success of this request and mimicked Charlotte's intonation and accent: 'Please pass the biscuits!' Charlotte's face grew dark as she whirled around and growled at Sofia: 'STOP COPYING ME!' Yet, not five minutes earlier, I had seen a Dutch student, Sanne, who was also learning English, do the same thing – parrot Charlotte's request for apples – to which Charlotte responded: 'Aww, good job, Sanne!' Putting a hand on Sanne's shoulder, Charlotte turned to another British student, beaming proudly: 'Did you hear Sanne say "apples"?'

I went home from teaching that day with the two exchanges playing in my mind. I worried about what each interaction meant for Sanne and Sofia socially and emotionally, but I also thought about their English learning. I wondered: If Sanne is encouraged to use English, but Sofia is told to 'Stop copying me,' what does that mean for their opportunities for learning? And if those patterns of interaction somehow repeat across a whole school year, could that mean that Sanne would learn a lot of English and Sofia just a little?

At the time, I was not sure how to find out and, like so many ideas I had that year, that one was lost in the myriad immediate worries of a first-year teacher. Yet, when I moved back to the United States and continued teaching preschool, I saw similar versions of the interactions between Charlotte, Sanne and Sofia play out again and again among other students, and I remembered my question. Four years after the interaction at the snack table, I applied to graduate school in the hope of gaining the tools I needed to find out. And four years after that, armed with quite a bit of theory, some methods, a video camera and a field notebook, I found myself in Padma's classroom in River City. This book is therefore about Padma and her classmates, but it is also about Charlotte, Sofia, Sanne, and the many children I taught and learned from in between.

Why Study Young Language Learners? Age and Second Language Learning

Conventional wisdom might say, however, that studying second language learning in young learners is less interesting or less useful than studying older learners. 'Children are like sponges' is a common refrain from parents and teachers, reflecting the belief that young children are naturally facile language learners. This idea is supported anecdotally, by adults who describe language learning woes in foreign language classes or who move abroad and struggle while marveling at how easily their children adapt. The idea is also pervasive in materials for teachers, as well as in policy initiatives, like the European Union's focus on early language learning. And at conferences like TESOL (Teachers of English to Speakers of Other Languages) and AAAL (American Association of Applied Linguistics), and in journals like *TESOL Quarterly* and *Applied Linguistics*, the under-representation of studies with young language learners suggests that those who study language teaching and learning may still see young students' second language (L2) acquisition as more natural and less problematic than learning by older children and adults.

The notion that 'younger is better' has roots in first language acquisition research, in the Critical Period Hypothesis [CPH] (Scovel, 2000). The CPH proposes that there is a window of time in childhood inside which first language learning can take place, and outside of which, it becomes very difficult, if not impossible, to acquire language. The CPH originated in accounts of children who, for reasons of abuse or isolation, passed into adolescence without learning to speak, and were never able to fully learn, a language (e.g. Curtiss, 1977). The CPH was later extended into second language research. Yet, some scholars, like Bialystok and Hakuta (1999) argue that this is a case of mistaking correlation for causation: Do younger learners have better eventual outcomes? Perhaps. Does this mean that age *causes* better outcomes?

Not necessarily. In fact, many scholars have found that being younger and being older are both better for some aspects of language learning (Krashen *et al.*, 1979). For instance, while older learners can draw on their first language to make faster gains, young children show advantages in perceiving and producing the sounds of a new language (Ellis, 2008). Other researchers have demonstrated how age simply serves as a proxy for other social, educational and environmental factors: for instance, young children have less language to learn before they catch up to peers, and interlocutors might have more generous and less judgmental expectations than they do for adults (Marinova-Todd *et al.*, 2000). Mounting evidence points to the improbability that age-related, neurological constraints predetermine the success of younger learners over older ones (Singleton & Ryan, 2004). And, importantly, by taking age as the criterion for comparison in the first place, studies of age-related factors in language acquisition obscure important differences in how young children learn new languages.

A More Complex Picture of Young Children Learning New Languages in School

Research with young L2 learners has shown that there can indeed be significant differences in the paths young children take to learning a second language. Wong Fillmore (1976, 1979), for instance, examined the interactions of five Spanish speakers who had recently arrived in the United States and who had just begun kindergarten, first or second grade. She found that the students varied widely in the kinds of cognitive and social strategies that they used for handling English interactions. Some students joined interactions and pretended they understood, using context to help them guess meaning. Others used key words and phrases in a 'fake it til you make it' approach. Still others jumped in with what little English they had, worrying less about getting it right than just communicating and then relying on friends for help. Wong Fillmore observed that these strategies, combined with students' personal characteristics, resulted in drastically different progress in the students' English over a year, so much so that one student, Nora, made more progress in the first three months of school than others made at all.

Wong Fillmore concluded that Nora's success stemmed from her identification with, and desire to be like, the English speakers in the class as well as her willingness to try new words and to speak even when she knew it would not be perfect. Wong Fillmore (1991a) later presented a model describing all of these 'ingredients' for second language learning: learners who want to learn, speakers to provide input, and social settings that allow enough interaction between the two. Wong Fillmore emphasized, however, that these ingredients can combine in many ways and that there is not one kind of ideal learner or situation for learning. Instead, individual traits, like sociability or communicative need, can combine with factors in the classroom environment, like activity structures, to produce different outcomes for students in the same classroom. A student who prefers to listen rather than jump into interactions may thrive in a highly structured classroom with lots of teacher talk, while a student who initiates and engages in peer interaction may do better in less structured spaces like playgrounds or play-based classrooms.

These ideas are clear in Genishi's ethnographic work (Genishi & Dyson, 2009), which set out to describe the paths six preK and kindergarten students took to learning English in school. Genishi illustrated that some students, like Tommy, a Cantonese speaker, immediately put to use any English words they learned, jumping into play and giving answers before they could even string together multi-word phrases. She contrasted this with accounts of students like Miguel and Luisa, Mixteco speakers who spent a lot of time watching on the sidelines (Luisa) or participating with actions (Miguel), before gradually becoming speakers in the classroom. Genishi found that language learning depended primarily upon students' desire to communicate and their recognition that they needed to use the new language to do so. Yet, their learning also depended on context, since need and desire to communicate shifted with activities and settings, and learning contexts supported students in different ways. Genishi attributed all of the students' eventual success to teachers' and peers' recognition of students' 'inner clocks' – whether to begin speaking in English right away or to wait and listen – and their accommodation of these different ways of participating. Similarly, Clarke (1999) followed four Vietnamese-speaking preschoolers and also found that students took different amounts of time to begin speaking English. She showed how the social dynamics of the classroom readily supported the interactional preferences and forays into English of some of the students, while, for others, the teacher had to experiment with ways to adapt to their preferences, allowing them to stay silent longer. For all the students, Clarke found quality interaction to be the key element in students' eventual English growth. She concluded, therefore, that having teachers who were responsive to the interactional needs of the students was crucial.

From a developmental perspective, Tabors and Snow (1994) outlined a sequence of L2 learning in young children: from a silent period to telegraphic speech to productive language use (a sequence that aligns with those found in other recent studies, e.g. Blum-Kulka & Gorbatt, 2014). They found that moving through this sequence depended at least in part on opportunities for peer interaction that provided comprehensible English input. They described an intervention in one preschool classroom where English-speaking peers were taught how to initiate interactions, speak slowly, provide recasts, repeat themselves, and to ask for clarification with emergent bilingual peers. They found that interactions between trained students and emergent bilingual students increased markedly and that emergent bilinguals' turns in these interactions also increased. They illustrated that social context is not fixed but can be changed with adult help. In later work (2003), Tabors and Snow added motivation, exposure and personality as additional factors found to cause variability in how quickly young children move through the L2 developmental sequence.

Together, these studies point to (some of the) differences in young children's L2 learning paths and processes, making clear that L2 learning is not uniform for young children. They show how an understanding of young children's paths to learning requires looking beyond young learners themselves to their classroom context, with its routines and patterns for interaction, and the way that young learners interact with peers and teachers in that classroom. Yet, these studies also point to the potential for children to have vastly different phenomenological experiences as language learners in school. In addition to obscuring inter-age group differences, another risk of seeing all children as sponges is that it can lead to the erroneous conclusion that being submersed in English at a young age – being asked to 'sink or swim' – is somehow easy or painless. When I ask my multilingual undergraduate students, all now competent speakers and writers of English on their way to becoming teachers, to tell about their experiences learning English in school, few recall their early English learning as painless. Many recount stories of frustration, of embarrassment, of not knowing what was happening or how to ask for help. And although they were in kindergarten or first grade when they began learning English, these memories remain vivid. Valdés (1999) describes her first day of school in the United States, in which she did not know how to ask where the bathroom was and ran from the room moments too late, with her classmates laughing. Valdés, now a professor with an endowed chair at Stanford, is, like my students, objectively a very successful language learner. Yet, focusing only on her ultimate success belies the struggle of those initial months of English learning.

Aims of the Book

Valdés's story, the stories of my college students, the stories of my preschool students and the findings of the studies above, highlight the importance of examining not just children's language learning outcomes but also their processes: both their paths to learning and their experiences along those paths. Additionally, these stories and studies point to the importance of looking at both experiences *and* outcomes to build an understanding of how the former shapes the latter.

In this book, I follow four prekindergarten students – Padma, Hande, Rashmi and Kritika – across their first year of school as they learn English as a new language. I aim to understand: (1) their experiences as language learners in a classroom for the first time, navigating language learning, academic expectations and social relationships, and (2) how those experiences shape language learning across the school year.

Padma, Hande, Rashmi and Kritika are a useful group of students to help answer these questions, because they began school under an objectively similar set of circumstances: All were four-years-old, all were from families that had come to the United States as refugees, all were born in the United States, all had a strong, immersive foundation in their families' languages – Nepali for Padma, Rashmi and Kritika; Turkish for Hande – all were new to school and all came to school knowing just a few words in English. Yet, this book will illustrate that as they became students in the same classroom, their classroom identities and their ways of participating diverged widely, resulting in very different kinds of language growth. Their stories will help to raise critical questions, not just about how we understand the processes of young children's language learning, but how we understand their outcomes and decide what counts as success.

Structure of the Book

Chapter 1 introduces research on the importance of interaction in second language learning, and, in particular, the importance of peer play interactions in young children's second language learning. It also introduces, however, research that shows that negotiating one's way into peer interactions is not always simple. I present this study's layered approach to bringing these two lines of work together.

Chapter 2 lays out some of the theoretical perspectives that frame this work: practice theory and the habitus (Bourdieu, 1977, 1990, 1991), positioning theory (Davies & Harré, 1990), speech acts (Austin, 1975), linguistic repertoires (Rymes, 2014) and translanguaging (García & Li Wei, 2014).

Chapter 3 introduces the four focal students – Kritika, Padma, Rashmi and Hande – and describes how they came to be together in a Head Start classroom in a suburb of River City. This chapter addresses the changing city context and refugee resettlement, as well as introduces the classroom context and the teachers. It answers the question of how two teachers, neither of whom had ever worked with multilingual students before, also found themselves in a class with one Turkish and 11 Nepali speakers. Finally, in this chapter, I tell the story of my arrival to the classroom and lay out my approach to the study.

Chapter 4 looks at teachers and parents as context-makers and shapers of students' experiences. This chapter connects the parents' and teachers' past experiences with language learning to their current views on the children's language learning, and explains how these views inform the adults' hopes and aspirations for the children.

Chapter 5 illustrates how the teachers' beliefs about language became language policy, shaping the practices of Classroom Three. It provides a detailed account of classroom practices, linguistic and otherwise, that are key to understanding the children's situated interactions outlined in subsequent chapters.

Chapter 6 turns to the classroom social lives of Padma, Hande, Rashmi and Kritika. Within the multiple, nested layers of context described in the prior chapters, I trace the social trajectory of the four girls across the year, describing how they were positioned in classroom peer interactions and by the teachers. I support this analysis with teacher interview data and social network data from student interviews.

In Chapter 7, I turn to the question of how the four students' different social positions and ways of participating shaped their language outcomes. I explore this question from three theoretical perspectives: through the on-the-ground theory-building of the teachers, through the perspective of language as a stable system of vocabulary and syntax, and through the lens of language as social action. A very different picture of success emerges from each perspective.

Chapters 8 and 9 offer detailed discussions of these various versions of success. In Chapter 8, I examine Kritika's success story, showing how her translingual repertoire and deft use of her multilingual and multimodal communicative resources allowed her to be positioned as a successful learner. In Chapter 9, I return to the ideas of social network analysis to examine Hande's success story. I suggest that a position on the periphery of the class, rather than constraining Hande's learning, might have afforded Hande her own version of success, by allowing peripheral, but linguistically productive, ways of participating. Her story raises questions about what counts – and what should count – as 'participation' in language learning.

Chapter 10, the conclusion, provides a brief summary of the book's main findings and explores possible explanations for why Kritika and Hande might have had such opposite versions of success in social positioning and language learning. It explores how the practices and policies of Classroom Three may have put linguistic and social aims 'at cross purposes' for the students and suggests what teachers and schools might do to support an alignment between those aims. I also return to the third and fourth focal students, Padma and Rashmi, suggesting the need for different definitions and methods in order to understand their successes.

Notes

(1) The names of all parents, children, and teachers are pseudonyms.
(2) In this book, I mainly refer to students learning a new language in school as 'emergent bilinguals,' highlighting my hope that their English learning will be additive, that they will maintain their home languages, and that they will continue to develop as bilingual speakers, rather than English speakers at the expense of Nepali and Turkish. While the term 'English learner' or 'English language learner' might technically be just as accurate, it shifts the focus to English, rather than all the students' languages.

1 Participation in Interaction and Language Learning: A Layered Approach

Introduction: Interaction in Language Learning

In the last chapter, I recounted the brief story of Sanne and Sofia, two preschool children who received very different kinds of reactions to their attempts to emulate a peer's English use. I described how, as their teacher, I wondered whether, over time, these differences in their participation might impact the two students' language learning. In this chapter, I present an overview of two complementary lines of research: one that helps to explain why different kinds of participation might lead to different kinds of learning and a second that shows how two students might end up participating in different ways to begin with.

While it seems like common sense that interacting with others in a new language is key to language learning, this was not always conventional wisdom. Prior to the 1970s, common methods of teaching language included asking students to translate written passages (the 'grammar-translation' method) or having students repeat correct utterances in the target languages (the 'audiolingual' method). These approaches viewed interaction as a *result* of learning – an outcome that could occur only after learning had taken place – rather than a part of learning itself. In 1978, however, a book edited by Evelyn Hatch, *Second Language Acquisition: A Book of Readings,* presented data showing young children acquiring a second language *through* interaction. Hatch found that, across a range of contexts and languages, interaction was not simply a place for children to display already-acquired language knowledge, but that, instead, interaction was itself the locus of learning. Hatch wrote: 'One learns how to do conversation, one learns how to interact verbally, and out of the interaction syntactic structures develop' (Hatch, 1978: 404). Around the same time, Stephen Krashen (1977) proposed the idea that comprehensible input – or language just beyond a speaker's competence level – was key to language learning, and that this input was best obtained through interaction. And just a few years later, Michael Long (1981) presented the first elements of his Interaction Hypothesis, which proposed that participation in interactions with native speakers supported language learning in multiple ways, including through the modified input that those speakers provide. In the intervening decades, research on interaction and language learning has proliferated. The next sections present research on interaction and language learning, particularly in young children, that helped to frame this study.

Participation in Interaction is Key to Language Learning

The first line of research that frames this work focuses on the importance of interaction as a mechanism for language learning. Quantitative research in this area, drawing primarily from cognitively-oriented research paradigms, has sought to understand in what ways and to what extent learners' participation in interaction is associated with language learning outcomes. In adults, evidence for the unique contribution of interaction to language learning continues to build (Ellis *et al.*, 1994; Nassaji, 2016; Russell & Spada, 2006; Storch, 2002; Swain & Lapkin, 2001). In a meta-analysis of more than 125 quantitative studies on interaction and language learning, Mackey and Goo (2007) found that, in the 28 studies that met their conditions of randomly assigned participant conditions and examination of specific language learning features, all 28 studies showed strong effects of interaction on language learning (mean effect sizes of Cohen's $d = 0.75$ for immediate effects and $d = 1.02$ for delayed effects). These effects held up for all contexts and all language features, as well as for both short-term and long-term outcomes.

With young second language learners, interaction is equally important. And while interactions with adults provide young learners with valuable interactional feedback (Mackey & Oliver, 2002; Mackey & Silver, 2005), for children learning a new language in school, peer interaction is particularly important (Genesee, 1994; Palermo *et al.*, 2014; Palermo & Mikulski, 2014; Pinter, 2007). For instance, Palermo and Mikulski (2014) and Palermo *et al.* (2014) examined the contributions of English exposure at home and at school, both from teachers and peers, to the English vocabulary development of 107 Spanish-speaking preschoolers across a school year. Controlling for children's age, gender, family income, and general cognitive abilities, they found that while the level of English that children were exposed to from teachers had no relationship to children's vocabulary outcomes, the quantity of peer-to-peer English they were exposed to in the fall was uniquely and positively associated with children's English expressive vocabulary in spring. (Exposure at home also made a unique and positive contribution to vocabulary growth.) Similarly, Rydland *et al.*'s (2014) mixed methods work in Norway examined the impact of peer talk during preschool playtime on vocabulary acquisition. Quantitatively, across 26 children, they found that playing with peers who use a rich vocabulary correlated with stronger L2 vocabulary knowledge at the end of preschool. Importantly, they found that these effects endured for the following five years, through age 10. In a different preschool context in Norway, Grøver Aukrust (2004) found a positive association between complex explanatory sequences by peers during play and Turkish speakers' Norwegian receptive vocabulary outcomes. Finally, examining effects of interaction on syntactic development, Chesterfield et al. (1982) observed the interactions and English production of six Spanish-speaking children in a bilingual classroom across a school year. Using a rank-order approach, they showed that the children who interacted most with English-speaking peers were also the children to show the strongest growth in the mean length of utterances in English. They did not find a consistent relationship between classroom interaction with teachers and English growth. Together, these quantitative findings provide compelling evidence that interaction, particularly peer interaction, supports children's L2 learning.

Qualitative work, drawing on conversation analytic traditions, provides insight into *how* those peer interactions support learning. In early work, Peck (1980) showed that peer language play provides an affectively-positive learning context, as well as draws learners' attention to form and phonology. Ervin-Tripp (1981, 1986, 1991) found that of many kinds of peer play, games in particular supported language learning, both through repetition and by having words that are often accompanied by a related action, making it easy to infer their referents. She showed how games allowed children to navigate successful entry by drawing on prior knowledge of game and play routines, even before they could speak the new language, and that even when games resulted in dispute, they provided a joint activity and a motivation for children to come to a mutual understanding. These findings are echoed by S. Long (1997), whose work illustrated how common play routines allowed interaction between three seven-year-olds in Iceland – two native Icelandic speakers and one novice – and allowed the Icelandic learner to have entry points into the language. In a later study, of Mexican-American students learning English in the United States, S. Long (2004) showed how, in play, young children in kindergarten acted intentionally as one another's language teachers, supporting emerging English through play interactions like collaborative peer reading, clarifying and translating for one another, modeling behavior, and 'playing school' together (taking turns pretending to be teachers and students). Piker (2013), too, showed that, for four Spanish-speaking children in a bilingual Head Start classroom, play served the dual function of providing the motivation for English use as well as input for building students' linguistic repertoires. And in the qualitative component of their mixed-methods study, introduced above, Rydland *et al.* (2014)

showed that peer imaginative play provides a unique context for word learning in two ways: first, by allowing the use of words that extend beyond the immediate context (like 'jellyfish') and second, by providing opportunities for words to be picked up and recycled by different players across an extended interaction. These findings are echoed by Bernstein (2016b), who showed how collaborative writing between preschoolers during play interactions could serve as a context for emergent bilinguals' English word learning – especially of words that would otherwise have no concrete classroom referent, like 'dragon' or 'ladder' – through repeated use by peer interlocutors.

Both quantitative and qualitative work on interaction and language learning, therefore, point to the importance of children's participation in interaction – particularly in peer play interaction – as a critical component of language learning. For young emergent bilinguals, these peer interactions serve as what Blum-Kulka *et al.* (2004) and later Cekaite (2017) called a 'double opportunity space.' That is, play functions 'both as a locus for the construction of children's social worlds and social relations and as an arena for the development of language skills' (Cekaite, 2017: 2), serving both social and linguistic aims.

But Getting into Interactions Involves Power and Positioning

Yet, as important as participation in peer interaction is for gaining language experience, getting into interactions is not always easy. A second line of research that informs this study focuses on the complexities of learners entering and navigating interactions. This qualitative and discourse analytic research draws on sociolinguistic and anthropological approaches to examine how power and positioning shape who gets to participate in interactions and in what ways. This line of work emerged in the 1990s, with Bonny Norton's proposal that social identity might be the missing factor in second language acquisition studies, mediating between individual variables (like motivation, aptitude, learner strategies) and social ones (like participation in interactions). She thought that social identity might explain why a highly motivated learner might still be denied access to an interaction, or why a learner might seem to be a competent speaker in one interaction but not another. Norton (Norton Peirce, 1995) showed, for instance, how Eva, an adult immigrant from Poland, was positioned as a foreigner by her coworkers at a fast food restaurant, who then used this positioning to justify Eva's exclusion from interactions, thereby depriving her of opportunities for language learning. Yet, when Eva was able to re-position herself as a multicultural European, she was accorded greater respect and greater access to language-providing conversations.

Preschoolers must also navigate and negotiate social positioning, and this positioning also shapes their participation. Piker's (2013) study, introduced above, illustrated the importance of play interactions for language learning. However, Piker provided the caveat that not all students in the study were sought out, or permitted into, interactions with English speakers and that this influenced how much students participated in English. She described how Carmen, a Spanish speaker and a popular, outgoing student and creative playmate, was able to sustain her presence in play with English-speakers in ways that supported her own English use. Meanwhile, David, a less popular student was allowed only to play quietly on the sidelines and his contributions were ignored. In addition, then, to highlighting the importance of play interactions to English acquisition, Piker's study also illuminates the way that students are afforded differential access to these interactions based on their classroom social status.

Similarly, while Rydland *et al*.'s (2014) work (discussed above) found both qualitative and quantitative evidence for the importance of peer play in language learning, the authors also found that peer-driven conversations are not always accommodating or inclusive. As they put it: 'becoming a ratified participant and gaining self-confidence as an L2 speaker in vocabulary-rich peer conversations in preschool may not be an easy task' (Rydland *et al.*, 2014: 233). Cekaite and Evaldsson (2017) found the same in their research in a Swedish preschool. They showed how Felis, a 3½-year-old Somali speaker, regularly tried, and was rejected from, entering her Swedish-speaking peers' interactions. The authors illustrate how Felis's lack of Swedish was a barrier to entry and that her non-verbal or pretend-Swedish bids for entry were ignored, mocked or outright rejected. Yet, when the teachers intervened with language help, it only further served to marginalize Felis within the class, 'positioning her as a "non-competent language user"' (Cekaite & Evaldsson, 2017: 465) and cementing her exclusion from peer play. The authors point out that while peer interaction during free play can be beneficial for young emergent bi/multilinguals, it can also act as a gatekeeper, excluding new learners from accessing the very input they need to grow linguistically.

Beyond the binary of participating or not, students' social positioning can also allow access to different *kinds* of participation. Toohey (2000, 2018) illustrated this in her multi-year study of six emergent bilingual students beginning elementary school in Canada. One student, Amy, a petite girl who had gone through kindergarten in Hong Kong, came to school speaking no English but had a tidy appearance and an array of school skills, like sitting still, using scissors and raising her hand. She quickly earned the identity of being academically competent ('for such a little girl'), and other students saw her as pleasant and quiet and welcomed her into play. Yet, her size and quietness also led other students to make her play 'baby' or 'pet' in games and to treat her as such. Meanwhile, another student,

Harvey, who came from a Chinese family, was constantly disheveled with a runny nose and unclear speech, and was often excluded from play entirely. Yet, he discovered that by taking on a peripheral 'helper' role, he was allowed to join. Given that participating in different kinds of conversations meant practicing very different kinds of English, Toohey wondered (as I wondered about Sanne and Sofia) about the long-term learning effects of always being made to be the baby or the helper.

Hawkins (2005) also explored differing participation, through the cases of two kindergartners, Anton from Peru and William from China. Anton arrived at school with many academic skills from his older sister and came to be seen as a valuable work partner, though not a preferred playmate. William, who was skilled socially, was likely to be chosen by peers as a fun playmate but not a good schoolwork collaborator. Hawkins showed how these different positions led William and Anton to diverge in the kinds of language they were exposed to over the year. These cases – Hawkins' Anton and William, Toohey's Amy and Harvey and Piker's example of David's play on the sidelines of interaction – show that participation in interaction is not an all-or-nothing achievement. Speakers' social positions might allow their participation in some types of interactions and not others, or might allow them to participate in certain ways and not in others.

Importantly, students' classroom positioning *itself* is not all or nothing. Day (2002) illustrated how positioning and participation can shift, not just across the school year but across various classroom activities. In her study of Hari, a Punjabi-speaking kindergartner learning English in a Canadian kindergarten, she found that Hari appeared differently competent across the day and that he was positioned as most competent in activities in which he had an ally. During whole-class activities, the teacher often took on this role, asking Hari if he wanted to say anything and recasting and expanding upon his speech, thus positioning him as a ratified speaker with valuable contributions to make. Midway through the year, a new student, Casey, joined the class and Hari took him under his wing. Casey, an English speaker, positioned Hari as an expert on classroom matters as well as a desirable playmate and interlocutor, thereby elevating Hari's status in the classroom. Additionally, when Hari's comments to peers were ignored or not heard, Casey repeated them, and in this way functioned as an amplifier for Hari's voice. Hari's case illustrates how, beyond what students themselves know or can do, activities and interlocutors combine in different ways to shift students' access to participation and ways of interacting, as well as to make students seem more or less linguistically competent.

Willett (1995) provides another clear example of how emergent bilinguals' positioning and participation can depend on the whole ecology of the classroom – activity structures, materials, teacher policies and teacher perceptions – and beyond. In the first-grade classroom in the United States that Willett studied, the teacher normally alternated 'boy-girl-boy-girl' student seating in the classroom to prevent socializing during desk work, but she allowed three female emergent bilingual students to sit together in order to facilitate Willett's research. This meant that the three female emergent bilingual students were able to work together extensively and undetected, while the fourth student, Xavier – the only male emergent bilingual student – worked alone like everyone else. The girls were thus able to take turns asking for help and then sharing answers, so none of them looked like she needed too much assistance, while Xavier was left to ask all his questions himself. This arrangement, which allowed the three female students to pool resources and appear competent, left Xavier looking needy and incompetent by comparison. The teacher was also unconvinced that Xavier's father, a stable hand in the university stables, could help him at home, and she decided to have Xavier do special pull-out English as a Second Language (ESL) sessions. But when Xavier came back to class he was often lost and would become frustrated to the point of tears. The teacher also replaced his phonics workbook – a high status item in the class – with an ESL workbook, further cementing his position as incompetent. Over the year, these identities had profound effects on the four students' learning opportunities, as well as eventually on the teacher's placement decisions for students. At the end of the year, while all four students scored within the same range on an English placement test, Xavier's negative identity led the teacher to recommend that only he remain in ESL for second grade.

Willett's study highlights the importance of examining students' negotiation of social positions and participation within the larger sociocultural context. It also makes the point that institutional perceptions of what counts as successful learning for young children may have little to do with language learning itself and a lot to do with students' performance of doing school. In Toohey's (2000) study, the same was true: being identified as competent was tied up with physical appearance and skill, academic ability, and social and behavioral competence. As in Willett's work, the teacher's decision of who to keep in ESL (Harvey) and who to mainstream (Amy) was less about the two students' current linguistic competence and more about who was seen as having the social skills to become more competent without help.

Together, the studies in this section illustrate the complexity of negotiating a classroom social position that permits 'enough access to experienced members of the community of practice and to their mediating means to be able to appropriate those means' (Toohey, 2000: 71). Entry into interaction with peers is not a given: some students may be excluded, relegated to peripheral roles, or allowed into certain interactions, but not others. And while navigating entry and sustaining participation require deft negotiation on the part of any student, emergent bilingual students face an additional challenge of doing so in a new language. Tabors (2008) referred to this situation – needing language to make friends and participate in interactions, but needing friends and interactions to learn English – as the 'double bind' of any child starting school in a new language. This double bind has been noted by many: Rydland *et al.* point out that 'less proficient L2 learners may have problems becoming ratified participants' in interactions that would facilitate language learning (Rydland *et al.*, 2014: 215). Tabors and Snow's (1994) intervention, described in the Introduction, came out of the observation that preschool students who were learning English went largely ignored until they could produce some English. Blum-Kulka and Gorbatt (2014), in their study of 32 children from immigrant backgrounds starting preschool or kindergarten in Israel, emphasize 'the crucial role of peer interaction in language socialization,' but point out that learners 'need to have at least rudimentary communicative skills' in their L2 to gain entry to, and benefit from, those interactions (Blum-Kulka & Gorbatt, 2014: 170-171, italics in original). As Kanno put it:

> For language minority students, acquiring the L2 is a key to increased participation although it is by no means the sufficient condition. However, learners are often blocked from the very resource that is vital to their acquisition of the L2: opportunities to interact with native speakers. (Kanno, 1999: 129)

Peer interaction is a crucial context for learning a new language, yet it takes both social and linguistic skill to enter, sustain and maintain a desirable position with those very interactions.

A Layered Approach to Examining Positioning, Participation and Learning

Taken together, the two lines of work presented in this chapter make clear that: (1) Interactions are important. Participating in interactions, particularly peer interactions, provides a critical context for young children's language learning. (2) Interactions are complex. Getting into interactions is tied up with power and positioning, which are partially, but not fully, in a learner's control, and are shaped by interlocutors, context and history. Additionally, not all interactions and ways of participating are equal. Different ways of participating can lead to different opportunities for learning.

Bringing these ideas together leads to the logical assumption that, over time, those different opportunities will lead to different learning. This assumption has been important in justifying and making sense of research into positioning and differential participation in interaction. One example of this sense-making comes from Zappa-Hollman and Duff (2015). In their study of how students' social networks shape their learning, they review another a study, by Dewey *et al.*, writing:

> Although no conclusions can be drawn in [Dewey *et al.*'s] study regarding the impact of the social network membership on the students' linguistic development *(which is assumed to be beneficial based on other research)*, one of the findings suggests that 'the quality of the linguistic interaction that a learner obtains in apparently similar social networks can be rather uneven. Some friends and contacts help to provide a much richer learning environment than others.' (Dewey *et al.*, 2013: 279, italics mine)

The italicized portion of the text conveys that while Dewey and colleagues themselves only examined differential participation, it was safe to assume, based on other research, that that participation in interaction would produce beneficial effects (see italics). Zappa-Hollman and Duff thus make explicit what is often implicit in studies of how students get into and participate in interactions: that while those studies show empirically how positioning shapes participation and how participation matters for students' learning *opportunities,* they then assume that students' participation will also matter for language *outcomes,* because other studies have shown how interaction shapes learning. I point this out not to critique this assumption: on the contrary, not only is this type of cross-study extrapolation important for drawing conclusions about phenomena within a field, it allows researchers to limit the scope of their work to manageable aims and approaches. At the same time, with few studies bringing these two lines of inquiry together within the same study, the assumption that 'different participation means different opportunities for learning, which mean different learning' remains an assumption, if a well-justified one.

This study brings both these lines of research together in what King and Mackey called 'layering.' They wrote: 'A layering approach goes beyond integration of techniques, but rather, demands the explicit consideration of research problems from a range of distinct epistemological perspectives' (King & Mackey, 2016: 210). I draw, therefore, on the logic and methods of both lines of interaction research introduced in this chapter – on the importance of interaction for language outcomes and on the complexity of interaction as a process – to examine positioning, participation and language learning for the four students in this study. In doing so, I take what the Douglas Fir Group (2016) called a problem-oriented approach (rather than a discipline- or perspective-oriented approach), bringing multiple methodological and epistemological orientations to bear on understanding one phenomenon. In this study, I use the approaches of both lines of research that inform this work, to examine how students negotiate positions and participation within the complex classroom learning context AND how their English grows across the year. In doing so, I hope to illuminate whether and how, for these four children, different participation affords different opportunities for learning, which means different learning.

2 Language and Language Learning as Social Practice

Chapter 1 provided an overview of what makes young children's language learning in school so complex: it is bound up with becoming a student and a classmate; it depends on interactions with teachers and peers, which are not always simple to navigate; it involves using existing semiotic resources in strategic ways, and it means simultaneously working to become more competent and working to be seen as more competent in a new language. This chapter introduces some of the theoretical and methodological tools that I use in this study to make sense of that complexity, beginning with how I understand context.

What's in a Context?

The studies in Chapter 1 illustrated the importance of understanding children's language learning, as well as their negotiation of positions and participation, in context. Yet, what exactly *is* their context? To be sure, it is their classroom, but to think on a smaller scale, each interaction in which they participate is its own context. And to think on a larger scale, their classroom was shaped by the history of preschools as particular kinds of institutions, but was unique in that it formed in response to the large number of new residents to the area, due to refugee resettlement. This attention to multiple facets of students' context is evident in Uri Bronfenbrenner's famous Ecological Systems Theory of Development (Bronfenbrenner, 1979). See Figure 2.1. In this model, Bronfenbrenner situated the child – the star of the developmental show – at the center, immediately surrounded by the microsystems in which she participates: home, school, playground, place of worship, grandmother's house, etc. The next ring shows the mesosystems, or how all of the child's microsystems interconnect. For example, her mother might take her from their home to the playground for a playdate with her friend from school and, when they get in a fight, her friend might remind her of the sharing rules from their classroom. The exosystem represents contexts in which the child is not a participant, but which can effect changes in the systems in which she does participate. For instance, when her mother's boss is cranky and her mother has to stay late at work, she may be less patient when she gets home. The macrosystem consists of less concrete contexts,

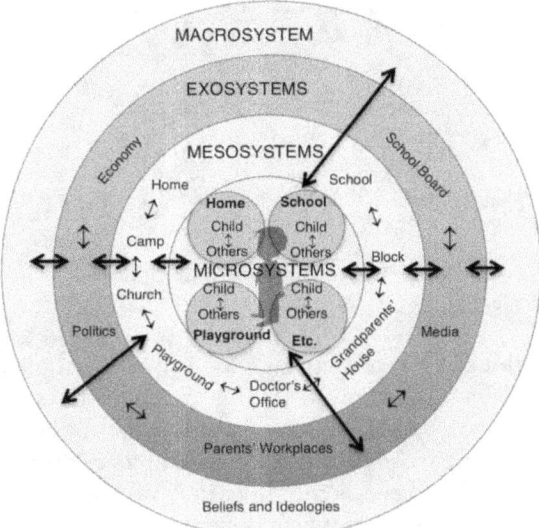

Figure 2.1 Bronfenbrenner's model

like beliefs and ideologies, which pervade all of the other systems. For example, perhaps the child's mother lives in the United States and feels guilty for not spending more time with her daughter, but only has two weeks of paid vacation time, and, even though she co-slept with her daughter as a baby so that she would be securely attached, this was also stressful because they live on Long Island, not in Berkeley, so she was the only one in her mothers' group that did it, and she felt judged. In Bronfenbrenner's model, each system interacts with the others that are both 'inside' and 'outside' of it.

While Bronfenbrenner's model was revolutionary in developmental science, and continues to be influential, it also lends itself to the temptation of unwrapping, that is, removing ring after ring 'of context' to reach the true object of study: the kid in the middle. Leo van Lier, an educational linguist who was instrumental in developing an ecological theory of language learning, also used a concentric circles model to discuss context, yet he cautioned:

> An ecological theory holds that if you take away the context, there's no language left to be studied. It's like an onion. You can't peel away the layers and hope to get at the real onion underneath; it's layers all the way down. (Van Lier, 2004: 20)

Michael Cole, a cultural psychologist, also cautioned about the allure of 'peeling away.' Cole (1998) wrote that the concentric circles model presents a view of context as 'that which surrounds' and prompts one

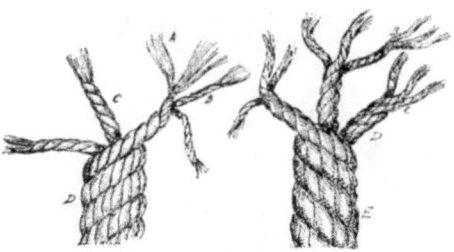

Figure 2.2 The construction of a rope

to see an individual or a certain task as 'in the middle.' Cole used the example of language to show why this makes little sense: phonemes only exist as part of words, but words only exist by being made up of phonemes. Similarly, words only have meaning in discourse, but they make up discourse. There is no linearity, no causality; 'that which surrounds' is not prior to that which it surrounds. Cole proposed instead that we take the *Oxford English Dictionary*'s definition of context, 'the connected whole that gives coherence to its parts,' which comes closer to the etymology of 'context', the Latin *contexere*, meaning 'to weave together.' This definition evokes a rope, in which small fibers combine to make small strands, which are then combined into larger and larger strands, and then into a rope (see Figure 2.2). The rope's strands are given meaning by their place in the rope, at the same time that the rope only exists if these strands are in place. In this sense, to think of a class of children, the class is both composed of students and at the same time, being in the class *makes* them students. In this view of context, what holds the threads together? Cole suggests both activity theory, which draws on the work of Lev Vygotsky, and practice theory, originating in the work of Pierre Bourdieu, as approaches to studying human interaction that are compatible with this view of context. Both help to frame this project.

Learning as Social Activity: A Sociocultural View of Language Acquisition

While interaction plays a role in nearly all theories of second language acquisition, the view that interaction is both a place for language learning as well as for the construction of social relationships and structures is a broadly sociocultural one. Vygotskian sociocultural theory, which was brought to the field of Second Language Acquisition through the work of Rick Donato, Jim Lantolf, Merrill Swain and Steve Thorne, among others, theorizes that learning is a process of internalization and appropriation. Any new skill appears first on the social plane, through participation in interaction with others, and then, later, on the individual plane (Vygotsky, 1978). Through interaction, children learn to use artifacts, or cultural tools – more concrete ones, like spoons or markers, to more abstract ones, such as language and gesture – to mediate their goal-driven activity. For second language researchers who draw on Vygotskian sociocultural theory, interaction is at the core of language learning, which takes place through participation in 'cultural, linguistic, and historically formed settings such as family life and peer group interaction' (Lantolf & Thorne, 2007: 197). Far from simply providing input, interaction is the location of learning itself.

Specifically, Lantolf (2000, 2013; Lantolf & Thorne, 2006, 2007) described interaction as mediating L2 learning in two important ways. First, it provides opportunities to understand and appropriate others' intentional ways of using language to participate in activity. Second, it enables learners to use language in ways that are just beyond their individual capabilities, in their zones of proximal development, or the range of activities that a person cannot yet complete independently, but can in cooperation with another person. Donato (1994, 2000) and Swain (1997; Swain et al., 2002) described similar learning processes, which they called 'collective scaffolding' and 'collaborative dialogue,' respectively. Through these interactions with others, learners appropriate language that they can then rehearse in private speech or use productively in other interactions. Importantly, from a sociocultural perspective, development and learning are not individual processes. Instead, they involve appropriation and internalization of intro-individual social activity. Sociocultural theory thus dispenses with the dichotomy between the individual and the social, as well as between the cognitive and the cultural. All development, and the learning that precedes it, is both social and cultural. There is no 'that which surrounds.' This is also true in the second theoretical perspective Cole mentioned: practice theory.

Language – and Human Activity – as Social Practice

Practice theory was developed by sociologist Pierre Bourdieu (1977, 1990), as a way to overcome what he saw as three related and false dichotomies in sociological and anthropological research: objectivity and subjectivity, positivism and phenomenology, and structure and agency. The first in each set come together in the researcher striving to view human activity as an outsider, looking down from above in order to create a stable account of patterns and routines, by, for example, mapping the daily schedule in a prekindergarten classroom. The latter in each pair convene in attempts to understand the 'native perspective,' or personal experience of, say, being the new kid in school or the parent of a child with a disability. For Bourdieu, the former approach reduces human activity to acting out predetermined roles on stage or to executing prewritten plans, while the latter ignores everything outside individual experience, including the conditions, such as relations of power, that made that experience possible. With practice theory, Bourdieu sought to bridge the two and to understand how structure sets the conditions for human activity without determining it and how activity (re)produces those structures. He accomplished this through the notions of habitus and field.

Habitus

A person's habitus is the embodied accumulation of her past experiences, which gives her an unconscious sense of how to interpret the present and how to *act* in it. It is both a product of the social structures in which a person has participated, as well as a producer of present (and future) participation and structure. To give an example, imagine a high school classroom on the first day of school. The students know (perhaps without being able to articulate it) how to enter the room, sit in their chairs, raise their hands, speak and not speak. Their new teacher might give class rules but no one has to explain to the students which way to face their chairs, when to talk, or how to ask questions. These 'rules' have long ago been internalized and are now part of the students' habitus. Now, imagine a preschool classroom. Students are told to 'sit criss-cross applesauce, snowball hands in your lap,' to 'keep your hands to yourself,' and to 'raise a quiet hand and wait to be called on *before* you talk.' Throughout the day, they are reminded that, 'we walk in school, not run,' 'we wait our turn,' and 'we tell a teacher when we have to go to the bathroom.' This is because when children start preschool, they have not yet incorporated (literally in the sense of *corpus*, body) these schooled ways of moving, speaking and being. Yet, by the time they get to high school, these bodily practices will be so ingrained in students that students will not think about how to sit or how to volunteer answers, because they will see those as simply the natural things to do. And if they become preschool teachers one day, they too will participate in reproducing those ways of being in their students, likely without ever wondering how they know that raising a hand is the 'correct' way to ask a question. To give a more detailed definition, habitus (the same word in singular and plural) are:

> systems of durable, transposable dispositions, structured structures predisposed to function as structuring structures, that is, as principles which generate and organize practices and representations that can be objectively adapted to their outcomes without presupposing a conscious aiming at ends or an express mastery of the operations necessary to obtain them. Objectively regulated and regular without being in any way the product of obedience to rules, they can be collectively orchestrated without being the product of the organizing action of the conductor. (Bourdieu, 1990: 53)

Teasing apart this quotation is to tease apart Bourdieu's theory of the habitus:

Systems... Habitus are 'systems' in that they are not singular like a habit (generating one kind of behavior) but are constellations of possibilities for action. While a student's habitus makes it probable that she will sit a certain way, other elements like her clothing or the teacher's gaze, may incline her to draw on another way of sitting (e.g. slouching, turning around to talk to a classmate). Yet, there are certainly ways of sitting (squatting, kneeling on her seat) that her habitus makes her unable to think of as even possible.

...of durable... Habitus are neither temporary nor quickly shed and rebuilt, but are formed over years of social experience. They give disproportionate weight to early experiences, so that later experiences, rather than serving to revise or recalibrate the habitus, are instead understood *through* the habitus. In this manner, later experiences cannot but help to reinforce the habitus, as it is impossible to step outside one's habitus and experience things in another way.

...transposable... Habitus endure across space and time, even in contexts other than those in which they were formed. Thus, not only do American high school students raise their hands in class, American adults raise their hands in work meetings, in restaurants ('Who had the fish?'), and at the doctor's office ('Who's Katherine Bernstein?'). While Europeans raise a finger or a pen, Americans raise hands. And, that Europeans and Americans think to raise anything, shows that the American and European social fields of school are more similar than different.

...dispositions... Habitus are tendencies to think or act in certain ways. Note that being disposed to do something does not mean determined or destined. Despite my inclination, I may intentionally *not* raise my hand in a meeting when I am the youngest person in the room for the associations of student-ness that come with hand-raising.

...structured structures... Habitus have been shaped though past experiences, both implicit experiences, such as watching adults in social encounters, and explicit ones, like being told not to run in school.

...predisposed to function as structuring structures... Once formed, habitus in turn frame how we understand and act throughout our lives. Through these actions, we then help to recreate the social contexts, or as Bourdieu called them, *fields*, that formed us and that will form the habitus of our children. In other words, these structures are *'principles which generate and organize practices and representations.'*

...objectively adapted to their outcomes without presupposing a conscious aiming at ends or an express mastery of the operations necessary to obtain them. When the conditions, or field, in which a person finds herself closely

resemble the field in which her habitus was formed, she is at ease. It might look to an observer as if her ability to maneuver successfully or her social graces are the result of explicit strategizing or gaming the system on her part, but, for Bourdieu, this 'feel for the game' is instead a result of a match between habitus and social context, or in other words, of 'having dispositions compatible with the conditions and in a sense pre-adapted to their demands' (Bourdieu, 1990: 54).

> ...*Objectively regulated and regular without being in any way the product of obedience to rules...* A person's habitus predisposes certain actions while making others less likely and others still unthinkable. Thus while an 'objective observer' might conclude that a person is carefully following particular social rules, the habitus produces practices that are patterned but not conscious, like water running down a groove worn in rock.

> ...*they can be collectively orchestrated without being the product of the organizing action of the conductor.* Habitus is both an individual and collective concept (Bourdieu wrote often about 'class habitus'), so the idea of habitus matching field applies to groups of people as well. When several people's habitus were formed in similar conditions, it might appear that they are coordinating their behavior or following the same rules, but it is simply that they have been set on a path which disposes them to act in similar ways when facing similar contexts. Bourdieu borrowed Liebniz's analogy of two watches that are perfectly in sync, not through mutual influence or outside correction but that were crafted with 'such art and precision that one can be assured of their subsequent agreement' (Bourdieu, 1990: 59).

Thus, when a person's current social conditions closely resemble those under which her habitus was formed, her resulting practices are perfectly adapted, a priori, to those conditions:

> Native membership in a field implies a feel for the game in the sense of a capacity for practical anticipation of the 'upcoming' future contained in the present, everything that takes place in it seems *sensible*: full of sense and objectively directed in a judicious direction. (Bourdieu, 1990: 66)

In a theory of practice, therefore, beliefs are not simple cognitive phenomena or mental states, but a part of the body. Beliefs – our 'practical sense' for what is right, just, beautiful – are built into bodies through social participation, 'instilled by the childhood learning that treats the body as a living memory pad ... and as a repository for the most precious values' (Bourdieu, 1990: 68). These beliefs are just as much part of the body and the habitus as ways of talking and sitting. They are what give practices their sense and make them seem *common sense*. It is through this 'misrecognition' – the taking of what is socially learned and historically situated, and thus arbitrary, to be sensible and *natural* – that practices as mundane as hand-raising or as significant as class divisions come to be seen as self-evident. In this self-evident-ness, the social order is reproduced (Bourdieu, 1977).

Practice theory, then, like sociocultural theory, dispenses with the divide between the social and the individual, by incorporating the social *into* the individual, through the habitus. Although practice theory and sociocultural theory originated in different academic fields (and at different times and places) and focus on different phenomena, or perhaps different aspects of the same phenomena, they both serve as useful frameworks for viewing human activity as not just situated *within* a social and cultural context but as always already social and cultural, even when carried out by one person alone. In my work within both theoretical paradigms, as well as related paradigms such as cultural-historical activity theory (Cole, 1998; Engeström, 1991), communities of practice and situated learning (Lave & Wenger, 1991), cultural worlds (Holland *et al.*, 2001), cultural theories of human development (Rogoff, 2003), I have found no contradictions between these theories, only that they are useful for explaining different things. When focusing on interaction as a locus for language learning, for instance, sociocultural perspectives hold explanatory power; when focusing on interaction as a locus for using language to exclude or dominate, practice theory may be more useful. It is fair, then, to call this study sociocultural, as well as a study of practice.

Practice Theory Continued: Social Fields

One additional way in which practice theory provides an escape from the view of context as concentric circles is through the idea of *field*. Hanks (2006) explained that Bourdieu's notion of field differs from other definitions of context in several important ways. First, a field's scope is not tied to a single location and its organization is non-radial (not concentric circles surrounding a person or utterance). Thus a field's boundaries are not spatial ones but, instead, are marked by social cut-offs and credentials. For example, the field of Head Start has multiple centers spread across the United States and has boundaries marked by regulations, income caps and age requirements. Similarly, a family might be spread across the world with clusters in various locations, but membership remains clearly marked by blood relations and marriage, and boundaries are reinforced through traditions, inside knowledge, jokes and turns of phrase. Importantly, fields are spaces in which discourses and values circulate, endowing particular individuals with capital and power on the basis of their practices, since the same practice can be valued in one field and not another. For instance, a four-year-old who reminds her parents of the rules and tells her siblings what to do at home may be quickly put in her place, but at school she might be viewed as an obedient student and helper. Yet other practices, like following directions, might be valued in both places. Bourdieu sometimes called fields 'markets' to emphasize how a trait or action could bring 'profit' in certain fields, particularly through scarcity. For instance, at the start of the school year, when only one emergent bilingual student in Classroom Three, Dinesh, spoke some English, he secured a profit from it in the form of special tasks from teachers and friendships with English speakers. As the year went on and other students began to speak English, his profits diminished and he had to work harder for the positive attention of teachers and peers.

Positioning in a Theory of Practice

A final characteristic of fields is that the roles or positions available within a field outlast any individual that temporarily occupies them. In a classroom, the positions of 'teacher' and 'student' remain stable year after year, despite being filled by different people. Yet, these positions are not freely available to all and are enforced through degrees, titles, abilities (like literacy) and age: Students can vie for positions as *kinds* of students, but they cannot be teacher. Importantly, the positions available in classrooms are not limited to generic 'teacher' and 'student': there are good students, jokers, slow learners, squirmers, talkers, quiet kids and mean kids. While these students may not all exist in a particular classroom, they are all recognizable kinds of students within the field of schools.

In this project, I examine how students position themselves and are positioned by others as a certain, recognizable kind of people. This perspective moves away from an understanding of identity either as solely situated in a person's view of him or herself or as a stable constellation of individual characteristics (like race, gender, age, class). Instead, it is a shared social achievement, negotiated, and perhaps battled over, through language and interaction. Davies and Harré describe this process:

> An individual emerges through the processes of social interaction, not as a relatively fixed end product, but as one who is constituted and reconstituted through the various discursive practices in which they participate. Accordingly, who one *is* is always an open question with a shifting answer depending upon the positions made available within one's own and others' discursive practices and within those practices, the stories through which we make sense of our own and others' lives. (Davies & Harré, 1990: 46)

From this perspective, the ways in which students are positioned depend not only on their own intentions and desires but on which discursive positions are made available by others and by the larger context. Importantly, while positioning happens in moment-to-moment interactions, these fragmentary positions can, over time and repetition, become more stable identities. This process has been described through the metaphors of 'sedimentation' (Holland & Lave, 2001; Kramsch, 2012), 'lamination' (Leander, 2002) and 'thickening' (Wortham, 2006).

Language in a Theory of Practice

A final way in which practice theory informs this project is in understanding what language *is*. In a theory of human activity as practice, ways of speaking are just as much a part of the habitus as ways of walking or believing. A person's primary linguistic habitus develops through participation in the field of the family and continues to form through participation in other fields, such as school. Just as a match between habitus and social field produces practices perfectly adapted to that field, a match between linguistic habitus and social field produces language practices to the same effect, giving speakers a feeling of ease and fluency. This phenomenon was shown in the work of Shirley Brice Heath (1983) and Sarah Michaels (1981), who contrasted the easy experiences of White middle-class children starting school, having language that 'matched' that of the classroom, with the confusing and frustrating experience of starting school as a Black working-class student, whose language practices were mismatched with what Bourdieu called the 'legitimate language' of the market. According to Bourdieu, when a speaker finds herself with language unsuited for the market, she must either exert immense effort to either control her language or simply be silenced, like some of the Black children that Michaels (1981) studied.

Viewing language as social practice has three implications in this project:

(1) Because linguistic practice emerges as an interaction between habitus and field, a given utterance might work perfectly well to accomplish a social action for one person in one context, but it might be ignored in a different context, or even in the same context but in the mouth of another speaker.
(2) Because practice emerges as an interaction between habitus and field, people with a multilingual habitus interacting in a multilingual field will produce multilingual practices.
(3) Because the habitus is embodied, so too are a person's practices, including language practices.

I address each in turn.

Linguistic Practice is Social Action

In a theory of practice, 'the all-purpose word of the dictionary, a product of the neutralization of the practical relations within which it functions, has no social existence' (Bourdieu, 1991: 34). Speakers and listeners bring with them the whole social structure in which they participate, so that while anyone can technically say anything – a student can command his teacher to sit down, a teacher can say, 'We only speak English here!' – whether those words are obeyed or laughed at or even heard is another question. Thus, in this work, I am interested in both what students learn of the stable, codified system of English, as well as what they can do with it, in real time.

In order to study language as social practice, that is, to understand what Kritika, Padma, Rashmi and Hande learned to *do* with English, I draw on the notion of *speech acts*. In his 1975 book, *How to Do Things With Words*, philosopher of language, John Austin, proposed that utterances like, 'I pronounce you man and wife' or 'I apologize,' create change in the world, rather than simply conveying information about it. Austin called these utterances performatives, because they perform an action. He wrote that each performative could, for the purposes of analysis, be broken into three parts. First, the performative's *locutionary form*[1] consists of the words themselves (for example, a preschool student pronounces the words, 'More milk'). Second, the performative's *illocutionary force* is what is being carried out *in* saying the words (i.e. the student is making a request). Finally, the performative's *perlocutionary effect* is the result, or what happens *by* saying the words (perhaps that the teacher brings milk to the student). Austin argued that performative utterances, such as commands, pronouncements, requests or promises, cannot be true or false but are, instead, *felicitous* (they work) or *infelicitous* (they fail). He outlined several conditions for the felicity of a performative: Most importantly, a procedure has to exist (e.g. marriage; sentencing) and it has to been done with the right words ('I do,' 'I find you guilty'). Additionally, it has to be said completely (not just 'I'), said in the right circumstances (at an altar perhaps or in a courtroom), by and to the right persons (an officiant and two unmarried adults; a judge and a defendant), and with the right intentions (no fingers crossed behind the back). While Austin's theory of language as social action therefore accounts for some aspects of social context (e.g. the right people, the right place) in the success or failure of a performative, it focuses primarily on the power of particular linguistic construction to effect change in the world.

Bourdieu (1991) argued that Austin's theory falls short of accounting for the power of institutions in shaping the success of performatives. He pointed out that Austin's work fell into the trap of misrecognition: Austin placed the power of performatives in the words themselves, when really, argued Bourdieu, the force behind a great many performatives comes from the social position of a speaker. The speaker's social position is what gives her the institutional backing, as well as the access to the legitimate language of the institution, needed to execute a performative. While the locutionary form of a performative might be perfectly correct, therein conveying an appropriate illocutionary force, social (institutional) conditions may mean that it has no effect. As Bourdieu put it: 'Only a hopeless soldier (or a "pure" linguist) could imagine that it was possible to give his captain an order' (Bourdieu, 1991: 75). Thus, in the 'milk' example from above, Bourdieu might say that 'More milk!' in and of itself has no greater or lesser potential to bring the teacher with milk than, 'Could I have some more milk, please?' The effect comes from who says it, in what context and to whom: "More milk!" might be met with a reprimand as rude coming from an older English speaker, or met with praise coming from an emergent very young bilingual student.

Yet, rather than invalidating Austin's work, Bourdieu's critique brings Austin's work into the realm of social practice. In this project, Austin's three-part notion of speech acts provides a useful heuristic for breaking down students' talk in order to analyze not only whether students could produce grammatical utterances, but also whether they could produce utterances that were listened to and obeyed. Separating students' speech into locutionary form, illocutionary force, and perlocutionary effect allows the teasing apart of each student's capacity for correctness, her ability to convey intent, and her success at achieving the desired effects. This teasing apart permits the measurement of each student's relative success in accomplishing social action through language. As Bourdieu pointed out, it is perfectly possible to have correct form and force, but to have no effect; and as I will show in Chapter 7, it is also possible to have the desired effect without correct form.

Participation frameworks

Importantly, speech acts occur within speech events. In any speech event, individuals are not only positioned as kinds of people but also as kinds of participants. In many theories of communication, these participants are a dyad: one speaker and one hearer. Yet, this does not often reflect the complex organization of face-to-face communication, particularly in multi-party interactions. Recognizing this, Goffman (1981) deconstructed these roles. Rather than just 'hearers,' he proposed to distinguish between the official audience (addressee(s), unaddressed intended hearers, intended hearers who are not listening, etc.) and unofficial hearers (such as overhearers, eavesdroppers, bystanders). He also dissected the role of speaker, arguing that speakers can say things they do not mean, give speeches they did not write, or argue for positions they do not really support. He proposed to distinguish between these production formats by dividing the speaker into: animator (the mouthpiece), author (the creator of the words being spoken), and principal (the person whose interests are at stake in the words being spoken). All three can be found in one person (as when a preschool student declares, 'I don't like carrots'), or different people (as when she scolds a classmate: 'We share with our friends,' citing the classroom rule written by the teacher). These ways of being speaker and hearer are participant statuses that, when configured in various ways, form different participation frameworks.

Goodwin and Goodwin (C. Goodwin, 1981, 2000, 2006; Goodwin & Goodwin, 2005) argued that speakers and hearers collaboratively engage in creating and sustaining these participation frameworks and in actively negotiating and managing participant roles through gaze, body language and gesture. The Goodwins pointed out, for instance, that a speaker will typically cease to speak if no one is looking at her. She will also restart her speech, often with a recast (rephrasing), once a listener's status is reinstated by returning their gaze to the speaker. The Goodwins also illustrated that within an interaction, more than one person can inhabit a role, and that one person can inhabit more than one role. For instance, C. Goodwin (2004) showed that a man who had severe aphasia after a stroke could successfully participate in interactions by distributing the role of speaker over multiple people and turns, through gesturing or pointing toward a place or object, having another speaker make a guess as to the detail he wanted to contribute, and then confirming with one of his three words (*yes*, *no*, and *and*) whether that was the comment he intended. This type of research shifts the focus from typologies of *kinds* of speakers and hearers toward an understanding of the social practice of collaboratively constituting speech events. It views participation frameworks as actively constructed through participants' demonstrating to one another their understanding of what each other is doing and the events they are engaged in together. Through both vocal and nonvocal actions, participants *create* the social field: 'a multi-party, interactively-sustained, embodied field within which utterances are collaboratively shaped as meaningful, locally relevant action' (C. Goodwin, 2006: 45).

Within a theory of language as social practice, then, I understand participant frameworks as particular versions of social practice ('what we are doing here now') and speech acts as kinds of action taken within a particular participation framework. In order for a particular speech act to 'work,' participants in the interaction must more or less agree on what sort of framework they are participating in. For instance, the speech act 'expressing an opinion' might be felicitous if a student and teacher both believe they are participating in a class discussion, but if the teacher instead sees the current participation framework as one of lecturer+listener, the opinion may instead be seen as a disruption. Thus, the same sequence of words might convey a very different force and have very different effects as part of a different participation framework.

Linguistic Practice as Translingual

In addition to viewing language as social action, a second implication of seeing language as social practice is that because practice emerges as an interaction between habitus and field, people with a multilingual habitus interacting in a multilingual field will produce multilingual practices. While this might seem obvious, it has often been ignored in research and bears restating: People with a multilingual habitus interacting in a multilingual field produce multilingual practices. Members of a multilingual community of practice may use their languages in certain ways for certain activities, or use one language or another at particular times. (See decades of research on code-switching, for instance Gal, 1979; Hill & Hill, 1986.) Yet, the language *practices* in such a space cannot easily be divided into 'English practices' or 'Spanish practices' or 'Nepali practices.' This was clear even in early work on code-switching, for instance when Hill and Hill (1986) showed speakers of Nahuatl and Spanish using Nahuatl words imposed onto Spanish grammatical structures.

This idea – that a speaker's language practices are not made up of English practices and Nepali practices, or Spanish practices and Nahuatl practices, but are always inherently multilingual, even when interacting with speakers of just one of their languages – is captured in the notion of translanguaging (García & Li Wei, 2014). Translanguaging was a term originally coined in Welsh by Cen Williams to describe an approach to bilingual language teaching that utilizes both languages within a single lesson, allowing students to receive input in one language, say, through reading, and produce work in the other language, like through writing. The term, eventually translated to English by Baker (2001), has come to be used to describe the way that multilingual speakers operate in the world. Rather than viewing bilingual people as two monolinguals put together, who might switch one language 'off' and the other 'on' as needed, a translanguaging perspective views bilingual speakers as having one linguistic system, encompassing all their languages, upon which they draw to accomplish various cognitive and social tasks (García, 2009; García & Li Wei, 2014). Otheguy (2016) explains the difference between translanguaging and code-switching as a difference in perspective: While code-switching is how an outsider, taking the dominant societal view of languages as discrete systems, sees a multilingual person's practices, translanguaging is how an insider sees her own multilingual practices. The translanguaging perspective has been fruitful in three ways: (1) as a theory, to understand multilingual speakers through a multilingual lens; (2) as a pedagogy, to transform monolingual classrooms – and dual language classrooms that practice language separation – into more flexibly multilingual spaces; and (3) as a political stance, used to advocate for a view of multilingualism as natural and to push against hegemonic practices and ideologies, including monolingual assessments and policies.

While much work with a translanguaging lens has taken place with older speakers, the translanguaging perspective has also been helpful in understanding bilingual early childhood speakers. For instance, researchers have shown that by preschool, many multilingual speakers easily wield their repertoires, using translanguaging to mediate understanding, co-construct meaning, and to share knowledge (García et al., 2011; Portolés & Martí, 2017). Children also demonstrate adept recognition and critical consideration of peers' preferences and proficiencies, and they deploy their languages as strategic social tools, to convey social solidarity with peers, to include, as well as to exclude (García et al., 2011; Sanders-Smith & Dávila, 2019). Additionally, children's translanguaging happens whether it is sanctioned by the teachers or not (García et al., 2011). In classes that practice strict language separation, translanguaging is often part of what Larson and Gatto (2004, after Goffman, 1961) called the *underlife* of the classroom – practices taking place under the institutional and pedagogical radar. Yet, teachers' participation in translingual practice has the power to create a disruptive underlife: Through strategies such as language brokering, recasting, translation, revoicing, code-switching and parallel monolingual language production, with teachers conversing or reading by each using one language, teachers can transform what counts as acceptable language use (Gort & Pontier, 2013). Axelrod (2017) showed that when teachers support hybrid language practices, preK children engage in expansive, playful language exploration. And encouraging translingual practices both supports metalinguistic knowledge as well as children's development of multilingual identities (García-Mateus & Palmer, 2017; Kirsch, 2017; Sanders-Smith & Dávila, 2019; Sayer, 2011; Velasco & Fialais, 2018). Indeed, teacher support matters for children's translingual skill. Axelrod and Cole (2018) studied students' language use in a K-5 before-school bilingual writing program in the United States that aimed to support students' Spanish. They found that while students across ages naturally worked translingually, and that they used knowledge from one to support the other, their metalinguistic knowledge and translingual writing skills increased with age and, importantly, with support from the facilitators. In Sanders-Smith and Dávila's (2019) work at a trilingual preK in Hong Kong, they noted that Cantonese and English, each supported by a specific teacher, were used frequently and fluidly by students, but without a teacher to explicitly support Mandarin, it was rarely used.

Across this work, researchers emphasize that even very young multilingual children are capable of attending to and analyzing phonological, semantic and orthographic dimensions of languages, *and* of using those dimensions as resources to accomplish social aims in sophisticated ways. Yet, most work on translanguaging in early childhood has been undertaken in places that are explicitly multilingual, whether they separated languages or not. As this study will show, translanguaging and the translingual underlife of Classroom Three were alive and well. And although I set out to understand the English learning of the students in this study, Kritika's story in particular will show that examining English learning in separation from the other elements of children's repertoires only tells part of the story.

Linguistic Practice as Embodied

A third and final implication of viewing language as practice is that because the habitus is embodied, so too are a person's practices, including language practices. To study language as a stand-alone verbal phenomenon is to ignore that 'language is a body technique' (Bourdieu, 1991: 86) and that gesturing, laughing, sitting and moving all co-contribute to creating meaning. One notion that aligns well with both language-as-social action and translanguaging, and which captures *both* the multilingual and the multimodal nature of linguistic practice, is the notion of 'repertoire.'

In the 1950s and 1960s, John Gumperz observed the way that multilingual speakers in marketplaces in India seemed to pay little attention to which named language they were using, instead moving fluidly between the several languages they shared, in order to negotiate, buy and sell (Gumperz, 1958, 1964). Gumperz (1965) later wrote that, for communities, distinguishing between language X and language Y is not nearly as relevant as making best use of their shared *communicative repertoire* to accomplish social action. Later, in a separate project in the UK, Gumperz (1979; see also Twitchin with Gumperz, 1996/1979) used close analysis of interactions to illuminate a phenomenon that he called cross-talk: when two people from different cultural backgrounds, such as from India and the UK, might speak the same language but misread and misunderstand each other nonetheless. Gumperz showed that elements like intonation, word choice, body position, and volume all provide cues to a listener that she and a speaker are indeed participating in the same activity and that they are reading the interaction in the same way. He illustrated how the smallest deviations in these cues from what a hearer expects can lead the hearer to doubt everything about the interaction and to come away with a feeling of dislike and distrust for the speaker. In one famous example, Gumperz was brought in to help the managers at Heathrow Airport in London understand why the British airport employees did not like the newly hired Indian workers in the cafeteria. After observing and recording, Gumperz realized that when British cafeteria workers offered each item, they pronounced the word with a rising intonation – 'Gravy?' – indicating a question, like 'Would you like gravy?' The Indian workers, however, used a downward or flat tone to offer each item – 'Gravy' – which diners heard as, 'Here, it's gravy. Take it or leave it,' leading them to perceive the server as not very hospitable, or even rude. Gumperz (1982, 1992) later called these small, frequently-under-the-level-of-consciousness indicators of 'what we are doing here' *contextualization cues*, or cues that help to both indicate and create the context of an interaction. When interlocutors share contextualization cues, an interaction goes smoothly; when they do not, they can leave feeling dissatisfied, yet without knowing exactly what went wrong.

Betsy Rymes (2014), looking back over Gumperz's work, argued that as important as Gumperz's ideas of repertoires and contextualization cues were separately, together they might provide a different kind of analytical power. By folding contextualization cues into communicative repertoires, she proposed an understanding of repertoires as built from both linguistic and non-linguistic features. In other words, within a speech community, speakers acquire not only a shared repertoire of phonology, vocabulary and syntax needed to accomplish social action, but they also learn an accompanying repertoire of intonations, rhythms, gestures, body positions and ways of using eye gaze. Rymes defined repertoires as 'the collection of ways individuals use language and other means of communication (gestures, dress, posture, accessories) to function effectively in the multiple communities in which they participate' (Rymes, 2010: 528). In this definition, Rymes makes two moves that distinguish her approach from Gumperz's. First, as discussed above, rather than focusing just on language, she included in repertoires all the elements that Gumperz saw as 'cues' – intonation, timing, interactional scripts – as well as other elements like dress or accent that also cue listeners as to what a speaker is up to. Second, rather than focusing on the communicative repertoires of communities, she focused on repertoires that individuals develop through participation *in* communities. These two moves enabled her to shift from examining repertoire use within a single community (such as the speakers in the Indian marketplace) or examining cross-cultural communication between two communities (such as the British and South Asian airport workers), and instead to study how individuals use their repertoires to interact across a range of diverse contexts and to find common ground with many different people. In other words, Rymes focused on how speakers come to choose not only the right languages but also the right intonation *and* body position *and* tempo to cue their interlocutor as to what they are doing here and now.

For Rymes, then, repertoires are products of participation in communities: in other words, social practices. But because individuals rarely participate in just one community, they acquire multiple ways of speaking, moving, interacting, dressing and eating that reflect their multiple kinds of participation. In a sense, Rymes wrote, 'an individual's repertoire can be seen as something like an accumulation of archeological layers' (Rymes, 2014: 10). The challenge for speakers, then, is to know which of these layers or elements to use when, where, and with whom to find common ground. Rymes, drawing on Erickson and Schultz (1982), called this achievement of common ground *comembership*. Many people who leave home for another part of the country or world, recount coming back and having their accent return. Others tell embarrassing stories of unconsciously taking on a speaker's accent. Just as our habitus produce practices that are strategically adapted to our social field without our having actually strategized about them, when elements of our repertoire overlap with our interlocutor's, we may deploy them without thinking that what we are doing is seeking comembership.

A theory of communicative repertoires fits very comfortably, therefore, with a theory of practice. First, repertoires are a collection of practices. Second, these practices are developed through participation in various communities. Third, the elements in one's repertoire are not just verbal but are embodied. Fourth, just as a person looks most competent when her habitus aligns with the field of practice in which she finds herself, a speaker can best achieve co-membership when her repertoire aligns with her interlocutor's. Finally, whether a repertoire element is useful or beneficial or not depends entirely on where and with whom a person is interacting. A theory of repertoires, like a theory of the habitus, then, is a relational one.

Linguistic Practice as both Stable and Emergent

In this chapter, I have theorized a view of language as social practice. In this view, language is understood as emergent, embodied social action that draws on speakers' full communicative repertoires to respond, under real-time pressures, to the shifting social field. Yet, viewing language as practice means seeing language not only as emergent but also stable. Language is stable because of the work of institutions, like schools, in whose interest it is to maintain a codified, legitimate language in order to secure their own survival (Bourdieu, 1991). Language is also stable in the eyes of assessments that students are given to determine their placement in particular classes, like ESL, and to assign them with particular labels, such as English learner. Although speakers themselves might not understand their practices through vocabulary counts and measures of syntactic complexity, the school system in which they are embedded certainly does. Additionally, one of the bodies of literature in which this study is grounded – quantitative work on the importance of interaction in language learning – also places value on understanding language growth as growth in the stable systems called 'English' or 'Norwegian' or 'Hebrew' or 'Nepali.' In this project, therefore, I examine language in both ways: as social action and as a system of words and structures. It is precisely because those two views seem incommensurable – because they place such different value on what language *is* and what success might look like – that I examine both. Understanding how each view might provide a different account of learning in Classroom Three, and how those views relate to one another, is an important outcome of the layering approach described in Chapter 1.

Note

(1) Austin called all three of these 'acts.' His student, John Searle, who extended Austin's work, made the useful distinction between them by calling them 'form,' 'force,' and 'effect,' respectively (Searle, 1969), a terminology I will take up.

3 From Bhutan, Uzbekistan and Berkeley to River City: Arrival Stories

Welcome to River City

This chapter addresses how the four focal students, their peers, their teachers and I all came to be together in a classroom in a suburb of River City, Pennsylvania. Although this is a study about Padma and her peers, it is also about River City and who lives there. Demographics researchers at the Brookings Institution have characterized River City as 'mostly white; slow growing' (Frey, 2000) and 'a former immigration gateway' (Hall *et al.*, 2011). River City's last great wave of immigration took place in the 1880s and 1900s, bringing Italian, Polish, Croatian, Hungarian, Greek and German speakers to the city. While several neighborhoods are still identified by the groups that built them, it is no longer common to hear these languages in the streets, nor has recent immigration kept pace with the rest of the United States. In 2010, River City ranked 98 out of 100 major metropolitan areas in recent immigration, with recent immigrants making up just 1% of its total population (Singer, 2010). Yet, River City also had the highest ratio (4:1) of highly skilled immigrants to unskilled immigrants in the nation (Hall *et al.*, 2011).

To explain these two patterns, it helps to look back to the collapse of heavy industry in the city. River City's steel industry, built at the turn of the 20th century, attracted the last wave of immigration to the city and sustained the city's economy for nearly a century. In the late 1970s and early 1980s, the steel industry began a rapid decline, and the city lost 130,000 manufacturing jobs in two decades (Giarratani *et al.*, 2003). Christopher Briem, a demographer at a local university, explains the lack of low-skilled immigration to the city in the past 30 years as follows: When the steel industry collapsed, many of the workers who would have been in heavy industry were forced to find other work that did not require a college degree. They became the low-wage, low-skilled workforce in the city, taking any jobs that might have drawn low-skilled immigrants (cited in Roth, 2014). Briem put it anecdotally:

> I was standing in front of a bus stop in [a certain River City neighborhood] the other day and I watched 20 buses go by. If you were anywhere

else in the country, a decent chunk of those drivers would probably be immigrants or minorities, and I swear to God, every one of them was a 55-year-old white guy, that barring historical events would have been working in a mill. (quoted in Roth, 2014, n.p.)

The same events explain River City's high-skilled immigration. After steel's disappearance, the city focused on developing its tech, education and medicine industries (Isaacson, 2014, 2015), often recruiting from overseas.

Refugee Resettlement: River City and Beyond

Yet in the last decade, there has been another shift in River City, driven by refugee resettlement. Resettlement is a technical term that refers to the permanent relocation of refugees to a third country, when neither repatriation to their country of origin (first country) or integration into the country of refuge (second country) is possible (United Nations High Commissioner for Refugees, 2011, 2017). It is considered a last resort, the best option for those 'whose life, liberty, safety, health or fundamental human rights are at risk' in both their country of origin and of refuge (United Nations High Commissioner for Refugees, 2011: 2). Refugees cannot apply for resettlement; instead, they must be recommended by the UN Refugee Agency, or United Nations High Commissioner for Refugees (UNHCR), who applies on their behalf to one of the approximately 25 resettlement states – countries who have agreed to regularly accept refugees.

The UNHCR considers for resettlement people who meet two criteria. First, they must qualify for refugee status under the 1951 *UN Convention Relating to the Status of Refugees*, which defines a refugee as:

> a person who ... owing to a well-founded fear of being persecuted for reasons of race, religion, nationality, membership in a particular social group or political opinion, is outside the country of nationality and is unable or, owing to such fear, is unwilling to avail himself of the protection of that country; or who, not having a nationality and being outside the country of his former habitual residence as a result of such events, is unable or unwilling to return to it. (United Nations General Assembly, 1951: 137, Article 1A (2))[1]

Second, repatriation and local integration must have been assessed and rejected as viable solutions. This is determined through a Needs Assessment, which consists primarily of an in-depth interview but which can also consist of home visits to assess living conditions (United Nations High Commissioner for Refugees, 2011). A case file is composed for each refugee or family based on the needs assessment, and if it is determined that resettlement is the best option, a Resettlement

Registration Form is prepared and submitted to potential countries of resettlement. This serves as a representation of a refugee's story and needs (United Nations High Commissioner for Refugees, 2011).

A refugee does not get to decide the country of application. The UNHCR chooses the country of application based on several criteria, such as language, culture, family connections, health needs and treatment options, the urgency of the request combined with processing speeds of potential resettlement states, as well as the selection criteria and annual quotas of those states. Once UNHCR submits the application to a resettlement state, that country takes over the process.

In the case of the United States, resettlement is jointly administered by the Department of State (Bureau of Population, Refugees and Migration), the Department of Homeland Security (US Citizenship and Immigration Services (USCIS)), and the Office of Refugee Resettlement. Applicants first undergo a security clearance to make sure that they have no criminal activity or association with groups considered to be terrorist groups by the United States (Government of the United States of America, 2016). Applicants then undergo a face-to-face interview with an officer from USCIS/DHS to confirm the history and needs portrayed in the Resettlement Registration Form and to determine eligibility for admission to the United States as a refugee (Government of the United States of America, 2016). At that interview, applicants provide testimony of persecution or fear of persecution, as well as any supporting documents that may exist.

Applicants who are determined as eligible for resettlement in the United States are assigned a resettlement agency in a US city. These resettlement agencies, sometimes called VOLAGS or voluntary agencies, partner with the US government to facilitate refugees' transitions to life in the United States. Refugees cannot choose their city or agency, although immediate family reunification is prioritized and requests to be near extended family or friends may be considered (Center for Applied Linguistics, 2012a). Typically, refugees wait 6–12 months from approval of their application to departure for the United States.

Before departure, refugees are given an orientation to life in the United States. All are given the handbook, *Welcome to the United States: A Guidebook for Refugees*[2] (Center for Applied Linguistics, 2012a), in one of 17 languages, and most also watch a video depicting the resettlement process[3] (Center for Applied Linguistics, 2012b). Travel arrangements, including airfare and immigration documents are arranged by the International Organization for Migration. An interest-free loan is made for each person's airfare and all adults sign a promissory note that they will pay off the loan within 3½ years (Government of the United States of America, 2016). They are expected to start making payments on the loan approximately 6 months after arrival in the United States.

When refugees arrive in the United States, they are met by someone from a local resettlement agency and taken to an apartment or house that has been prepared ahead of time, usually with donated furniture and kitchen equipment. Single adult refugees may be placed in an apartment with other single adult refugees. Rent and utilities are covered by the agency, in part through federal support, for up to 90 days, after which time a refugee or family is expected to be financially self-sufficient (Center for Applied Linguistics, 2012a). The US office of refugee resettlement can also provide assistance for up to eight months (Government of the United States of America, 2016). Within the first 30 days of arrival, the resettlement agency also helps refugees to enroll in English classes, enroll children in school, and apply for social security cards and government assistance such as the Supplemental Nutrition Assistance Program (SNAP), Temporary Assistance to Needy Families (TANF), Refugee Cash Assistance, Refugee Medical Assistance or Medicaid. The agency also provides pocket money, as well as transportation and interpretation for medical appointments and job interviews. Generally, guidance is also provided in things like doing laundry, using appliances, calling for police, fire and ambulance, understanding a lease, reading a utility bill, and writing and mailing a check. Refugee status lasts for one year, after which refugees must apply for a green card (permanent residence). After 5 years, they can apply for citizenship (Government of the United States of America, 2016).

Resettlement in River City

The families in this study each came to the United States through the resettlement process. In the decade before I arrived in River City for this project, the number of former refugees in River City had grown steadily, from 109 families in 2003 to 434 families in 2012[4] (Demographics and Arrival Statistics, n.d). The first refugees to arrive were mostly Bantu Somali, then Nepali Bhutanese, and, more recently, from Syria and the Democratic Republic of Congo. While refugees do not have a say over where they are initially resettled, they can decide whether to stay or move. Many families who are resettled in River City stay, citing a combination of affordability, plentiful housing, and growth in job sectors like hospitality, wholesale trade, mining and construction (Grant, 2013; America's Most Affordable Cities, 2013). Additionally, many refugees who are resettled in other cities choose to come to River City as a secondary resettlement location, after hearing of low costs and plentiful jobs (Director of Community Assistance and Refugee Resettlement at local VOLAG, personal communication). In particular, many Nepali Bhutanese families, including several in this study, moved to River City after having initially lived in other states, in order to be with a large community from the same country of origin (Director of Community Assistance and

Refugee Resettlement, personal communication; Story of the Bhutanese community, n.d.). I also heard from more than one Bhutanese Nepali River City dweller that in addition to the economic and cultural factors, River City's steep hills, summer greenery and winter snow are reminiscent of southern Bhutan's landscape. For an account of the specific ethnic conflicts that brought the families in Classroom Three to River City, as well as parents' accounts of the displacement and resettlement process, see Appendix 1.

With secondary relocation, the population of Bhutanese Nepali residents in River City was estimated in 2017 to be 6000–7000, the largest in the United States (personal communication, Director of Bhutanese Community Association, 22 August 2017). The languages of emergent bilinguals in the River City Public Schools reflect this: Of the 34 languages spoken, the top four are Spanish (25% of emergent bilingual students), Nepali (20%), Arabic (15%) and Swahili (15%) (ESL Services, District Level at RCPS, personal communication, 19 September 2017). The overall number of emergent bilingual students has also increased from approximately 300 in 2004 to 825 in 2014 to 1024 in 2017 (ESL Services, District Level at RCPS, personal communication, 10 July 2012, 29 July 2014, 19 September 2017).

Starting School

The Nepali-speaking parents in this study mostly found out about the Head Start program through friends or neighbors or via the family center in their neighborhood, where many parents attended adult English classes. Some parents used friends to help them enroll. One focal child's mother tried to enroll her daughter in a community school for refugees but it was full, so they suggested Head Start.

The school's neighborhood was made up of asphalt roads flanked by orange brick houses with green lawns, American flags and aluminum awnings over front porches. On a hill at the edge of the neighborhood sat the large apartment complex where most of the refugee-origin families lived. The complex, with its three- and four-story brick buildings, white shutters and green lawns, looked more like a tired college campus than the urban housing developments the families might have inhabited in larger cities. The school itself – a one-story, pale yellow brick building surrounded by parking lots and green lawns – had once been an elementary school but now housed several Head Start classrooms, an Easter Seals classroom for severely disabled children, a DART early intervention classroom for children with moderate developmental delays, a public library, a tax office and a district magistrate's office. In the center courtyard of the building was a playground, which all the classes shared. The library meant stories and songs with the children's librarian each Thursday. The magistrate's office meant that on the day that the magistrate heard cases in the afternoon, parents and children leaving the school wended their way through police, lawyers and clients waiting to see the judge. Thus, in many ways, the school was more like a community center than a school. There was no cafeteria, so food was delivered each morning, and teachers heated and served it at breakfast, lunch and snack. Also, there was no principal or supervisor on location. Instead, a supervisor came every few weeks to observe the three classes, and teachers had to call or email if they needed help or advice.

The school was unique in other ways, too. When I came to the school in 2012, a local outreach program had been working to identify eligible children who lived in the area and was helping their parents with the Head Start application process. As a result, significant numbers of parents who had come to the United States as refugees had applied to the local Head Start program, increasing demand for places in the classrooms. Thus, while one of the Head Start classrooms had been in operation for several years, the other two had just opened in response to the demand. (One of the teachers, who still works at the school, told me in summer of 2017 that this demand has continued and that three more classrooms were slated to open there in fall 2017.) Approximately two-thirds of the students in each class spoke Nepali, around one-third spoke English, and a handful – also children of families who had come as refugees – spoke Swahili, Somali, and Arabic. While multilingual populations of students are not unique in Head Start classrooms, what was unique was the sudden population shift and growth. The county responded quickly to accommodate this growth, but the teachers and administrators had no experience with multilingual populations. In many ways, the school was a microcosm of River City: a place with a population that had been stable for a long time but that was undergoing rapid changes, and where people were improvising and adapting in response.

The Teachers

The teachers in Classroom Three, Ellen and Lucia, were at the front line of this improvisation and adaptation. Both teachers were White women from lower-middle-class or working-class backgrounds, who had come to Head Start later in life. Ellen, the lead teacher, grew up in New York and had always wanted to be a teacher: 'I had a friend who had a chalkboard in her basement, like this big chalkboard and I just loved writing on it and I just always wanted to be a teacher. I never wanted to be anything else' (Interview, 16 November 2012). In college, Ellen had studied elementary education but could not get a job right away, so she worked in a bank for several years. She then had three daughters and stayed home with them. When the youngest started school, Ellen began substitute teaching in a nearby Catholic school and was offered a full-time job there. She taught first grade at the school for nearly 10 years before her family moved to River City. In River City, she had several part-time jobs before finding a job in a daycare center, where she worked for 2½ years. Her youngest daughter, who had been working for Head Start, then told her that she should try to get a job there instead. Ellen got an Early Childhood certificate easily, based on her degree and experience, and got a job as a traveling substitute teacher in April of 2012. In summer 2012, she entered the teaching lottery and was offered her own classroom (Classroom Three), which would be opening in fall 2012.

Lucia, the assistant teacher, had grown up in River City. She described herself as a 'Jack of all trades', having worked as a secretary in an engineering company, then for a foot doctor, then as a medical assistant. When her son, now 14, was a baby, she took a job in a daycare center, where she could put him in the infant classroom for free while she worked. What started as a convenient arrangement turned out to be a calling:

> I did some other professions before this, but once I did start working in daycares, I was very comfortable working with the kids and doing what needed to be done in this environment. I knew I had the patience; I knew I had things that I can contribute: ideas, suggestions, love, understanding, patience. (Lucia, Interview, 16 November 2012)

When her son got older, Lucia left to work as an aid for a family center. While her job involved working with and supporting parents, there was a Head Start classroom across the hall where she would occasionally fill in. There, she experienced the same realization that she had in the day care – that this was the work she should be doing:

> I always liked it. I really wasn't supposed to work with [the children]. I was supposed to stay more with the family center, but it was okay. And it all clicked, like having the puzzle that all came together (Lucia, Interview, 16 November 2012).

In 2003, she got her first position as an assistant teacher in a Head Start classroom. When that classroom downsized to two teachers, she worked as a traveling assistant teacher, where she experienced many classrooms and met many kinds of staff. Finally, hoping to settle into one classroom close to her home, she applied and was accepted to work in the new Classroom Three. She and Ellen met each other a few weeks before school started, to prepare their new classroom.

Ellen and Lucia both reported that they only spoke English, although each had some experiences with other languages. Ellen had studied French for seven years in school but had not been able to make much progress. She recounted her father's disbelief when, on a family trip to Montreal in high school, she had barely been able to help with French. 'I remember there was a sign there: *Chien Chaud*. It was "hot dog" and I remember that to this day. [I said,] "Ok, I can order you a hot dog" (*laughing*). But that was it. I can't do it.'" (Ellen, Interview, 16 November 2012). Ellen also mentioned her grandparents: 'Growing up my grandparents spoke Italian and you'd think for all those years of listening to it, I would have known, but no. I just- no.' Ellen had, therefore, not experienced personal success in learning a second language. Additionally, prior to this year, she had also never worked with emergent bilingual students, nor had she had any training to prepare. While the district had given the teachers an iPad with a Nepali translation app, the app was limited to one word at a time, and Google Translate did not offer Nepali as a language option at the time (it does now), so the iPad was not very useful. In our fall interview, Ellen expressed that some training would have been helpful:

> It would have been nice to have a little workshop on it (*laughing*) [...] I mean it's just- it's just, 'Here you are!' They gave me an iPad with some translating thing. Pssht (*throws hand up*). You know, it's just like, you have to figure it out on your own, how to do it, and I think Lucia and I are trying our best, you know? (Ellen, Interview, 16 November 2012)

Lucia, when asked about whether she had any experience with English learners said:

> I've NEVER had- I mean I had a situation where I had more Spanish kids (.) than normal one particular year and I had children who were from like Puerto Rico and Mexico and it was great. But I mean I mighta had five kids [not 11]! And I know that it's not easy for the children and we look at visuals and we use our hands and we try to talk slower and we try to go with the basics. (Lucia, Interview, 16 November 2012)

I asked her if she had just figured these things out on her own or if she had any training, either then or recently. Lucia replied:

> No, I've never had a special training on it. (.) U:::m I'm lucky enough to come from [a particular River City neighborhood], full of different kinds of people. I used to call it an international (.) place. So I have that background. I grew up with a father who was born in another country. (Lucia, Interview, 16 November 2012)

Both Ellen and Lucia felt thrown in to teaching the emergent bilinguals in Classroom Three, but drew on intuition and their own experiences to make sense of their students and of how to support them. The next chapter will focus on this sense-making, particularly around the students' language learning.

The Classroom

Ellen and Lucia's room, Classroom Three, sat at the end of a long hall, past the gym, the bathrooms and many unused lockers. On the lockers closest to the classroom, the bright new labels with children's names on them contrasted with the old green paint. In the classroom, too, the new birthday chart on the wall and alphabet border stood out against the well-worn carpet and furniture. The layout of the classroom was typical for preschool classrooms in the United States, organized into well-defined areas named after the activities that took place there throughout the day: the Library Corner was for reading, the Block Area for playing with blocks, the Writing Center for writing. In the Housekeeping Area, students could cook in the pretend kitchen, put on dress-up clothes and care for baby dolls. In the Art Area, students could use markers, paint, stickers, scissors, paper and glue. At certain times of the day, these areas changed functions and titles. Several times during the day, the block area became the space for whole group meetings, called Circle Time, when students might hear stories, talk about the day ahead, discuss the calendar and weather, or work on the letter of the week. Additionally, for breakfast, lunch and afternoon snack, the tables were wiped down and set with plates, cups and napkins rather than toys or art materials. At these times of day, the teachers signaled the shift by pulling pieces of fabric down over the surrounding shelves, lest students be tempted to create a creative lunch-art or circle-time-block hybrid space.

The Children

All of the students in the class were three or four years old and their families met the income requirements for Head Start, earning at or below the federal poverty line. There were 17 students in Ellen and Lucia's class, although some of the students changed across the year. Because Head Start is a free program, there is a minimum attendance policy and several students were asked to leave the program in the first few months after missing too many days of school. The parents of one student withdrew her after deciding that she was not ready for preschool and that they would wait until she was four. Table 3.1 shows the class at the beginning and end of the year, by students' gender, language, race/ethnicity (European/European American, African/African American, or Nepali Bhutanese), and approximate age at the start of school (3, 3½, or 4 [going to kindergarten the following year]). Table 3.2 summarizes the shifts in class demographics across the year.

The shifting demographics of students in the class – from mostly English speakers to mostly Nepali speakers – came to be seen by the teachers as an important factor in the year, and I will argue that it was significant for the students as well. Because the class had mostly stabilized by early December, unless otherwise specified, when I refer to the class, I mean the class as it looked from December to June.

Table 3.1 Classroom Three at the beginning and end of the year

	Start of Year					End of Year			
Student	Gen.	Lang.	Race/Ethn.	Age		Student	Gen.	Lang.	Race/Ethn.	Age
Kelsey	F	English	EA	4		Kelsey	F	English	EA	4
Luke	M	English	EA	4		Luke	M	English	EA	4
Joey	M	English	EA	4		Joey	M	English	EA	4
Alyssa	F	English	AA	4	→	Pooja	F	Nepali	NB	4
Hande	F	Turkish	EA	4		Hande	F	Turkish	EA	4
Brady	M	English	EA	4	→	Sreya	F	Nepali	NB	3
Joy	F	English	AA	3.5		Joy	F	English	AA	3.5
Tommy	M	English	EA	3		Tommy	M	English	EA	3
Elise	F	English	EA	3	→	Anita	F	Nepali	NB	3
Emanuela	F	English	AA	3.5	→	Caleb	M	English	EA	3
Padma	F	Nepali	NB	3.5		Padma	F	Nepali	NB	3.5
Kritika	F	Nepali	NB	3.5		Kritika	F	Nepali	NB	3.5
Rashmi	F	Nepali	NB	3.5		Rashmi	F	Nepali	NB	3.5
Dinesh	M	Nepali	NB	3.5		Dinesh	M	Nepali	NB	3.5
Prakesh	M	Nepali	NB	3.5		Prakesh	M	Nepali	NB	3.5
Monal	M	Nepali	NB	3		Monal	M	Nepali	NB	3
Kabita	F	Nepali	NB	3	→	Maiya	F	Nepali	NB	3

Note: '→' denotes a student leaving and being replaced by another student.

Table 3.2 Shifts in class demographics for Classroom Three

	Start of Year		End of Year	
Home language	English	9	English	6
	Nepali	7	Nepali	10
	Turkish	1	Turkish	1
Race/ethnicity	European American	7	European American	6
	African American	3	African American	1
	Nepali Bhutanese	7	Nepali Bhutanese	10
Gender	Female	10	Female	10
	Male	7	Male	7
Age	4 going to K	6	4 going to K	5
	Turning 4	7	Turning 4	6
	Just 3	4	Just 3	6

The Focal Students

I chose four students to focus on to help me answer my questions about how social positioning and participation might shape language learning. My focal students each met four criteria. First, all four students were in the class from the start of the school year and stayed until the end. Second, since previous researchers have shown that gender positioning and socialization are strong factors in early education settings and schools in general, I wanted to make sure that this did not overshadow other, more subtle differences in school identity work, so all four students chosen were the same gender. I also chose students who were close in age – all turned four in the same six-month period around the start of the school year – so that outcomes could not be attributed to developmental differences. Finally, I chose students who had similar, very beginning levels of English (based on my observations and recordings in the first few weeks of school). Three of these students spoke Nepali and one spoke Turkish, which are both Level III languages on the Foreign Service Institute's scale of languages' similarity to English (where Spanish is Level I and Japanese is level IV), meaning that the amount of potential transfer from these languages to English would be comparable, (DLIFLC.edu - Languages at DLI, n.d.).

Padma

Padma was a tiny-framed Nepali speaker who lived with her parents, seven-year-old sister, and grandmother. Padma's grandmother was her primary caregiver, as both of Padma's parents worked. As described in the opening scene of this book, Padma's grandmother brought her to school each day. Padma's favorite place to play at school was in Housekeeping, with the baby dolls ('babies'), and she could often be heard narrating in Nepali the preparation of elaborate meals in the pretend kitchen. She was quick to laugh as she wiggled across her day, but also to whine about an injustice. Many of her conversations were about her *didi*, or older sister, whose wardrobe of dresses Padma had inherited. Padma often wore one of these now paint-spotted dresses over a long-sleeved shirt and pants, always accompanied by socks and sparkly sandals, except when it snowed, when she switched to pink cowboy boots. Padma turned four in the beginning of October.

Rashmi

Tall and wiry, Rashmi, another Nepali speaker, seemed like she had grown too fast for herself. Her jeans and hooded sweatshirts were just a tad small and her arms and legs sometimes appeared to be slightly out of her control. Her energy was boundless and she buzzed around the room. Her favorite place to play was the sand table and she sometimes spent all of play time running over to check if she could have a turn. Her cousin, Prakesh, was also in the class and he was her favorite playmate at the sand table or outside. She also liked to be in Housekeeping, where she enjoyed 'cooking' and playing with the babies. Rashmi lived with her father, her mother and a new (actual) baby. She lived across the hall from

Prakesh's family, and the doors to both apartments were always open as Rashmi and Prakesh went back and forth. Their fathers, who were brothers, alternated in bringing the children to school and picking them up. Rashmi turned four in early November.

Kritika

Tall and serious, Kritika also spoke Nepali. She lived alone with her mother, whom I only met once, since she worked all day. Kritika came to school and went home with a different friend or neighbor each day. Kritika rarely missed a day of school. She loved to draw, to play with the sand, and to build with the small toys, but no matter where she played, a group of girls went with her. Kritika wore dresses over pants, generally with socks and sandals, but her outfits were never as colorful, flouncy or as brightly mismatched as Padma's. Kritika's hair was always combed and she repositioned her headband throughout the day to make sure her hair was neat. She was less likely than the other children to talk about her family and was stoic in the first weeks of school when other children cried for their parents. Kritika turned four in late September, a few days before Padma did.

Hande

Hande was a Turkish speaker whose parents had lived in the USSR, as part of a Turkish minority in what became Uzbekistan (see Appendix 1 for more). Hande loved Mickey and Minnie Mouse and often wore T-shirts with their picture, along with sweatpants or jeans. She grinned when she smiled and usually had her short curly hair in two pigtails on top of her head. When I think of Hande, I see her at one moment, quiet and serious, drawing intently, or singing softly to herself. The next I see her shaking her head back and forth, making silly noises, rolling her eyes, and then collapsing into giggles. Hande loved the Art Area and spent long periods of time drawing alone, but was a friendly and attentive playmate when invited. She lived with her mother, father, and very boisterous younger sister, along with 13 other relatives in an apartment near the school. Hande was the oldest of the focal students, having turned four in August, and would be the only one going to kindergarten the following year, according to the district's 1 September birthday cutoff.

A Final Arrival Story: The Researcher

I have told the stories of how the children's families came to the United States and how they came to enroll their children in Head Start. I have told about how Classroom Three was born, and how Ellen and

Lucia came to teach there. But how did *I*, the researcher, come to be seated on a brightly colored rug with Ellen, Lucia, Kritika, Padma, Rashmi and Hande, one fall day in 2012, singing the Good Morning song? And what role did I play in the classroom once I was there?

I grew up in River City but moved away for college. After college, I was a preschool teacher in Belgium and then San Francisco, and when I decided to go to graduate school to learn more, crossing the bridge to Berkeley was a logical choice. But just before I began my dissertation research, as so often happens, life circumstances took me back to River City, so although I had planned to study young language learners in California, instead I found myself re-discovering my native city and all the ways it had changed in the decade since I had left.

When I went looking for a classroom in River City in which to carry out this project, I wanted a classroom that reflected the changing demographics of the city. I asked the director of early childhood programs for the region for a recommendation. She brought me to the school where Ellen and Lucia worked and took me to both of the new classrooms opening that fall. Each of the new rooms had a high number of emergent bilingual students, and both sets of teachers invited me to join their classes. Yet, as a former preschool teacher, I quickly recognized that the teachers in Classroom Two needed a third pair of hands more than they needed a researcher. The dynamics between the teachers and within the particular group of students were difficult that year, and I could not in good conscience add a camera to the room. Instead, I chose Classroom Three across the hall, which was busy and noisy in more typical ways, and I spent each Monday of the 26-week school year there as a researcher. I also spent another full day per week volunteering in Classroom Two, in a sort of unofficial reciprocity, in a more teacher-like role.

Approach to the Project

This ethnographic study spanned Padma, Rashmi, Kritika and Hande's full year of prekindergarten. Data collection involved spending a full day a week with the students. During my time in the classroom, I became a participating observer, alternating between watching, taking field notes and being drawn into play or conversation with the students. I also helped the teachers before and after school and during nap time, cutting up oranges for snack, wiping tables or preparing art materials. In these ways, I learned the practices of Classroom Three. Because I had been a preschool teacher, many of these practices were familiar to me. But as I looked at them through the eyes of students and parents who had never participated in such a setting before, I saw them anew.

In addition to participant observation, I video-recorded for about two hours a day: circle time, which provided teacher and student interactions; one meal (snack or lunch), which provided student interactions with some teacher involvement; and an hour of free play activities (the sand table, the art table, the dress up area, the block corner, etc.), which provided long unstructured periods of peer interaction. These videos served the dual purpose of providing transcribable interaction data to analyze the micro-interactional work of students positioning themselves and each other, as well as linguistic data for analyses of students' growth in both language as a stable system and language as social action. I also interviewed the teachers at the start and at the end of the year, the parents in the middle of the year, and the children themselves at the end. More detail about each of these approaches will be presented as necessary to understand my analysis throughout the book.

Interacting with the students

Although my experience as a teacher brought me to this project and informed how I saw events there, when I was in Classroom Three, I tried very hard *not* be a teacher. I wanted the students to view me as different from the teachers, because I wanted to be able to watch them interact even when they were breaking classroom rules. Following the approach of Corsaro (1985), I used two strategies to accomplish this. First, I was intentionally reactive. Unlike teachers, who actively initiate and direct activity, I placed myself in areas of activity and let students decide how and when, if at all, to interact with me. Second, I maintained peripheral participation, never trying to intervene, settle disputes, repair interactions or direct or coordinate play. I sat quietly on the edge of action but was friendly and responsive to requests for help or invitations to play.

Even as a reactive participant, I was often recruited as a babysitter of dolls or a customer in both 'Restaurant' and 'Hair Salon.' Joining in play helped students see me as different from a teacher, since Ellen and Lucia were sometimes watchers of and commenters on, but never participants *in*, the children's play. I also never acted as an arbiter of disputes and I always pleaded ignorance of the rules, telling the students they would have to ask a teacher. I intentionally referred to 'the teachers' as others, carefully positioning myself as separate from them. I let students see me *see them* breaking rules, as well, especially ones that I thought were a bit silly, like 'No taking toys from one area to another.' One day, as some of the Nepali speakers were playing 'Wedding,' the girls drew all over their hands with markers, breaking the rule, 'No drawing on yourself with markers.' 'Mehndi!' they showed me proudly. I knew from Indian friends' weddings that brides' hands and feet are decorated with henna and that this is called *mehndi* in Hindi (and apparently also in Nepali, a closely related language.) I agreed that it was very, very beautiful and their play continued.

One final and significant way that I was different from the teachers was the nature of my interest in the children's languages. Hande never spoke Turkish at school, realizing right away that no one understood, but the Nepali speakers in the class frequently spoke Nepali to one another. Although I did not speak Nepali, I had studied Hindi briefly so, when there were potatoes for lunch, I could identify the word *aloo* and when the children were fighting over a toy or baby doll, I recognized *mero* (my/mine), *timro* (your/yours), and *usko* (his/hers), all the same as in Hindi. Over the year, I made sure that the students saw me listening in on their Nepali conversations and laughing when they laughed. Sometimes, I had hunches about what a word might mean, and I either asked a parent after school or looked it up later. For instance, one day, the teacher asked children at circle time to identify a picture of a butterfly and Kritika yelled, '*Putali!*' When I got home I looked it up and, sure enough, it was Nepali for butterfly. Once I knew some words, I also made sure that students saw me responding to requests made to other children in Nepali, passing the milk when I heard *dudh*, pointing in the right place when someone asking where her doll (*mero nani*) had gone, or baring my teeth and showing my claws and chasing students around the playground when someone suggested I was a *gunda* (monster/bad guy).

Interacting with the teachers

When I interacted with the teachers, rather than emphasizing my non-teacherness, I instead highlighted my former role as a teacher. I empathized about paperwork and policies and low pay. I shared songs that I knew that were relevant to current curricular themes. I cut oranges to the perfect size and shared knowing smiles when a student said something amusing. I started a lot of stories with, 'When I had a student who...' or 'I once had a parent that....' I tried not to make the teachers feel watched. My role as a classroom volunteer across the hall, in a classroom that both teachers in Classroom Three considered in need of support, helped with this positioning.

Interacting with the parents

Day to day, I used different strategies to align with parents. With the long-time River Cityers (white, English-speaking), I played up my own native River Cityer status. I talked about growing up there and missing it during all my years in California. I talked about it being nice to see my grandmother more and how my grandfather had worked the steel mills for 30 years. With the Nepali- and Turkish-speaking parents, there was not a lot of talk, as just one mother and two fathers spoke English.

It was not until January, when I conducted parent interviews, that my relationship with the parents deepened. Not all parents chose to do an interview and there was a noticeable difference from January onward in my relationship with parents whom I had interviewed and those I had not. The long-time River Cityers were much more interested than I had anticipated in talking about language and classroom dynamics. They were excited to have me listen to their thoughts and were grateful that, as a thank you for the interview, I had specifically chosen a children's book based on what I knew each child liked. This difference was even more pronounced with the refugee families, because we had not been able to talk much before. I brought interpreters with me to these meetings, and when the female interpreters and I spoke with the mothers and grandmothers in particular (as opposed to fathers), the conversation took on the feeling of an intimate social event, rather than an interview. The mothers and interpreter and I were all around the same age, which added to this feeling. Afterwards, much to my surprise, even before I told them I had books for them, they thanked us again and again, hugging both me and my interpreter. When I gave them copies of the English-Nepali bilingual book, *The Story of a Pumpkin* (Tiwari & Rai, 2013), a folktale written down and illustrated by a group of Bhutanese refugees in New England, one began to cry. After the interviews, we went back to not talking much, but we did a lot more smiling and waving. One mother, who spoke some English, would sit down with her daughter and me when she came to pick her up during snack time, and we would make small talk.

Ethical Research in Contexts like Classroom Three

In general, with parents, teachers, and students, my first aim was to be a friend. I knew that I did not want to be the kind of researcher who surgically extracts data and then disappears, only taking and not giving anything in return. As part of this effort, in addition to helping in Classroom Three, I also volunteered with one of the local resettlement agencies as a home educator, teaching newly arrived families how to navigate using stoves, paying rent, calling 911, etc. This often brought me to the apartment complex near the school, where I occasionally saw children from the class, and it helped me better understand the process of resettlement. Even given that work, I also knew that I would only be 'in the field' in River City for a few years and that eventually I would leave. I wanted, at minimum, to have been useful in my time there. I think, overall, I succeeded. I cut oranges for snack, tied shoes, brought coffee, commiserated over assessments, offered rides, gave out books, and on more than one occasion was hugged by a student, a teacher or a parent. Parents smiled broadly when they saw me around their apartment complex in my capacity as a volunteer, the students cheered when I returned for visits after completing my data collection, and the teachers, when we had lunch most recently, still expressed surprise that I had taken such an active role in the classroom ('I don't know, we thought you would just sit there and watch or something').

In a recent chapter (Bernstein, 2019) in Warriner and Bigelow's (2019) volume on research ethics in complex contexts, I wrote about the special vulnerabilities of each of the participants in my study. Teachers are always vulnerable to researchers' portrayals of them. Inviting a researcher into the classroom is an act of both generosity and risk on the part of the teacher, who has no guarantee that the researcher will write about him or her in ways that are favorable. Like any workplace study, classroom studies could threaten a teachers' livelihood. Early childhood teachers can also be economically vulnerable. Head Start paraprofessionals, like Lucia, make an hourly wage lower than the minimum starting hourly wage at Target (a US 'big box' retailer), which at the time of writing was $13/hour. Lucia, in 2012, when this study was carried out, made significantly less than that. I always tried to imagine myself in the teachers' shoes – I would want a researcher in my classroom to be helpful and to express solidarity with me, and occasionally to make me laugh and bring me caffeine; I would want a researcher to write about me honestly but compassionately – and I tried to conduct myself accordingly. Similarly, I was aware of the parents' vulnerabilities as not-yet-citizens, as immigrants, as (former) refugees and as parents. I was careful not to demand accounts of traumatic stories – stories that had likely been told and retold in the many interviews and background checks required for resettlement. The children, too, were vulnerable in this work. Children in general have little choice over where researchers find them and whether they will participate or not in research. Although their parents indeed gave informed consent for their participation, I looked for continual assent from the children. If they asked me not to record them at a given moment, or they turned their backs and quieted their voices, I did not continue to listen or record. It was important that they feel respected and autonomous.

In writing this book, I am acutely aware of my continued power to (re)present (Green & Stewart, 2012) those with whom I spent that year. In this book, when I talk about parents, I have tried to portray them as the competent, resilient and thoughtful people that they were and are. In describing the children and in making decisions such as how to transcribe their talk, I avoid both descriptions and transcriptions that position them as little or cute (for instance, writing 'scabetti' for 'spaghetti,' or 'wabbit' for 'rabbit') and have tried to convey them as the complex, multidimensional, multilingual, savvy, sophisticated, mischievous, hilarious, smart people that I knew them to be. Finally, I have also tried to write about the teachers with compassion. Teaching is difficult and complex work. Ellen and Lucia were navigating a new set of teaching circumstances and working to get to know families whose experiences and languages and histories they had never encountered. To make sense of these circumstances and families, they drew on the resources they had available to them – past experiences with teaching, their own stories of language learning, their families' immigration stories. While across the year, these strategies led them to miss opportunities and miss seeing students' skills or learning, the purpose of including Ellen and Lucia in this book is not to judge them but to understand how their decisions and perceptions helped to shape the students' experiences and trajectories across the year, and to learn from this analysis. I ask readers to read about Ellen and Lucia with compassion, as well.

Notes

(1) A person meeting these criteria may be excluded from refugee status, however, if they have ever been found guilty of war crimes or serious non-political crimes.
(2) Downloadable at http://www.culturalorientation.net/providing-orientation/toolkit/welcome/welcome-to-the-united-states-guidebook.
(3) Viewable at http://www.culturalorientation.net/providing-orientation/toolkit/welcome/english-welcome-to-the-united-states-dvd.
(4) This trend continued through the 2015–2016 year, with 651 families arriving in River City. It did not, however, continue in 2016–2017, as President Trump's cap of 50,000 refugees for the entirety of the United States for fiscal year 2017 was reached in July of that year (Kamarck *et al.*, 2017). Refugee resettlement has been strictly curtailed under the current administration. Just 202 families arrived in River City in 2017–2018 and 235 in 2018–2019.

4 Adults as Context-makers: Parents' and Teachers' Beliefs about Language

This chapter focuses on teachers and parents, the adults who shape preschool students' experiences. I examine the adults' beliefs about language and language learning, as well as their goals for the students' year in preschool. I explore how these are shaped by parents' and teachers' histories. I begin by reviewing what beliefs about language are, what counts as policy, and how teachers and parents serve as policy makers. By exploring teachers' beliefs in this chapter, I lay the groundwork for understanding teachers' classroom language policy decisions in Chapter 5.

Language Ideologies

Whether we realize it or not, all of us hold beliefs about how language works and how people should use language. These beliefs, or language ideologies, come from our experiences as language users, and they shape not only the ways we use language but our reactions to and opinions about others' language use. For instance, when a person instructs a child to say, 'Yes, ma'am,' or when she hears a British accent and thinks it sounds sophisticated, or when she is wildly impressed by a multilingual person from the United States but not a multilingual person from India, her language ideologies are at work.

The concept of language ideologies originates in Michael Silverstein's work, where he defined 'linguistic ideologies' as 'any sets of beliefs about language articulated by users as a rationalization or justification of perceived language structure and use' (Silverstein, 1979: 193). In the following decade, scholars like Judith Irvine, Susan Gal and Paul Kroskrity elaborated on Silverstein's work. Irvine (1989) emphasized the shared, cultural nature of beliefs about language, as well as the ways that these beliefs intersect with political and moral interests. For example, the common view in the United States that Black English is 'slang-y' or inappropriate for places like school or in professional contexts is both widespread, as well as bound up with the history of structural racism in this country. Gal (1989) showed that language ideologies can be both conscious and unconscious and that speakers need not be able to articulate their beliefs in order for beliefs to shape practices. For instance, most people in the United States would not be able to articulate that they think multilingualism is only 'good' if you speak English first, or that there is a hierarchy of what constitutes a high-status second language, but, as a society, our reactions to the white, L1 English speaker who speaks mediocre French, in contrast to the Latino, L1 Spanish speaker who speaks mediocre English, reveal this implicit ideology. Importantly, as Kroskrity (2004) underlined, there is never just one language ideology circulating in a given time and place. As groups and as individuals, people hold many different ideologies, including some that may be contradictory.

Language Ideologies and Language Policy

Language ideologies play an important role in language policy. While the most common understanding of language policy is a narrow one – that policy consists of official written rules or laws – those who study language policy and planning (LPP), see policy as much broader. Spolsky defined language policy as 'all the language practices, beliefs, and management decisions of a community or polity' (Spolsky, 2004: 10), or the ways that people use language, their beliefs about language and its use, and any attempts to direct other people's language practices. Language management can be done explicitly, through things as far-reaching as state laws or as local as the sign in my high school French classroom that said, 'Ici on parle français.' Management can also be done implicitly, through more subtle actions, such as a bartender learning sign language to better serve deaf customers, or a grocery store clerk rolling her eyes when a Spanish-speaker customer doesn't understand her question in English. In all of those cases, the French teacher, the bartender, and the store clerk are all making (very different kinds of) language policy. By this definition, then, written codes and law (the most explicit types of management) are just one part of policy. As Spolsky pointed out: 'language policy exists even where it has not been made explicit or established by authority' (Spolsky, 2004: 8). Language policy is 'overt and covert, top-down and bottom-up, de jure and de facto' (McCarty, 2011: 2). Often, policy cannot be identified by looking for a posted rule, but can instead be inferred from observing practice.

Teachers and Parents as Policymakers

While parents and teachers may not think of themselves as policymakers, they are some of the most common policymakers that children encounter. When children are taught, for instance, to say 'Yes' rather than 'Yeah,' or to ask 'May I?' rather than 'Can I?', this is language policy at work (Blum-Kulka, 1997; Burdelski, 2011; Ochs & Schieffelin,

1984). Any time teachers or parents try to shape the language practices of the children in their care, according to their beliefs about how children should use language, they engage in language management. Whether these adults engage in explicit and overt language management decisions, or more subtle socialization into valued language practices (Schieffelin & Ochs, 1986), all parents and teachers shape the language practices of their children.

In multilingual homes, parents' language policymaking policy often addresses which language will be used when and by whom. In places like the United States, parents who are bilingual may decide to only speak the family heritage language at home and leave the societal language to be learned at school (De Houwer, 2007). Some families, particularly those in which only one parent is bilingual, might implement a 'one parent, one language' management plan, so that the children are exposed to both languages at home (Caldas, 2012; King et al., 2008). Parents may also choose to send their children to complementary schools – weekend classes in the family's heritage language – or enroll them in bilingual or trilingual schools during the week (Caldas, 2012; Slavkov, 2017). In all of these cases, parents' decisions are shaped by the political, social and cultural context in which families live (King et al., 2008; Spolsky, 2012), but also by parents' language ideologies, such as their belief that bilingualism is a positive thing, that language is important for preserving identity, or that certain languages can provide upward mobility and economic opportunities later in life (Curdt-Christiansen, 2009; De Houwer, 1999; Gogonas & Kirsch, 2018; Kirsch, 2012).

In multilingual classrooms, policy often also addresses which language(s) will be used when and by whom. In a Spanish-English bilingual school, for instance, teachers might use Spanish 90% of the time in the first year of school and English 10%, eventually evening out the languages to 50-50 by the end of elementary school; or they might use 50-50 from the start (Howard et al., 2018). They may alternate languages by week, day, half-day or even by subject (e.g. both languages for language arts, English for social studies and art, Spanish for science and math) (Lindholm-Leary, 2012). Yet, even in schools with clear school-wide language management plans, 'implementation, by definition, involves policymaking, with educators acting as policy-makers' (Menken & García, 2010b: 2). This is because, whether at home or in school, language management also includes hundreds of tiny decisions each day: If a child answers in the 'wrong' language, do you pretend not to understand? If the child has a friend over, do you switch to English for the benefit of the friend?

These tiny, daily policy decisions are not limited to bilingual classrooms and families, however. They are just as relevant to teachers who teach in classrooms that are not officially multilingual but which include multilingual children. While these classrooms may not have an official language plan, teachers use their own judgement to shape language practices, such as encouraging students to express themselves in their home languages (Hélot, 2010; Volk & Angelova, 2007) or reminding them to using English only (Razfar & Rumenapp, 2012). Even when classes do have an official, monolingual language policy, teachers' strict adherence or flexible bending of that policy – how they 'appropriate, resist, and/or change dominant and alternative policy discourses' (Johnson, 2010: 6) – is shaped by teachers' own beliefs (Auerbach, 1993; Menken & García, 2010a; Pettit, 2011; Ramanathan, 2005). Yet, as discussed above, these beliefs are not always conscious, and teachers may not be able to articulate the reasons for their own practices or their management decisions. Additionally, in a theory of practice, beliefs are embodied, built into a person's habitus through participation in social fields across time. This notion of habitus as embodied belief helps to explain how teachers come to make unconscious and sometimes unspoken language policy decisions in their classroom – decisions that have powerful consequences for students' language learning as well as for their navigation of identities as learners.

The remainder of this chapter describes the language ideologies held by the Classroom Three parents and teachers, as well as how their own histories shaped those ideologies. The data for this chapter come from interviews with parents and teachers, as well as field notes and video transcripts from across my year in Classroom Three. (See Appendix 2 for more detail about data collection and analysis for this chapter.)

Parents' Beliefs about Language: Additive Bilingualism and Biculturalism

In interviews, I asked parents what they hoped their children would get out of the school year. All parents listed academic goals, like learning shapes, colors and letters, as well as social and emotional goals, like patience, cooperation, listening to teachers and learning to follow rules and routines. Yet, the parents of emergent bilinguals listed language as the primary reason for sending their children to preschool. Prakesh's dad wanted his son to 'learn English, cope up with [get along with] his friends, and learn about the American community' (Interview, 28 January 2013). Anita's mother said of her daughter: 'She is learning English so I'm very happy. English will be difficult if she were to learn later when she's grown up, but if she starts now then it will be easy' (Through interpreter, interview, 30 January 2013).

To make sense of the parents' desires for, and beliefs about, language learning for their children, it helps to understand their own histories with language learning. While some of the parents reported studying English prior to arriving in the United States, many had not. All the parents expressed that the need to improve their English increased significantly after their arrival in River City, and they hoped that learning English now would help their children avoid the discomfort that many of them had experienced around learning English as adults. Anita's mother and Pooja's mother both talked about how difficult it had been for them to learn English as adults and that they hoped it would be easier for their young children. Pooja's mother told me that, if they still lived at the refugee camp, 'She [Pooja] would learn in Nepali and then it would be difficult later to learn English' (through interpreter, Interview, 30 January 2013). Prakesh's father explained, in English: 'Actually I too can't speak American English. I don't have pronunciation like the people of America. They speak very politely. (*shaking head*) I hate to speak like this (*points to self*)' (Prakesh's Father, Interview, 28 January 2013). Padma's grandmother, through the interpreter, also expressed dismay at her own English: 'I hope the children can understand people, that they can talk with people. I feel bad that I need an interpreter to talk' (Through interpreter, Interview, 30 January 2013). When I tried to reassure her, saying: 'No, it's okay- it's really hard to learn a new language. I mean I can't speak Nepali, and I hear the children speak it all day long,' she countered: 'It's okay for you to not know Nepali but I have to know English because everybody talks in English here.' The response of Padma's grandmother illustrates a common refrain among the emergent bilinguals' parents: We live in America; we need to speak (American) English[1].

Yet, as much as the parents of emergent bilinguals in the class wanted their children to learn good 'American English,' they did not want this learning to happen at the expense of their home languages. All of the emergent bilinguals' parents reported speaking exclusively Nepali or Turkish at home. Hande's mother framed this balancing act in terms of her own language loss:

> I'm really glad that she [Hande] is learning English because we live in this country and she needs it, but I was born in Uzbekistan, studying there up until grade three, and I knew the local languages. Now I can understand them, but I do not speak them. So if my daughter speaks more other languages, that's better. (Hande's mother, through interpreter, interview, 19 February 2013)

Pooja's mother echoed this, saying that she would even consider sending Pooja to an English-Nepali bilingual school, if there were one: 'Maybe not from the beginning, but later, maybe I would send [her], because I also don't want her to forget the [Nepali] language' (Interview, 28 January 2013). Prakesh's father said he, too, would like a bilingual program 'because, you know, we should not forget our culture, too. It's important' (Interview, 28 January 2013). Monal's father, however, felt that school should be for learning English, while home should be for learning Nepali:

> The native tongue, he can learn at home with his parents, with his relative, with his friend cause he's in- he's affiliated with the mother tongue.

It's the language he speaks at home or at his community, 'cause many of his friends speak [Nepali] and his parents speak and his relatives speak. (Interview, 30 January 2013)

I wondered if parents like Monal's father therefore worried that too much Nepali was being spoken in the classroom among the 11 Nepali-speaking children. I asked each parent whether they were happy to have so many Nepali speakers in the class. Pooja's mother answered that, for now, she would prefer *not* to have other Nepali speakers, so 'that way she won't be distracted speaking Nepali' (Interview, 28 January 2013). Hande's mother (the Turkish-speaking family) said the class was fine as it was and that it was 'no problem' if Hande picked up some Nepali from her peers (Interview, 19 February 2013). Prakesh's father suggested maybe 'less Nepali' would be best, and Anita's mother also suggested one or two as the ideal number. Padma's grandmother thought maybe fewer Nepali speakers would be better, but not none at all. She explained: 'One, two Nepali would be better because she also doesn't totally know English, so maybe some friends would be better' (Through interpreter, interview, 30 January 2013), suggesting that Nepali-speaking friends could be important for social support. Monal's father sighed deeply when I asked him this question:

> It doesn't matter, doesn't matter. 'Cause at least there are one or two staff to guide them who speak in English all the time. So the language he gets, the English speech he gets from the teacher is enough I feel in that age. 'Cause at least he's gonna learn some kind of command, some kind of vocabulary, some kind of description from the teacher. It's enough for the kid of like three, four years. (Monal's father, interview, 30 January 2013)

This response implied that while his son might learn more with fewer Nepali speakers, for a three- or four-year-old, the initial exposure provided by the teachers was enough. Monal's father continued, however, about the risks of being completely immersed in English:

> 'Cause always being with English-speaking children may make him confused sometimes or might make him depressed sometimes. But at least if he learns [English] slowly, that doesn't make him feel shocked. I mean, linguistic suffocation. How like the woman who's sitting here[2] might feel when we speak. We are speaking here and if she is sitting there – how she would feel? Monal might feel afraid or discouraged to go to school. I think there is another term like 'inferiority complex,' like as if they feel like inferior in the mass [of English speakers]. So, if they are unable to communicate, at least if there are some students speaking the same language, it may avoid inferiority complex. Cause if he can't merge with the English speakers at that time, at least he can communicate with the Nepali-speaking children. (Monal's father, interview, 30 January 2013)

Monal's father's term, 'linguistic suffocation,' reflects his own deeply emotional experiences of arriving in the United States, but also the comfort and support he drew from the close-knit Bhutanese Nepali community, both in exile in Nepal and now in River City. When I told him I liked the term and asked if he had invented it, he apologized: 'That's- that's- yeah my own term, this is. WE (*pointing to self*) feel linguistic suffocation, so like in that situation, I'm using this term "linguistic suffocation"' (Interview, 30 January 2013). Monal's father, switching to 'we,' expressed what I saw across my year in the school and the neighborhood around it: that the large, strong Bhutanese Nepali community was what many Bhutanese Nepali people liked about River City, and it was what had brought them there to begin with. Monal's father told me that he loved River City, because:

> I'm in a similar community. We have a lot of people who have known each other, a lot of who speak same language, a lot of people having similar culture, so it doesn't make us feel that we are away from the original land. So it makes us as if we are in our original land 'cause all of our kins, relatives, friends, similar cultured people, are here so we feel it as if we are born here (*smiles*). (Interview, 30 January 2013)

Being 'born here,' for Monal's father, did not mean being just like the English-speaking Americans around them: it meant feeling at home and at ease. Although he and the other parents of the emergent bilingual children in Classroom Three wanted their children to learn English and to therefore learn to get along in America, no one felt that those things meant giving up their home language, culture or community (or in Hande's case, being afraid to learn other languages, like Nepali). The Bhutanese Nepali parents sent their children to school with red rice on their foreheads for Diwali and insisted that they not eat beef (and in Hande's case, pork), despite Lucia's attempts to convince them to take a 'When in Rome' stance on school lunches. The parents instead hoped to raise children who were tied to their community through their language and who *also* spoke good American English. Their goals were additive ones, rather than goals of replacement or assimilation.

Ellen's Beliefs about Language: 'English Above All Else'

These additive goals differed from the teachers' goals, particularly Ellen's. In the fall, when I asked Ellen to tell me about her class, language was the first thing that she mentioned:

> This is the first time I have <u>EVER</u> dealt with the language. You know, the second language. Having children that absolutely do not speak <u>any</u> English, parents that do not speak <u>any</u> English. It's been a real challenge

for me. Like trying to get them – parents – to understand things, having the children understand our routines. (Ellen, interview, 16 November 2012)

Ellen also emphasized that during her home visits before school started, when she asked parents about their goals, they all talked about language, too. She told me: 'Of course the Nepali children's parents said: "For them to learn English." That's their main goal and it's true, I mean how are they gonna do anything in this school if they don't know English?' (Ellen, interview, 16 November 2012).

In contrast to the parents, who saw English as a way to get along in their new country, Ellen understood the need for English through the lens of academic preparation and success ('how are they gonna do anything **in this school**'). When I asked what her goals for the year were for the students, she responded:

> Well for the Nepali children getting them to speak English. And being able to write their names um being able to know the alph- I mean I would like them to at least be able to learn the alphabet, you know and not just ABC song, <u>know</u> mixed up that's an A, that's a B, upper- and lowercase. And maybe some numbers. Um the colors, the shapes, the usual things that you would teach any preschooler ... (1.0) that's what I would like them to know by the time they go to kindergarten. (Interview, 16 November 2012)

For Ellen – who had always wanted to be a teacher, who as a little girl played with a chalkboard in the basement, who had been a first-grade teacher in Catholic schools for many years, and who organized each week around a letter – the focus was academic preparation. At times, Ellen even expressed frustration with all the non-academic routines of Head Start, like naps, meals, tooth-brushing:

> I think that the day is too long. I would rather have two classes and they go home half day. Because really, after lunch, they're napping, they're eating, and they're doing some puzzles or something. There's no time to really get started on something else. (Ellen, interview, 11 June 2013)

It only made sense, then, that Ellen also thought of English acquisition within this narrative of academic learning and kindergarten readiness.

Yet, despite Ellen's agreement with parents that the most important part of school was to learn English, Ellen felt strongly that helping the children learn English should be a job for parents, too. She marveled that even the parents who spoke English well did not help their children to learn it:

> No matter what you would say to the parents, even if you could just have an hour at home where you just used English, I don't think it was happening. Little Monal, you know Dad would come in – he speaks

great English! – but he would come in and he'd speak in (1.0) his native tongue. (Ellen, interview, 11 June 2013)

Ellen was not concerned about the children's competence as bilinguals, but as English speakers. For her, time in Nepali meant time taken away from English, so she could not understand why the parents, who claimed English as a priority, would continue speaking Nepali, even at school. As Ellen listed all the supports that she and Lucia provided for her emergent bilinguals at school – gestures, visuals – I asked her if there was any support that she thought the students needed that they were not getting. She replied:

I am told that they [the parents] do not speak English to them at home. There is usually one person in the family that speaks some English and they apparently don't want them [the children] to uh get any kind of an accent from them so they don't speak English to them, which I think that, you know, you gotta reinforce. If they're only here, what, five, six hours, four days a week – and an hour of that they're napping! – we're not really talking much [...] and then they're going home and they're speaking Nepali for the whole rest of the weekend. I think that it would be nice if the parents would speak some English to them but you know, that's how it is. (*throws hands up*) That's what I'm told, that's how it is so. I think that would help a lot. (Ellen, interview, 16 November 2012)

In addition to worrying about the students not learning English at home, Ellen also worried about having so many emergent bilinguals in one class. As she put it: 'There's not enough English speakers to go around! (*laughing*) You know we only have (*counting on fingers*) 1-2-3-4-5 (2.0) 6-7-8 English [speakers] out of the- the- I mean, the foreign children exceed the American children in here!' (Ellen, interview, 16 November 2012). Ignoring, for the moment, Ellen's framing of the emergent bilingual students as 'foreign' despite all 11 of them having been born in the United States, Ellen expressed here an implicit theory of language learning: that interacting with speakers of a target language is important and that there is some ideal ratio of students that would support emergent bilinguals' interaction with those speakers. This theory held across the year for Ellen. In June, reflecting on students' language growth, she concluded that the high concentration of Nepali speakers was likely an important factor, if not the most important factor, in students' language outcomes, which were not as strong as she had hoped:

Were they using as much [English] as I would have liked them to be using? No. And that's because there were so many of them in the classroom. No matter when we would sit down, if there were two or three of them together, they would start speaking in Nepali. And I'd say to them

'Speak English! Try to speak English!' and they just- just would not or could not do it, I don't know which. I just think I think that it helped them to feel comfortable having so many in there. You know, because I think that it would have been scary for a lot of them: You're in a country where you don't speak English, there's nobody, there's nobody that- but, I just think we had- I think we had more [Nepali speakers] than [we should have had] for them to really have learned English well. (Ellen, interview, 11 June 2013)

Although she recognized that having many Nepali speakers might have helped the Nepali speakers socially – to feel comfortable and to adjust to school – Ellen felt that the costs for learning outweighed the social benefits. This is clear from the structure of her comment: Nepali speakers detracted from English learning (cost), Nepali speakers served as a social support (benefit), Nepali speakers detracted from English learning (cost).

Understanding Ellen's beliefs: Reasoning through the habitus

To make sense of Ellen's beliefs about language learning in her classroom, it helps to understand Ellen's own history with language learning. Ellen started learning French in middle school, yet, as she recounted in Chapter 3, she could barely order a hot dog in French by her senior year. Ellen told me that maybe she just had not had enough exposure, and she hoped that because her current students were starting early and in an immersion setting, they would not have the same failure that she had had. Yet, at the same time, she worried that they, too, would not reach some critical mass of exposure that they needed to really learn English:

I know they're gonna pick it up once they start making other friends. It does seem like where they live though, it's- they're just surrounded with their own (2.0) you know, language, and that's *it*. So I think it is gonna be a little more difficult for them to learn it. But you know I think they will. I think they will. I hope before they go to kindergarten they'll be speaking. (Ellen, interview, 16 November 2012)

This tension in her thinking can be seen in this quotation through her frequently shifting epistemic stance – from the certain, 'I know,' to the less certain, 'It seems like,' to a more certain, 'I think,' to a less certain, 'I hope.' Her uncertainty reflects another contradictory experience in her own past – that she herself was exposed from a young age to the language her grandparents spoke, but she never learned it. She told me: 'Growing up, my grandparents spoke Italian and you'd think for all those years of listening to it I would have known, but no. I just, no.' (Ellen, interview, 16 November 2012). Echoes of this narrative – in meaning

Table 4.1 Structural parallels between Ellen's descriptions of the children's language learning and her own

Structure	November comment (about self)	June comment (about students)
Expectation...	You'd think	And don't **(you)** think they're gonna learn
...that **input**...	for all those years of **listening to it**	just because you're **speaking it**
...*would* mean **learning**...	I *would* have **known**	that they're gonna **pick it up** (*snaps*) like that
...but contradictory, actual outcome. **(Repetition with expansion, for emphasis.)**	No. **I just, no.**	I thought they *would*. I really thought the kids would.

but also in structure and word choice – can be seen seven months later when I asked what advice she would give to new teachers about teaching emergent bilinguals:

> And don't think they're gonna learn just because you're speaking it, that they're gonna pick it up (*snaps*) like that. I thought they would. I really thought the kids would. And again, was there too many of them? That should be your next thesis. (Ellen, interview, 11 June 2013)

In addition to offering some unsolicited advice to me about my next research project, the structure of this comment parallels the way Ellen described her own counterintuitive experience. Table 4.1 illustrates these structural parallels. In Ellen's own experience, simply being exposed to Italian was not enough and she worried that the same would be true for her students who heard English but spent a lot of time at school still playing in Nepali. The solution for her was immersion in as much English as possible. In our spring interview, as we sat in the room across the hall where teachers had placed labels in Nepali around the room, she looked around:

> Here! They put up Nepali signs or something (*looks around, then points*). They [the kids] can't read it anyway, so what's the difference? I can't read it, they can't read it, so why don't we just teach them the American one? That's what the parents want them to learn anyway. To me labeling things in Nepali makes no sense and I didn't do it. I'm doing English. I mean when I went to every house [and asked], 'What do you want them to get out of this year?' [The parents said,] 'Learn English.' Every single one. So I'm speaking English. I'm putting things in English. Everything is English. (Ellen, interview, 11 June 2013)

Ellen's task, in her eyes, was to make sure students got as much English as possible under her watch, and for her, this logically included discouraging Nepali in the classroom and pushing for parents to speak English at home.

Lucia's Beliefs about Language: 'You're in America; Speak English (But Schools Should Accommodate, and Family Languages Are Ok, too)'

In our fall interview, when I asked Lucia what she thought parents hoped for in sending their children to the school, like Ellen, she began with English: 'I think for our kids who can't speak English and don't speak English at home, to learn English' (Lucia, interview, 16 November 2012). At the same time, she was not personally as concerned with this goal as Ellen was. When I asked Lucia what she wanted the children to learn in their year with her, she interrupted before I finished the question, answering excitedly:

> Oh the love of learning! The love of the- the- the- you know they want to wake up, they want to come to school! It's great when we hear some families who tell us that they [the children] were sad they didn't go to school [on Saturday and Sunday]. And it's like, yeah, we're sad too bu::::t (*laughing*) [...] But to learn, to grow. And um I- I love to see certain children who are more insecure become more secure and kids who are more mean become much bigger hearted. (Lucia, interview, 16 November 2012)

These social goals were evident throughout our interviews, our casual conversations across the year, and her interactions with children. At the beginning and end of the day, for example, Lucia often sat with children while they played on the rug, reminding them to share and be good friends, asking them what they were making or doing, telling them that they looked nice that day. For Lucia, who had developed a professional habitus in daycares and in social work with families, caring for children was central to teaching. Lucia once explained to me that you never know which children brush their teeth at home, have healthy food or a quiet place to rest and that it was great that Head Start makes sure kids have these things. Part of Lucia's job as assistant teacher, since there was no cafeteria in the school, was to prepare breakfast, lunch and snack. Thus, while Ellen spent the nap hour preparing lessons or doing paperwork, Lucia spent the time preparing food or cleaning up. And while Ellen would sometimes eat with the children and sometimes not, Lucia always did. She saw mealtime as a key learning time for students:

> I gotta teach 'em patience and I think it's a good thing to learn. You know. Instant gratification isn't always so good. You know, you're a::::ll gonna eat at the same time. They come in and we serve breakfast and 'Come on' and 'I want you to eat, I want you to have breakfast.' I like that part of our routine. (Lucia, interview, 16 November 2012)

Lucia's idea of kindergarten readiness also looked very different from Ellen's. She said:

I think [patience and sharing] are very much absolutely what helps a child get ready for kindergarten, 3rd grade, 4th grade, college! I can't stress enough how much social-emotional outweighs everything else. So when I talk to- I went to Rashmi's house and her mother told me, 'She is so smart.' Yes, she is, but we want to help her stay focused. (Lucia, interview, 16 November 2012)

For Lucia, the learning that she envisioned for the children was not completely dependent on English, as it was for Ellen, and the goal of English learning was always in tandem with and even subservient to her social and emotional goals for the children. Yet, like Ellen, Lucia did want the children to learn English and she, too, wondered about the apparent contradiction between parents' desire for their children to learn English in school and their use of their home languages with their children, even when in the classroom:

Some of the parents have asked us: 'Are they speaking English?' But they [the parents] have told us and they've showed us even when they're here in the classroom that they speak their own language. I understand that's what they know, but.... (Lucia, interview, 16 November 2012)

Later in the interview, Lucia also explained how one Nepali-speaking emergent bilingual in the class was struggling with some behavior issues: 'I think that she had trouble understanding us because they probably don't speak English at home' (Lucia, interview, 16 November 2012). Lucia also talked about how the parents' language could get in the way at school:

It is a little more difficult in some respects having a language barrier. There's no doubt when we're trying to fill out paperwork, when we're trying to communicate to them. You know, I was talking to a family the other day on the phone. I had a situation where u:::m, it was two weeks ago when the big storm came. And from home, I called every one of our families to let them know the following day that our school was canceled. So here's a prime example of not being able to <u>look</u> at them, not being able to <u>visually</u> show them by pointing to a calendar or something else and to have to verbally tell them that there is <u>no</u> school tomorrow [...] You know school's canceled with the weather. You know you have to <u>repeat</u> yourself. (Lucia, interview 16 November 2012)

Lucia repeatedly referred to this 'language barrier' throughout our interview, and commented on how this barrier could compound other challenges, like informing parents about school cancelations or behavior issues.

Lucia recognized, however, that from the perspective of parents, the barrier was difficult for them as well: 'There were no ands, ifs or buts: I thought it was more difficult for them [parents] than it was for me'

(Lucia, interview, 11 June 2013). She also felt that both parties – parents *and* schools – should bear the burden of facilitating communication. When I asked her in the spring what she would change for the next year, she said that the district should translate the parent handbook into Nepali: 'Just like in today's world, you can call anybody, like Verizon [a US telecommunications company], you'll see everything in English and Spanish. We should provide that, too.' She also suggested that perhaps teachers could enlist parents who already spoke some English, to help with day-to-day communication for other parents who spoke less (Lucia, interview, 11 June 2013). At the same time, Lucia expressed admiration in both fall and spring for the few parents who seemed to her to make an effort to use English as much as possible. Citing the example of parents who requested my consent forms in English rather than Nepali or Turkish, she said:

> We have a couple of families who, if I can give an example of your paperwork, who came to say: 'We'd like to see it in English.' That said a lot! I took that as: 'You know what, we really want to adapt to your environment. Thank you, but let me see it in English so I can learn how to get along better here.' (Lucia, interview, 9 November 2012)

Thus, while Lucia wanted to support families in their first language, her vision was that they would use the support to transition to English. Her ideal model was not one of additive bilingualism but one in which the parents' first language served as training wheels that would eventually be shed on the way to monolingual English use. She saw no possibility of an outcome in which parents or the school developed an intentional and permanent bilingual way of being. Lucia's comment about the permission forms also implied that the parents in question – those who asked for the paperwork in English – were the exception, not the norm, and that, while the school could do more to facilitate communication, the other parents could make more of an effort to 'adapt to the environment' and 'get along better here,' that is, by learning English.

Understanding Lucia's beliefs: Reasoning through the habitus

To make sense of Lucia's beliefs about language learning, it helps to understand her own history with language. Objectively, Lucia had a strikingly similar language experience to Ellen's. Lucia's father spoke Italian much better than he spoke English, and Lucia was therefore often in immersive situations where only Italian was spoken around her. Yet, like Ellen, she never learned more than a few phrases.

However, the narrative that Lucia built around those facts, and the stance she took toward them, was quite different from Ellen's. Lucia explained:

I grew up with a father who was born in another country. Who had a deep accent. Who I never had trouble of course understanding- that's your parent. Other people would say, 'What did your dad say?' (.) and I'd look at them like they're cra::zy. CAN'T YOU UNDERSTAND ENGLISH? And it was funny cause he himself didn't like the term broken English, he didn't like some of these slang words that they would have for our different nationalities or like for Italians or any other ones that we know of, black Jewish or whatever. We didn't- we didn't do that. We didn't grow up with that kind of (1.0) communication. We didn't grow up with um any kind of (2.0) bias you know. I remember my father had a construction company. Very commons with Italians. *(Long laughter)* And um what they can do with their hands in addition to cooking. *(laughter)* Let me tell you. Very true. Very true. And I remember when lot of Italians -and then he did have one black man- and it was nice. I remember having the guy come to our house which isn't too common back then and it was interesting cause I'd grow up where my father would have certain friends or relatives come over and then they would just speak Italian. I couldn't understand them and that was OKAY. And then of course=

Katie = Do you speak any Italian?=

Lucia: = Very little. *Poco.* Means little.

Katie: (laughing) Just the important words, *mangia*! (laughing)

Lucia: *Mangia*, eat! Yeah I teach the kids a little bit. I can teach them how to count to ten or say you know, *como stai::?* Which means How a::::re you? *Molto bene::*, very goo::d. You know, and we gotta watch our things cause we don't practice like holidays here with Head Start so where you know, pure Italians say *Buona Natale* at Christmas time. You know but I don't practice that [religion] here.

Although the basic facts of Lucia's story parallel Ellen's (close relatives who spoke Italian and lots of time immersed in the language with little acquisition of it), Lucia uses those facts to make some different points. Lucia emphasized that the way that her father spoke ('a deep accent') was okay with her, that she never minded putting in the work to understand him, that she was not bothered by being surrounded by a language she did not understand, and that she was not ashamed at only having learned some phrases in Italian. These experiences helped to form Lucia's view that communication with speakers of other languages was a two-way street, not just the burden of the person learning English. She also saw Italian as closely tied to family, history and culture and made this connection to her students: 'I don't want to infringe on your beliefs. My language is important to me, yours is important to you, and I want to tell you, I respect that' (Interview, 16 November 2012). Table 4.2 illustrates the parallels and differences in Ellen's and Lucia's family language narratives.

Table 4.2 Parallels and differences in Ellen's and Lucia's family language narratives

Ellen's narrative	Lucia's narrative	Both narratives show	Lucia's narrative also shows
Growing up, my grandparents spoke Italian	I grew up with a father who was born in another country. Who had a deep accent. Who I never had trouble of course understanding – that's your parent. Other people would say what did your dad say (.) and I'd look at them like they're cra::zy. CAN'T YOU UNDERSTAND ENGLISH?	Close relatives who spoke Italian (heritage language)	Stance toward immigration; stance toward imperfect English and those who are intolerant of it
	And it was funny 'cause he himself didn't like the term broken English, he didn't like some of these slang words that they would have for our different nationalities or like for Italians or any other ones that we know of, black Jewish or whatever. We didn't- we didn't do that. We didn't grow up with that kind of (1.0) communication. We didn't grow up with um any kind of (2.0) bias you know		Stance, learned from family, against bias, xenophobia or racism
	I remember my father had a construction company. Very common with Italians. (Long laughter) And um what they can do with their hands (.) in addition to cooking. (laughter) Let me tell you. Very true. Very true. And I remember when lot of Italians		Connection of culture to nationality
	– and then he did have one black man – and it was nice. I remember having the guy come to our house which isn't too common back then		Reiterates stance, learned from family, against bias, xenophobia or racism
and you'd think for all those years of listening to it	and it was interesting 'cause I'd grow up where my father would have certain friends or relatives come over and then they would just speak Italian.	Lots of time spent immersed in heritage language	to language
I would have known, but no. I just, no.	I couldn't understand them and that was okay. And then of course= Katie = Do you speak any Italian?= Lucia: =Very little. *Poco.* Means little.	But little acquisition of heritage language	Acceptance of ambiguity of not understanding. Acceptance of not having learned to speak Italian
	Katie: (*laughing*) Just the important words, *mangia!* (*laughing*) Lucia: *Mangia,* eat! Yeah I teach the kids a little bit. I can teach them how to count to ten or say you know, *come stai::?* Which means How a::::re you? *Molto bene::*, very goo::d. You know, and we gotta watch our things cause we don't practice like holidays here with Head Start so where you know, pure Italians say *Buona Natale* at Christmas time. You know but I don't practice that [religion] here.		Yet, acquisition of culture and key terms linked to culture. Stance that speaking some language counts, especially key cultural phrases

At the same time that Lucia's narrative framed culture and language and something to be maintained and respected, Lucia had also seen her father attempt to speak English with his family and in his community, in order to adapt to life in the United States. This American Dream-style narrative of persistence and hard work at assimilation is echoed in her continued comments about parents who ask to see school paperwork in English:

> And it was like you know, a very <u>good</u> thing. To me it was an advanced way of adapting. So they um, you know, want to learn, want them to have the opportunity of education so that hopefully they can succeed and better themselves you know, like I told you the story of the guy who was from India, and there's a lot out there who are very successful, be it from India or England or any other country. If you put your mind to it and you work real hard there's nothing you can't do. It's not easy but it's there for you. You know but you gotta <u>work</u> at it. (Lucia, interview, 9 November 2012)

For both Lucia and Ellen, then, the wish to see parents speaking English with the children was more than just a concern about immersion and acquisition. In a theory of practice, where belief is part of the habitus, Ellen and Lucia's thinking might stem from what Bourdieu called *doxa* – a collective sense for what is reasonable and appropriate, which comes from having habitus formed in similar conditions. Ellen and Lucia, both children/grandchildren of immigrants, had grown up with the ideal of the melting pot: their parents/grandparents wanted better for them and better meant English and assimilation. In a few generations, both of their families had seen a shift from being part of the Italian race in the eyes of their country to being unmarked, White Americans. And these experiences of assimilation as the model for successful immigration shaped their hopes for the families in Classroom Three. The teachers were impressed with the drive of refugee families, who showed up at school on snow days, who never had unexcused absences or attendance issues, who 'had alphabet flash cards up on the wall,' who valued education, and who 'want better for their child.' For the teachers, it seemed like common sense to also want English for them, even at the expense of their first language. In Ellen and Lucia's minds, the families were in River City for good and to become American. They did not consider that River City could be a temporary home[3] or that 'melting' was not the families' goal.

Conclusion

This chapter has shown that even adults who had no formal training in how language acquisition works have had experiences with language and that those experiences shape their beliefs. This shaping was evident in interviews with both parents and teachers, in which their own histories and the events that they chose to recount in their narration were echoed in their theories about the children's present language learning. This chapter highlights that all adults – parents and teachers, monolingual and multilingual – carry with them a sense for what is right and good about language learning and use, and that in the absence of evidence or research, and even at times despite it, adults reason through their own histories.

In the next chapter, Ellen and Lucia's beliefs, as well as their understanding of English as intertwined with academic and social progress, become important as I discuss the practices of Classroom Three, including language practices, shaped by Ellen and Lucia's policymaking.

Notes

(1) Several of the English-speaking, long-time River City residents whose children were also in the class agreed. One of the mothers told me: 'One thing is, you know, this is an English-speaking country and some of [the parents] don't speak English when they come into the classroom, and I think that as soon as you walk in the door you should try to speak English' (Interview, 19 February 2013).
(2) Padma's grandmother was sitting by the door waiting to be interviewed. Because Monal's father and I were speaking in English, Padma's grandmother could not understand us.
(3) In my work with the community, for example, I met two Bhutanese Nepali men in their early twenties who had come to the United States as refugees, but who were learning English and working as truck drivers in order to save enough money to return to Nepal, this time as immigrants rather than refugees, to open a tour company for Americans visiting the country.

5 The Social Field of Classroom Three: Policies and Practices

In many ways Classroom Three, as an institutional setting, resembled preschool classrooms across the United States. For readers familiar with Head Start or other public preschool programs, the details in the next two sections will feel familiar. Yet, in other ways, Ellen and Lucia's beliefs – about teaching and learning, about language and about language learning – interacted with the language practices of the children and families in ways that produced classroom language policies unique to Classroom Three. I begin with an account of the general practices and routines that made up the social field of the classroom, before turning to language practices and management in particular.

The Social Field of Classroom Three

Classroom Three looked much like many preschool classrooms in the United States, with areas separated by shelves to break up the space and named after the activities that took place there (see Figure 5.1). When children first entered the classroom, on the right near the door was the sand table, referred to by the students simply as 'Sand.' The table was covered in the morning but was open during playtime. Beyond the sand table was the sink for hand-washing and tooth-brushing, and just beyond that was the computer and then the 'Library,' where the books were kept, along with a beanbag chair and small armchair. Next to the library was the 'Writing Center,' a desk with two chairs and supplies of lined paper, fat #2 pencils, and a basket of colored pencils in varying states of sharpness. To the left of the classroom door was 'Housekeeping,' the area of the room where the dress-up clothes, baby dolls and carriages, pretend kitchen and food, little table and chairs and child-sized brooms were kept. Beyond that was the rug area, where students had 'Circle Time,' heard stories and sang songs. This was also where, during playtime, children could play with building blocks and pretend cars. In the center of the room were the tables. The two large tables were where students ate meals. During playtime, one of these

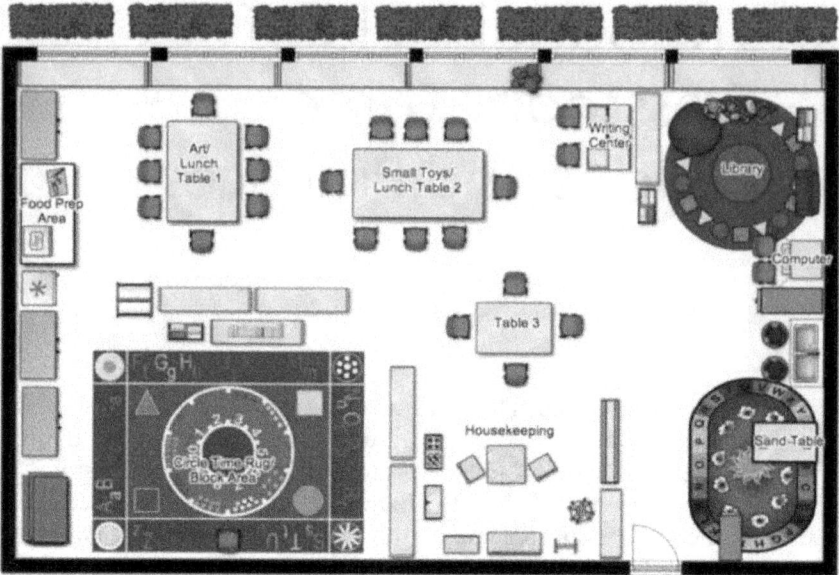

Figure 5.1 Classroom Three floorplan (reprinted with permission from Bernstein, 2018)

tables was for 'Small Toys' like puzzles or Lego and the other was for 'Art.' Nearby shelves were stocked with paper, scissors, markers, and glue, and an easel stood next to these. At the far corner of the room was the refrigerator and food preparation table, as well as teacher storage cabinets. The food table was differentiated from other tables in the room by its height, meant for adults not children, and its material, made of plastic not wood. Other spaces in the room were also marked as adult or child space in the same way. Everything on the long window ledge was in adult space, while the shelves below were kid space. Similarly, the tall filing cabinet with the printer on top, between the sink and computer, was adult space.

When students first arrived in Classroom Three at the start of the school year, one of the practices they had to learn was that the use of classroom space varied considerably throughout the day, and that the clock and the schedule determined the function of the spaces, as well as who could be in them.

Table 5.1 shows the schedule according to clock time and classroom time, as well as what teachers, students and parents typically did during those times, and what space belonged to whom.

In any preschool classroom, an important part of forming a school habitus is learning to live by the schedule of the class rather than by an individual schedule: to learn to eat (and perhaps even to be hungry) when food is served; to rest (and perhaps even be tired) when it is time to rest; to run when it is time to run; and to sit when it is time to sit.

Table 5.1 Schedule according to clock time and classroom time for Classroom Three

Clock Time	Classroom Time	Students do	Teachers do	Parents do	Teacher space (dark shaded area) and kid space (light shaded area)
8:30–8:50	Sign-In and Breakfast	Students write or trace their names with the help of parents, at Table 3 or the writing center. Students eat breakfast at Tables 1 and 2.	Teachers welcome students, chat with parents, help students with writing, help with breakfast. As students finish, Ellen helps them brush their teeth.	Parents help with writing and breakfast. Sit with children or stand and watch. Talk with one another or teachers.	
8:50–9:00	Good Morning Circle	Students come to carpet. Sing good morning song. Figure out who is missing. Hear what will happen that day. Line up to go outside.	Ellen leads circle. Lucia cleans up. Ellen calls students by name to go to line up.	Have left.	
9:00–9:30	Outside Time	Free play outside/in gym. Run, climb, kick balls. At end, line up for return to class	Supervise, chat. Ellen takes children to bathroom in small groups; Lucia stays with students.		

(Continued on next page)

78 (Re)defining Success in Language Learning

Table 5.1 Schedule according to clock time and classroom time for Classroom Three (Continued)

Clock Time	Classroom Time	Students do	Teachers do	Parents do	Teacher space (dark shaded area) and kid space (light shaded area)
9:30–9:40	Planning time	Seated again on the rug, one-by-one students decide and announce which area they plan to play in. Take name tag to chosen area.	Ellen sets up for playtime. Opens shelves, puts items out on tables. Lucia leads children in choosing and going to play.		
9:40–11:00	Free Play Time	Students play in chosen area. Can move between areas if they take their tag and there is room in new area.	Ellen sits at table 2, works one-on-one on assessments or projects with students, with one eye on Housekeeping, Small Toys, Sand and Library areas. Lucia prepares lunch with one eye on Art and the Rug.		

(Continued on next page)

Table 5.1 Schedule according to clock time and classroom time for Classroom Three (Continued)

Clock Time	Classroom Time	Students do	Teachers do	Parents do	Teacher space (dark shaded area) and kid space (light shaded area)
11:00–11:20	Story/Music	Students clean up and return to carpet to hear a book or sing songs. One or two help set the table.	Lucia leads on carpet. Ellen sets up lunch.		
11:20–12:00	Lunch	Students eat and talk.	Teachers sit with tables while children eat, then get up to set up nap mats. Loosely supervise, field requests for 'more.'		

(Continued on next page)

80 (Re)defining Success in Language Learning

Table 5.1 Schedule according to clock time and classroom time for Classroom Three (Continued)

Clock Time	Classroom Time	Students do	Teachers do	Parents do	Teacher space (dark shaded area) and kid space (light shaded area)
12:00–1:30	Nap	Students lie on mats and are supposed to sleep. No talking, no getting up.	Lucia cleans up lunch. Ellen does paperwork and watches students. Lucia sets up snack.		
1:30–2:00	Snack	Students wake up, come to snack table, are taken to bathroom in small groups as needed.	Teachers pick up nap mats, assist with opening/serving snack, take children to bathroom.	Parents start to arrive. Some wait while children finish snack.	
2:00–2:30	Play/pick up time	Students can do puzzles or read on rug.	Teachers clean up snack, greet parents, call children to door.	Parents chat with each other, teachers, wait by door.	

Language practices play an important role, as both the medium and the object of socialization practices. In addition to the shared lexicon of the classroom – 'sand,' 'choice time,' 'circle' – the students also learn *how* to talk in the classroom. In Classroom Three, students were reminded that during circle time, in order to speak they needed to raise a hand first. They were taught that talk inside the classroom takes place at a lower volume ('inside voice') than talk outside the classroom. They were told to 'use kind words' and not words like 'stupid' or 'I hate you.' Importantly, they also learned the value of talk in general in school. Students who raised hands and then gave answers were praised, even when the answer was not correct, while raising a hand and then not speaking, or worse, yelling an answer without raising a hand first, did not count. Students were thanked during activity choosing time for using language to indicate their choice rather than just pointing. And students were frequently reminded to 'use your words and not your hands' to solve problems with friends, such as who would get to use a particular toy.

Classroom Language Management and the Place of English in Learning

In addition to managing *how* language was used, Ellen and Lucia also activity managed *which* language was used. In this way, their beliefs, shaped by their own histories, became the basis for Classroom Three's language policies. For example, on each of the 26 Mondays I was in the classroom, I heard one or both teachers remind the students to use English. In March:

> Outside on the playground, Pooja was hanging from the jungle gym. Someone called to her from across the playground and she yelled back a long sentence in Nepali. Lucia approached her and reminded her, 'English, Pooja, English!' to which Pooja said, 'Hello?' Lucia smiled and gave her an enthusiastic thumbs up. 'That's better!' (Field notes, 11 March 2013)

And in May:

> Ellen: (*Comes over to the lunch table with her plate*) Let's speak English.
> Dinesh: Oh yeah!
> Ellen: Let's speak English at the table. (*Pulls over chair*)
> Dinesh: Yeah *I'm* speaking English!
> Ellen: I wanna hear your good English.
> (*Padma continues talking in Nepali to Kritika*)
> Dinesh: (*Loudly*) Yeah! Right, Tommy?
>
> (Video, 13 May 2013)

These reminders often reflected the teachers' own priorities for students. For instance, Ellen's reminders frequently linked English learning to kindergarten readiness:

> At lunch, Kritika was talking animatedly in Nepali to Pooja, telling what seemed to be a long story. As Ellen passed by to get more milk, she said, 'Kritika, speak English to her. She's going to Kindergarten next year.' Then, to the whole table, she added, 'English, let's speak English.' (Field notes, 14 January 2013)

Lucia, on the other hand, regularly linked English with social skills. In the following example, Lucia implied that not knowing one (English) is a cause for not knowing the other (sharing) and that helping a student to learn one will help her to learn the other.

> The children are playing on the rug after breakfast. Lucia is with them. Maiya, a younger Nepali speaker who joined the class mid-year, grabs a toy from Joey, an older, monolingual English speaker. 'Heeeeeeeeey!' Joey cries angrily. 'It's ok,' Lucia soothes him. 'She doesn't speak English too good yet, so we're gonna help her. Say, "Here Maiya, let's share." Yeah, we're gonna help her learn English, ok?' (Video, 3 March 2013)

On another day, Lucia linked English and sharing as related solutions for a fight over blocks and posed them as the two conditions necessary for successful play.

> A group of Nepali speakers are arguing about blocks. Lucia approaches and says gently, 'Pooja, English. Sh:::are.' (Field notes, 15 April 2013)

This linking of English with academics for Ellen and with social skills for Lucia would also come to color how each assessed progress in English across the year (see Chapter 7).

Yet, for as many times as the teachers reminded to the children to speak English, the reality was that the Nepali-speaking children spoke quite a lot of Nepali together, from the first day of the school year to the last day. And there were dozens of times in which the teachers commented in ways other than by asking them to switch languages. Ellen, particularly after a long stretch of talk, could be heard to exclaim: 'What are you saying?' to no one in particular. Once, she turned to me and said: 'Lotta jabbering going on over here. I wanna listen, but *(shrugs)*' (Field notes, 29 October 2012). On another occasion, Ellen passed by the sand table where Kritika, Pooja and Padma were talking and I was taking notes. As she walked by she said: 'Boy they are really jabbering away today! (.) What are you saying? *(laughs)*' (Field notes, 5 November 2012).

These reactions reflect Ellen's experiences with languages other than English. While the question, 'What are you saying?', might indicate a desire to understand the students, the term 'jabbering' implied impenetrable and unknowable nonsense, making her question, 'What are you saying?', just something to fill the air rather than a real inquiry. Lucia's responses, too, reflected her past. In contrast to Ellen, Lucia seemed both comfortable on the sidelines of Nepali conversation and genuinely curious about it. Each day as she prepared lunch, for example, she listened to the children's talk at the art table nearby, and she would stop to ask the Nepali speakers what they had said. One winter day, for instance, Pooja was enthusiastically explaining something to her friends in Nepali. Lucia asked:

Lucia:	Pooja, what does that mean? What you were saying?
Pooja:	I say 'snowman'!
Lucia:	'Snowman'?
Pooja:	One big ball, then one other big ball, then one small ball (*gesturing stacking motion with her hands*).
Lucia:	Oh making a snowman. Alright!

(Video, 25 February 2013)

This interest in and ease around Nepali aligned with what Lucia offered up in her narrative of her childhood: that she was comfortable around people of different races and backgrounds, like her father's Black colleague, as well as people she did not understand, like her father's Italian-speaking friends. For both Lucia and Ellen, management of language in the classroom was shaped both by their educational priorities (Ellen's academic ones and Lucia's social and emotional ones), and their own histories with language and learning.

Thus, officially, the language policy in Classroom Three was an English-only policy – as Lucia put it: 'We only speak English here' (Lucia, interview, 16 November 2012). The teachers reminded students of this policy regularly, through comments that linked English to academic and social aims. In practice, however, Ellen and Lucia both allowed a great deal of Nepali in the classroom – Ellen, with a cautious and perhaps suspicious tolerance, Lucia, with curiosity and a desire to see students practice English, too. At the same time, both also wished for the children to spend more time practicing English at home. These tensions in Classroom Three's language policy – a stated English-only policy and a *de fact*o policy of tolerance for Nepali – will become important as I look to how four focal students' social identities also took shape within the classroom and how these identities related to their English learning. Yet, before turning to the students' classroom identities, one more classroom practice bears noting.

Children as Socializers

In Classroom Three, the teachers did much of the socializing into classroom practices, linguistic and otherwise. But as children gained more expertise in these practices, they also reminded each other, through what Tholander and Aronsson (2003) called 'subteaching,' or children's engagement in teacher-like socialization of peers (see also Copp Mökkönen, 2012; Goodwin & Kyratzis, 2007). Children in Classroom Three often reminded one another to walk in the hall rather than run, to put a book away rather than leaving it on the floor, and to share rather than keeping the markers all to oneself. Subteaching extended to language as well: if a student knocked over another's blocks, a third was likely to instruct the offender: 'Say, "Sorry!"' And when one student barged into another's game, she might be told: 'You have to ask, "Can I play with you?"' And although all the instruction from the teachers into the practices of school took place in English, subteaching in Classroom Three also took place in Nepali.

In the following example, Kritika engaged in subteaching with Monal around the practice of nametags. In Classroom Three, the children each had a small Velcro nametag in the shape of a person. During free play time, the children took the nametag to their area of choice and attached it to a small piece of Velcro on the wall nearby to mark their official presence in the area. Since the teachers only permitted a limited number of children in each area, a free Velcro spot meant there was room to play. In this example, which took place at the sand table in late October during free play time, Monal left to play somewhere else but forgot to take his nametag with him. Kritika noticed and sought to remedy the situation (original speech in **bold**, original Nepali in ***bold italics***; English translation underneath in regular typeface):

Kritika: (*Notices that Monal's nametag has been left at the sand table, calls to Padma*)
Padma::: tyo sathi lai bolau bolau! Padma::: eh! Padma::: tyo sathi lai bolauna!
Padma::: call that friend, will you! Padma::::! Hey Padma::::! Please call that friend!

Kritika: (*Padma does not hear; Kritika calls to Monal herself*)
Aauna Monal!
Monal, come here!

Kritika: (*Monal does not materialize; Kritika brushes off her hands and yells in English*)
Missus! Missus! Missus! I am done.

Dinesh: (*Has been waiting for a turn, points to Kritika's nametag*)
Done *bhane nikaalnuni yo.*
If you are done you better take this out.
(*He tries to hand her nametag to her*)

Kritika: *(Puts her name back on the Velcro)*
Haat dhora garnu parchha haau. Haat dhora jarnu parchha.
You do it after washing hands, silly. You do it after washing hands.

(Video, 29 October 2012, reprinted with permission from Bernstein, 2018)

Here, Kritika not only showed that she knew the practices around nametag use; she also engaged in the teacher-like behavior of enlisting another student to retrieve Monal for her. Only when that did not work did she leave the sand table herself to return the tag to Monal. As she prepared to leave, Dinesh, who had been waiting nearby, tried to engage in subteaching with Kritika about taking her own nametag. Kritika, however, refuted this attempt, calling him 'silly' and reminding him that she had to wash her hands first. As this example shows, while subteaching was a way to socialize others into the practices of the classroom, it was also a way to demonstrate one's own competence in those practices. This highlights the closely intertwined nature of participation in the classroom practices and social positioning, and foreshadows the findings in the next chapter.

6 Becoming Students, Becoming Speakers: Positioning in the Social Field of Classroom Three

It is within the multiple layers of context described in the previous chapters that I turn to the cases of Padma, Hande, Rashmi and Kritika. This chapter traces the social trajectory of the four girls from the first fall day when I met them to the end of the school year. On paper, the four students looked quite similar: all were female, were four years old and were born in the United States to parents who had arrived as refugees. Each spoke a language other than English at home and none had been to school or daycare before their year in this classroom. Yet, once they began school, their social paths diverged sharply. In this chapter, I analyze how each student came to occupy a particular place in the social fabric of the class: for instance, how Kritika came to be seen as a leader, a competent student and a central figure in the classroom social network, while Rashmi came to be known as a troublemaker who remained on the periphery of the class.

In this chapter, I use three converging qualitative data sources – teacher interviews, field notes, and video transcripts of student interactions – to examine how students were discursively positioned within the classroom. Additionally, I use student interviews, in which students indicated whom they liked to play with, to quantify and visualize the social structure of the class through social network maps, a tool borrowed from Social Network Analysis. Social Network Analysis (SNA) is a theoretical framework for thinking about how members of social networks can influence each other in various ways, like providing support, information, or in this case, linguistic input. SNA uses quantitative data to map relationships among groups of people and to understand how those relationships affect the spread of resources. Because of this study's presumption that peer interaction, particularly with English speakers, is important for English learning, social network mapping provides a visual and numeric representation of how connected students are within the classroom peer network.

(See Appendix 2 for further details about data collection and analysis in this chapter.)

Kritika's Story

When I first met Kritika in September, she had just turned four. She spoke Nepali at home and in the community around her, though she watched some TV in English and could sing the first few lines of a popular South Asian ABC song, 'A for Apple, B for Ball' (https://tinyurl.com/nepaliABCsong). Kritika's round face wore a serious expression, and her height and posture gave her an air of someone older than just four, but the twinkle in her big brown eyes hinted at a mischievous streak. While other children cried as their parents left them at school during that first month, Kritika was stoic. From the beginning of the year, Kritika took everything in. She quickly learned how to assume a listening posture during circle time, when to speak or to be quiet, and how to perform the motions and then the words of the daily 'Good Morning' song. She was constantly watching other students and gauging teachers' reactions. Just a few weeks into the year, she could follow classroom procedures and routines and even enforce them among her less watchful Nepali-speaking peers, as in the example at the end of Chapter 5. In these reminders to her peers, Kritika positioned herself as competent and knowing with regard to classroom comportment. By November, Kritika's teachers also positioned her as a knower, a helper, and a sweet, socially competent child:

> And there's uh Kritika, who's also very loving. She likes to sing me happy birthday songs, she likes to walk over and give me a kiss on the cheek like nobody else. She too is actually from Nepal and um (4.0) kinda helps me with these other kids a little bit to redirect them 'cause she- she's pretty much on task. U:::m I would guess her only real weakness like other children who are from another country is their language barrier. But she is very very wonderful and pretty and very you know easy to get along with, so she's really at the top of her class. (Lucia, interview, 16 November 2012)

Lucia's assessment of Kritika is based on many things, including her demeanor, her behavior toward the teachers, her subteaching with other students, and her appearance. All of these contribute to her positioning as a competent student, despite her 'language barrier,' and place her, although I did not ask Lucia to rank the students, 'at the top of her class.'

Early in the fall, when Kritika and her classmates were just beginning to understand English, their teachers allowed them more leeway with classroom rules than they allowed the English speakers. Ellen and Lucia emphasized that the English speakers, as speakers of the classroom language, should be able to follow rules, telling them things like: 'Come on, you understand me.' Yet, as early as October, Kritika's teachers held expectations for her that were different from the other emergent bilingual students. In October, I documented at circle time:

> The teachers have tried to curb the practice [that had developed over the first month of school] of students jumping up and running to the middle of the circle when their name is called in the Good Morning song. Out of the first several students to be called, each of the Nepali speakers gets up anyway. Ellen, who seems tired this morning, sighs and shakes her head, laughing slightly, but ignoring it for today. But when Kritika stands up, Ellen gestures for her to sit down, shaking her head emphatically. 'No. Kritika you know better.' (Field notes, 22 October 2012)

These kinds of interactions further positioned Kritika as a rule-knower (if temporary forgetter), distinct from the other emergent bilingual students and more like the English speakers in the class.

Yet, Kritika was not all compliance and quiet and folded hands. As a person who knew the rules and was a careful observer of classroom practices, she also was adept at subverting them, like using the teachers' turned back to tickle a friend, or using the rules as a cover, as when she carried her nametag with her as she wandered the room, so that it looked as if she was simply switching play areas. During free play times, in a classroom where the teachers were swimming in new paperwork, in food preparation, and in working on individual projects with students, attention was often only given to more obvious instances of misbehavior, and Kritika had plenty of chances to capitalize on these tactics.

The space that the teachers allowed the children during play times also meant that rules were broken and disputes arose out of the view of the teachers. While for the English speakers this often meant running to the teacher to tattle, it was nearly impossible early in the year for emergent bilinguals to recount transgressions in English to their busy teachers, especially if they took place out of sight and thus could not be conveyed by pointing. Instead, the Nepali speakers often turned to Kritika, a rule-knower and enforcer, to whom they could recount incidents in their first language. Even once the Nepali-speaking students *could* tattle to teachers, Kritika was still often called to hear reports of transgressions, to intervene and to judge. Each request further solidified Kritika's position as a classroom authority figure and a teacher proxy.

A few months into the year, Kritika's Nepali-speaking peers also began to ask her for help in mediating interactions in English. In following transcript in Table 6.1, Hande (L1 = Turkish) and Prakesh (L1 = Nepali) have been playing together and having a good time making pretend ice cream at the sand table. As the transcript begins, Rashmi,

Becoming Students, Becoming Speakers 89

Table 6.1 Rashmi and Prakesh attempt to evict Hande from the sand table (Reprinted with permission from Bernstein, 2018)

Free Play Time – 19 November

 4:33 (*Prakesh and Hande are playing at the sand table and have been playing peacefully for 4 minutes*)	 4:43 (*Rashmi approaches and speaks from outside the camera shot*) **'Praku! Niskina sand bata?'** 'Praku! Will you come out of the sand?'
 4:44 (*Prakesh counters, looking at Hande*) **'Yeslai niski garta?'** 'Can't you get <u>her</u> [Hande] out?'	 4:47 (*Rashmi argues back*) **'Nai ta nai niskina'.** 'Why don't <u>you</u> come out?'
 4:48 (*Prakesh turns to Hande and tries to tell her to leave in English*) **'Get out! It the Rashmi!'** (*Hande doesn't look up*)	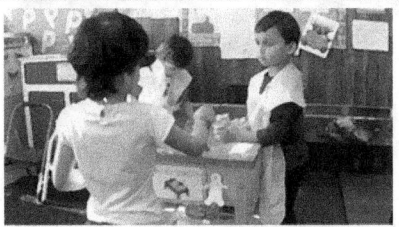 4:58 (*Rashmi tries again*) **'Prakesh, niskina!'** 'Prakesh, come out!'
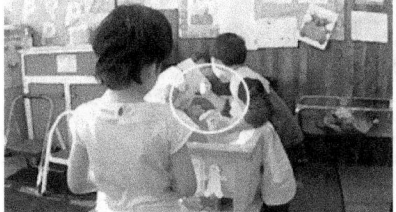 5:02 (Prakesh to Rashmi) **'Niskidina.'** 'I will not get out.' (*Prakesh turns to Hande, pointing away from the table and speaks in English*) **'Hey get out!!!'**	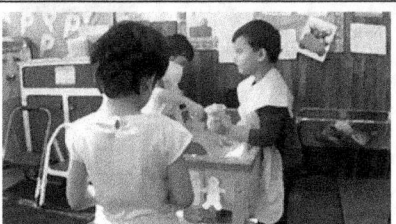 5:05 (*Hande doesn't acknowledge him. Prakesh looks ahead, brow furrowed*) **'Yellai bhaneko ki.'** 'I'm <u>telling</u> her.'

(*Continued on next page*)

90 (Re)defining Success in Language Learning

Table 6.1 Rashmi and Prakesh attempt to evict Hande from the sand table (Reprinted with permission from Bernstein 2018) (Continued)

Free Play Time – 19 November

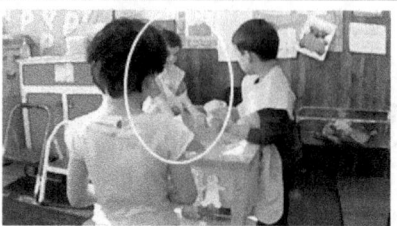

5:08 (*Hande, unaware of the plot against her, shows off her tower to Prakesh*) **'Ta da!'**

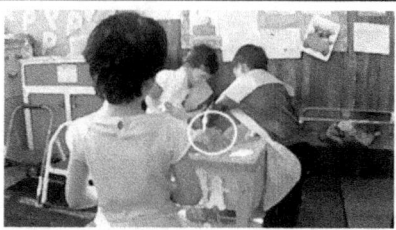

5:09 (*Prakesh knocks over her tower*)

5:13 (*Prakesh laughs*) **'Bigardeko yesko!'**
'I'm ruining hers!'

5:18 (*Rashmi tells Prakesh*)
'Yellai aaru bigar gardena, garta!'
'Ruin more of hers, ok?'

5:20 (*Rashmi hits Hande*)

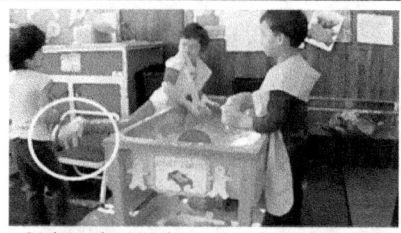

5:21 (*Hande, giggling, gives her a kick back*)

5:24 (*Rashmi tries to tell Hande to leave in English*)
'You outing from!'

5:28 (*Hande goes back to playing. Rashmi waits. Kritika comes over to peer into the video camera*)

(*Continued on next page*)

Table 6.1 Rashmi and Prakesh attempt to evict Hande from the sand table (Reprinted with permission from Bernstein 2018) (Continued)

Free Play Time – 19 November

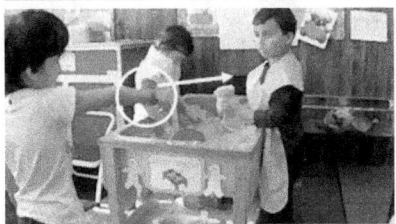

5:32 (*Rashmi asks Kritika for help, explaining*)
'Ma sandma aaune bhaneko ki herna! Yo niskidai niskidaina.'
'I am thinking of going in the sand, but this one's not coming out!'
(*Points first to Prakesh…*)

5:33 (*…then quickly moves her hand to point to Hande.*)

5:37 (*Kritika asks Prakesh*)
'Ta niskine ki naniskine?'
'Are you going to come out or not?'

5:38 (*Rashmi and Prakesh both point to Hande; Rashmi tells Kritika*)
'Yellai bhanna yellai! Yellai bhanna!'
'No, tell her! Tell her!'

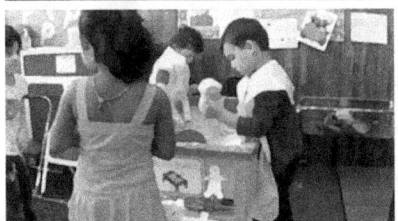

05:43 (*Kritika looks at Rashmi*)
'Ma bhandinani yellai chi.'
'I am not going to tell her.'

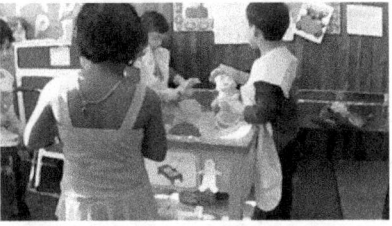

05:45 (*Prakesh tries again in English*)
'Hey, get out!'
(*Kritika examines her name tag in her hand*)

6:01 (*Kritika finally tells Hande*)
'Hey girl, go away!'
(*When Kritika speaks, Hande pays attention*)

Prakesh's cousin, comes to play at the table. Rashmi and Prakesh then try to get Hande to leave, recruiting Kritika for help.

The example in Table 6.1 illustrates that, as someone who was a rule follower, Kritika was reluctant to tell Hande to leave. Yet, it also highlights Kritika's peers' confidence that she could intervene on their behalf.

In general, Kritika preferred imaginative and highly verbal games like 'house', and it was in Nepali that her cleverness, articulateness and authority were clear. So, she chose to play mostly with the other Nepali-speaking girls, among whom she was a popular and in-demand playmate. Yet, Kritika's maturity, fairness and attention to rules made her a safe choice as a playmate for everyone, and she was sought out by English and Nepali speakers alike. By the spring, her centrality in the class overall was clear and, through repeated positioning, her overwhelmingly positive identity – as a competent and authoritative classmate, playmate and student – had solidified. In student interviews, Kritika was cited as a preferred playmate by more classmates than any other student and by both Nepali and English speakers. The social network map created from this interview data (see Figure 6.1) shows her central location in the classroom network. (Arrows toward Kritika mean a peer cited her as a friend; arrows away mean she cited another peer as a friend.)

Across the year, Kritika secured a similarly positive and authoritative position in the teachers' eyes. By spring, there were no recorded instances of teachers scolding Kritika, even when she was half of an offending pair

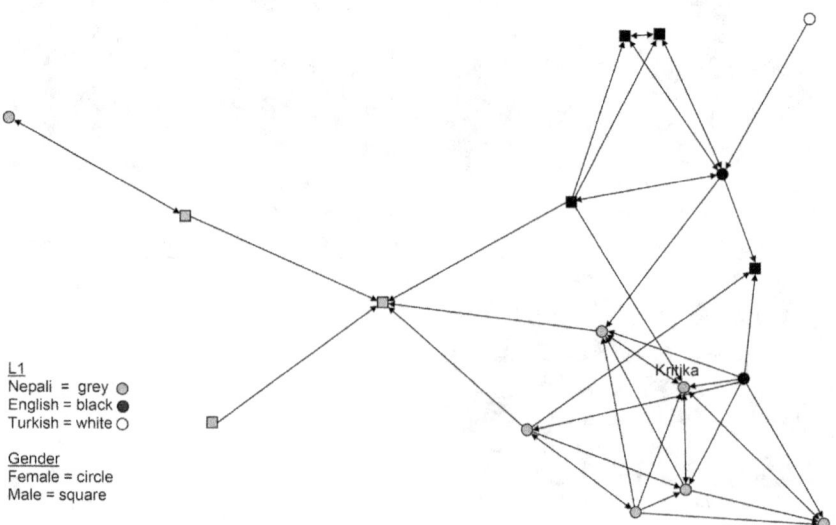

Figure 6.1 Social network map – Kritika

of students, and the teachers also spoke highly of her in their end-of-year interviews:

> **Katie (researcher)**: What do you think it means to be a successful kid in preK? To have a successful year?
>
> **Lucia**: To know that we want you to keep your hands to yourself. When we talk about rules and routines, that we want you to follow them. So when I have a child like Kritika and Kelsey[1] – to name some names, to give you the name with the face. This is what we call a successful child. That if we ask them clean up, they clean up, to sit down they sit down, to sit crisscross, to raise a quiet hand. To wait your turn and to share. That are able to possess or act on these behaviors that we are teaching you to do. (Lucia, Interview, 11 June 2013)

Ellen, interviewed separately and asked the same question, said:

> Kritika – Kritika was you know, she kind of got along with everybody I thought. She was a good little girl, she listened, she was very smart, I think she's gonna do really well next year. I think she could have gone to kindergarten this year I think. (Ellen, interview, 11 June 2013).

Padma's Story

Padma was 10 days younger than Kritika and had recently turned four when I met her. She was also a Nepali speaker. Each day in September, after Padma watched her grandmother walk out of the classroom, she spent the first ten minutes of the morning in tears, her tiny shoulders hunched over, staring down at her sock-and-sandal-covered feet. She usually allowed another parent to open her breakfast cereal and took a few half-hearted bites, her round black eyes looking mournfully at the door. Padma was the youngest in her household, composed of a sister in first grade, parents who worked full time, a young uncle and a grandmother. Her grandmother took care of her, walking her to and from school, even when it snowed. Where other children missed school when their parents had scheduling conflicts or had to work an odd shift, Padma's grandmother made sure that Padma never missed school. Padma was the student who showed up at 8:30 am when there was a two-hour snow delay that her grandma had not heard about, then walked home, and returned at 10:30. Although Padma was just ten days younger than Kritika, she was a full head shorter and at least 10 pounds lighter. In the fall, between her tears and her petite frame, she quickly became a student to whom the teachers used terms of endearment, like 'doll baby' and 'sweetheart.' One morning in October, for instance, I recorded Lucia saying to her: 'You're so sweet (*looks at Teacher Ellen*). Isn't she sweet? Little Padma, little doll baby. C'mere (*hugs her*)' (Video, 29 October

2012). Padma's positioning as 'little,' 'cute,' and 'sweet' in those first months of school made her a non-threatening (and thus tolerated and sometimes even welcomed) playmate among both English- and Nepali-speaking children, but also an easy target for other students to take dolls from or push out of the way. It was not usual to hear howls of 'Heeeey, *mero naaaaaani!*' ('Hey, my doll!') coming from her in the house corner. Often, Kritika came to her aid and, by October, the two had become close friends. Kritika kept track of Padma and helped Padma keep track of the rules, for which Padma did not have the same zeal as Kritika. The two played together frequently and, at lunch, chatted easily in Nepali, unbothered by conversations around them.

By mid-October, Padma did not mind coming to school so much. She rushed in to see Kritika, was excited to learn the letters that her older sister (her *didi*) talked about at home, and loved to take care of the baby dolls in the house corner. She darted around the room with quick movements and was a curious explorer. She was more interested than any of the other students in what I was doing in the classroom and whether she could write in my notebooks too. In October, she started to greet me with a loud, 'Hi Miss Katie!', when I came in on Mondays, and she began to find her voice throughout the day as well, singing loudly, standing up for herself and asking frequently, in both English and Nepali, 'What's that?' and '*Yu ke ho?*' As she became happier to be at school and found her voice in English and Nepali, her positioning shifted as well. Even by November, she was positioned less and less as sweet and more as spunky and stubborn. In my fall interview with Lucia, she described her thus:

> The:::n we have Padma (*downward tone*) who um (2.0) you know her strength is that um (2.0) she really clinged to Kritika, and I think Kritika has taken her under her wing. So she's got some good friendships and she's learned to speak up more and to I think accept us more, where [at first] she was more upset about being here, where I just don't think she really wanted to come. And I think that she had trouble understanding us 'cause they probably don't speak English at home and then it just might not have been home. ... But all and all she's done well. She is stubborn. But that's okay. That's her way of communicating. It's alright. Other than that, she's no problem. (Lucia, interview, 16 November 2012)

While teachers saw her as stubborn, and characterized her less positively than they did Kritika (in fact, her biggest strength was her friendship *with* Kritika), they also did not position her negatively. In fact, her stubbornness was not treated as defiance or lack of awareness of rules, but as an understandable boundary-testing from a tiny girl with a lot of spirit. Their reminders to her were often given with a smile and a shake of the head and were generally gentle. Though she was certainly not positioned by teachers (or students) as an authority on classroom rules, school knowledge or social norms, she was considered competent in them, if not always compliant. Over the year, her identity as Kritika's friend who was 'no problem,' solidified. She was not a student that teachers worried about or who caused trouble, nor was she a standout like Kritika or Kelsey. Spring interviews reflected this:

Padma::::? Padma Padma Padma. Yea::::h (2.0) Padma's um she got- she came along. You know she was very shy at first, she was crying every day. And then she stopped doing that, you know. And then she'd come in smiling. She:::- Yeah, I'd like to see her talk a little more English. She was not saying very much. But she got along well with the kids. She was a good little girl. (Ellen, interview, 11 June 2013)

Among her peers, as the year went on, Padma was welcomed into play as a friend of Kritika, but playing with her often required negotiation – over dolls, space, seats, etc. Her humor, energy and creativity (like the time she dotted red paint on two students' foreheads, drew *mendhi* on their hands, and staged a pretend wedding) seemed to make it worthwhile for her Nepali-speaking peers to take the time for these negotiations, but she was not a preferred playmate of her English-speaking classmates, with whom she had more trouble working things out. Nonetheless she had positive interactions with them, using humor to compensate for a lack of words. One day in the gym, for example, she caught Kelsey's runaway ball. Kelsey, expecting a struggle, approached confrontationally: 'Hey that's *my* ball.' Padma, laughing, insisted '*My* ball,' yet at the same time, tossed it back to Kelsey, who laughed, too (Field notes, 29 October 2012).

Padma's location in the social mapping of the classroom reflects her position as less central to the class overall (see Figure 6.2, in fact, by June, three of the six English-speaking children with whom she had spent the last nine months were unable to give her name in the interview.) Yet, she was still well connected within the cluster of Nepali-speaking girls. And although she cited only Kritika as a friend, three children, including one English speaker, cited her as a friend.

What the student map does not reflect is that Padma also enjoyed interactions with the adults in the room. 'Look Miss Ellen!' she could often be heard to say, and she enjoyed helping to set up for snack, as long as she could hold a baby doll in one hand. When I was in the room, she often invited me to play, and it was clear by the end of the year that she considered me a friend. She was the only child to ever climb onto my lap and she was often the last one at the snack table, forgetting to eat as she engaged me in repeating lines from 'Twinkle Twinkle Little Star' or pointing out things around the room, and then, later in the year, in conversation. Her teachers were never quite convinced that I enjoyed these interactions (although I did) and frequently chided her to 'Stop talking to Miss Katie and finish eating' or to 'Let Miss Katie write her notes.'

96 (Re)defining Success in Language Learning

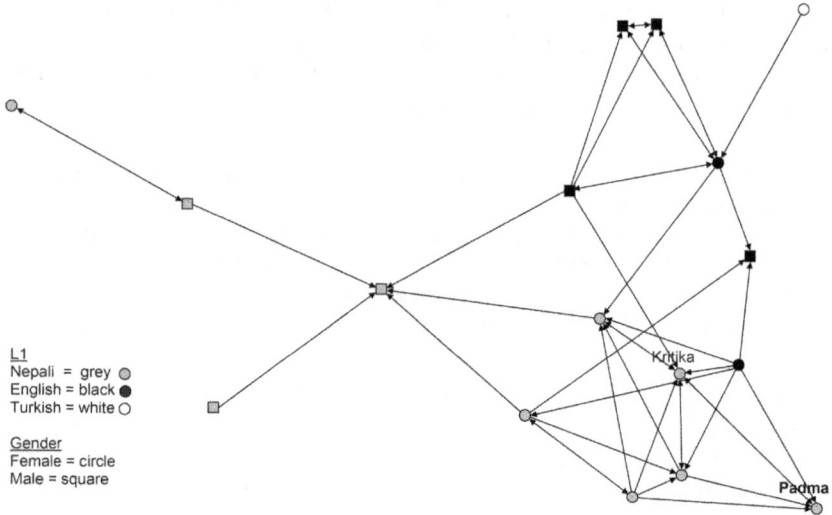

Figure 6.2 Social network map – Padma

Rashmi's Story

Rashmi was half a year younger than Kritika and Padma, with an early spring birthday, and also came from a Nepali-speaking family. She was tall and thin – all knees and elbows – and bright black eyes shone from her angular face. Unlike the other girls in the class, who wore a collection of pink and red and lace and frills, Rashmi preferred pants and sweatshirts, especially yellow ones – her favorite color. It is hard to tell her story without telling the story of her cousin, Prakesh, as well. She and Prakesh were one month apart in age, although their fathers, who were brothers, were nearly 15 years apart. Rashmi was therefore the youngest, and probably last, child in her family, while Prakesh was the first. They lived in apartments in the same building, and one of their fathers usually brought both children to school. They seemed to transition seamlessly from playing together at home to playing together at school, to the point where it seemed that they did not realize that the rules had changed. In the fall, the teachers spent a lot of time trying to get their attention and to have them focus on whatever the rest of the class was focused on.

Rashmi enjoyed meals and participated in conversations in Nepali with the other children, but free play time was Rashmi's favorite, when she could play with Prakesh undisturbed, preferably at the sand table. Circle time and nap time were the hardest times of day for her. These activities required her to do two things that she found very difficult – keep her body still and her mouth quiet. At circle time she fidgeted and talked continuously, sometimes in Nepali to Prakesh, sometimes singing, sometime repeating an interesting word in English over and over again. Scolding rarely helped, nor did having a teacher sit with her, so the teachers mostly ignored her and just carried on, talking over her. At nap, when the room was supposed to be silent, her talk was more problematic. Other students could be shushed with a sharp glance or word, a finger to the lips, or even just a teacher's presence nearby, but Rashmi could not be quieted. On more than one occasion, her teachers became so frustrated that they had to walk away. On other occasions, when they simply tried to ignore her and work on things in other parts of the room, they returned to find her mat dismantled with the blanket and pillows thrown a few feet in any direction, and once, nearly all of her clothes off. Yet, Rashmi seemed quite happy at school and could make her teachers and peers laugh at her antics. It was as if she simply did not realize that there was something else she was supposed to be doing and that everyone else was already doing it. And she was never positioned by her teachers as angry or intentionally defiant, just 'still learning.' As Lucia described her in the fall:

> Uh Rashmi is also from Nepal. She's our most hyper child. She's uh (.) in her own world. She's a wonderful girl though ... She has done some things that are quite funny but you can't laugh in front of them 'cause then you encourage it. So you really gotta keep a straight face and turn around and hide and laugh ... she needs a little more one-on-one. We have to help her family know that she needs a little more assistance knowing how to listen, follow the rules, stay on task ... this kind of environment isn't so easy for certain children. You know other children, they can grasp when we're doing planning, when we're going to work time and we want you to stay in an area and if you're playing in blocks, keep those items in block. Some of them may want to 'travel' and they don't get it yet. 'Cause this isn't Kansas, this isn't home. (Lucia, interview, 16 November 2012)

By late fall, although Rashmi was still always moving and often talking, she began to tune in at circle time. Videos show her sometimes paying attention to the stories teachers read and at times even commenting on them. Yet her teachers, used to ignoring her talk as irrelevant unless it disrupted others, seemed not to notice these comments as distinct from the rest of her talk, and they ignored them. And Rashmi, whose interest lay in the books and not the teacher talk, usually missed the sanctioned opportunities to talk that came after reading the text. During the reading of a book about seasons, for example, Rashmi commented on each page and was ignored by her teacher and classmates. Yet, when the teacher asked the very question that Rashmi had been answering all along, Rashmi was looking away and seemed not to hear:

Teacher: (*reads a page about apples*)
Rashmi: I like apple.

Teacher:	(*reads a page about pumpkins*)
Rashmi:	I like pumpkin.
Teacher:	(*reads a page about hungry squirrels*)
Rashmi:	I like hungry.
Teacher:	(*reads a page about snow, looks up to class*) Who likes snow?
Rashmi:	(*looking toward other side of circle, does not raise hand, or perhaps hear*)

(Video, 5 November 2012)

In March, as Ellen read a book about friends, Rashmi shouted '*Saati! Saati!*' over and over. The teachers shushed and then ignored her. When I later pointed out to the teachers that *saati* means friend in Nepali, Ellen was at first shocked that Rashmi might have been on-task, but then speculated that Rashmi's comment must have just been coincidental. By this point in the year, Rashmi's position as less competent academically and in school norms had been cemented.

Among her peers, Rashmi was often on the edge of action as well. Toward the middle of the year, Prakesh began to play with Joey, one of the English speakers in the class. When Prakesh was with Joey, Rashmi chose to play in the house corner, where she liked to take care of the baby dolls, wrapping them and unwrapping them in blankets, pushing them in the grocery cart, and cooking for them with the pretend food. She narrated in Nepali as she played, more alongside other children than with them, but her narration allowed them to come and go into her game, sometimes for extended time periods. While she was happy to engage as long as they were doing what she was already doing, she was not interested in collaboration or sharing, and often took other children by surprise by leaving mid-play or by making off with some item that they thought they had been using together *with* her.

Rashmi's unpredictability made her a tolerated, but never sought-out playmate among the Nepali-speaking girls, and she was one of the children regularly scolded by Kritika. Rashmi was also someone who was generally intentionally avoided by her English-speaking peers. On the rare occasion that she was invited into play in English, the lack of uptake on her part made it less likely that the other children would ask again any time soon. The following example from my field notes provides a contrast between the way Rashmi engaged with the ongoing play of Joy and Joey, two English-speaking students, and the way that two other Nepali-speaking girls did.

Joy, Joey, and I [Katie] are in the housekeeping corner one morning in April. Joy and Joey have lined up four chairs next to each other in a row. Joy holds out a baby to me and invites me to 'get in the car' with it. The three of us sit in the row of chairs with our babies on our laps and begin 'driving'.

Padma wanders over. Joy invites her to join us ('Do you want to come in our car?') and she gets in the car. I give Padma my baby. She thanks me and asks, 'Where we go?' Joy tells her, 'To the grocery store.' 'Okay!' she says. Joy lists some things we are going to buy and Padma nods along. When we get to the 'store' and get out of the car, Padma hands me my baby and leaves.

A little later, Maiya (a three-year-old Nepali speaker who joined the class mid-year) comes up to us. Joy says, 'Maiya, want to come in our car?' Maiya nods and comes to sit next to me. 'Want to hold my baby?' I ask, holding it out to her. She nods again. She stays for around 5 minutes, listening to Joy and Joey talk about going to work, etc. She leaves after a while.

Almost right after that, Rashmi comes in and tries to take Joy's baby from her. 'No!' Joy says sharply, jerking the baby away, eyebrows furrowed. Then she changes her tone, 'But you can come in our car,' she says gently. Rashmi looks at her blankly. 'Do you want to come in the car?' Joy asks again, with her eyebrows raised and in an even higher, almost mother-ese pitch. Rashmi doesn't seem to understand. She looks at Joy for a moment longer and then leaves. (Field notes, 15 April 2012)

Rashmi's entry into the scene was typical for her. She did not seem to realize that taking Joy's doll would make Joy angry. While Joy was more generous in this situation than most other students would have been, inviting Rashmi into play even after this transgression, the absence of any uptake on Rashmi's part – either from lack of interest or lack of understanding – eliminated the possibility for a positive interaction between Rashmi, Joey and Joy. Through the end of the year, Rashmi continued to be a tolerated playmate of the Nepali-speaking children, but never the preferred playmate of anyone but Prakesh. In interviews, she cited and was cited as a friend by only Prakesh. See Figure 6.3.

At the end of the year, too, the teachers' comments about Rashmi were strikingly similar to those that they made seven months earlier, highlighting the stability of Rashmi's identity from the initial positionings in the fall:

We gotta work on behavior. I mean she was hurting a lot of kids and even still though a lot of kids played with her which I thought was – 'cause she would you know she'd hit, she'd push, so I was surprised at that. She *does* have a good little personality. You know she just has to learn how to control herself. Um, 'cause you would tell her 'no' for something and she would- like when I [set up] that water table, she said, 'I want water table,' and I said, 'Yeah, you know, in your turn' and she then she just went over and put the toys in and started playing there. And I was like, 'N-n-n-n-no, you can't do that. Now you can't go there at all! You know you have to learn the rules.' So, she's gotta work on that. Working on learning the rules and calming down. Very hyper. Sometimes at nap time she's flipping flips and I mean ... (*deep sigh*) (Ellen, interview, 11 June 2013)

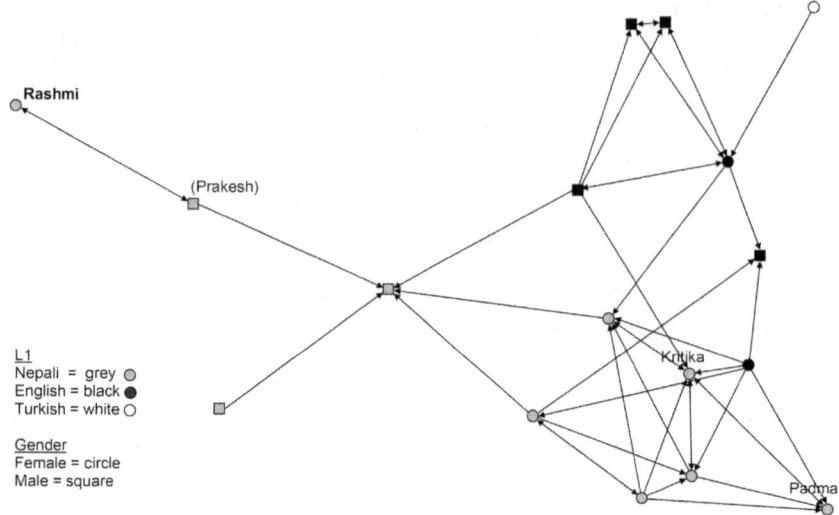

Figure 6.3 Social network map – Rashmi

Ellen and Lucia maintained deep affection for Rashmi across the year, although she continued to both shock and exhaust them. Both teachers were glad that Rashmi would be returning to their classroom for a second year of pre-kindergarten the following year, because neither teacher thought Rashmi was anywhere close to ready for kindergarten. They joked however, that they would need a lot of rest during the summer to get ready for a second year with her.

Hande's Story

When I met Hande, she had already been four years old since the spring. Of the four focal children, she was the only one who would make the September 1 birthday cutoff to start kindergarten the following fall. Hande was also the only Turkish speaker in the class. Hande lived with her parents, her sister and 13 other relatives in a small apartment not far from the school, where she spoke Turkish with everyone. Hande had wide, curious eyes and when she laughed, revealing a big toothy smile, her eyes laughed, too. Hande's short wavy hair was usually tied into two tiny pigtails that stood up on the top of her head, and she wore her favorite Minnie or Mickey Mouse shirts as often as possible. Hande came to the class a few weeks after school began, and, far into October, she still cried and clung to her mother in the morning, as her mother awkwardly stood next to the breakfast table, unable to talk with either the English-speaking teachers and parents or the Nepali-speaking ones. Hande was quiet during her first weeks, without a language in common with anyone in the class, and she did a lot of watching other children and drawing elaborate pictures alone at the art table. Although she was one of the oldest children, her teachers connected her quietness with being little, sweet and cute. Ellen told me in the fall:

> Um little Hande didn't come into the class until- I think towards the end of September she came in so she missed the first week and she was upset and crying in the beginning. And she has a different language – she's Turkish. So she's not even understanding the English *or* the Nepali children. So that's you know, but yet she starting to pick up- I just see them picking up little words here and there. The words that we keep saying over and over and over like 'milk,' 'breakfast,' 'bathroom,' you know, 'walk,' 'quiet' (*laughing*). (Ellen, interview, 16 November 2012)

Lucia explained:

> Hande who's our – probably our only – family from Turkey who too you know has a mom who can barely speak English. Her mom's really sweet. She's talking to me a little more. (2.0) Uh she [Hande] can barely speak English. She's a cutie. She's opening up, she's <u>very</u> artistic. She's very kind um we don't have any problems with her, so that's great (*rising tone*). (Lucia, interview, 16 November 2012)

Lucia connected Hande's quietness with her not causing any problems, which foreshadowed how Hande's positioning would change as she began to use more and more English. In the first few months, though, Hande sought connections with other students through close observation and carefully timed physical action. For example, during one interaction at the sand table (5 November 2012), she tried to add sand to her peer's sand tower and was first told, sharply: 'No that's mine!' She then spent almost a full minute carefully watching her peer pour sand onto his sand pile (Image 1) before making eye contact and offering him full cups of sand (Image 2). Eventually, the other student realized that she was helping and allowed her to participate in pouring sand on the tower.

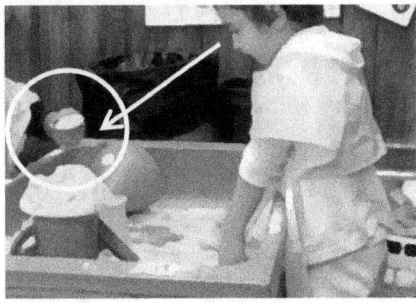 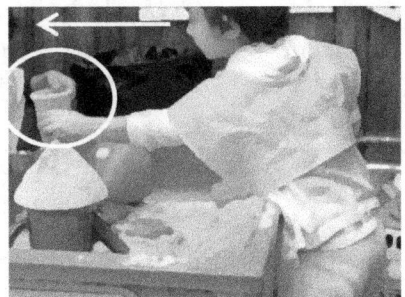

Image 1 Hande's close observation

Image 2 Hande's carefully timed physical action

In one-on-one interactions, Hande became successful at using similar strategies: showing her willingness to engage on peers' terms, being generous, and helping with ongoing activity rather than trying to direct play. While these strategies positioned her as a non-threat and allowed her entry into peers' interactions, they also positioned her as an expendable playmate who was easily ousted when a better option came along (as in the example when Kritika was enlisted to remove her from the sand table). Frequently, Hande would participate in a game, but when the roles or rules or players shifted, she would lose her place. On occasion, after being generous over and over again, Hande got angry and left an interaction. In the following example, Hande was playing at the playdough table with several students and was repeatedly asked for playdough or had it grabbed from her.

Kelsey: Hande, can I have some- a little bit more red? I'll give you more blue if you give me a little- a lot more red.
Hande: (*gives*)
...
Three minutes later.
Pooja: (*speaking in inaudible Nepali to Padma*) (*points to Hande*)
Padma: (*tries to take playdough from Hande*)
Hande: No! (*takes back*)
...
Two minutes later.
Tommy tries to take some of Hande's playdough
Hande: No, please no touch (*pulling his hand away*)
Tommy: Just a little.
Hande: Ok! I give it to you, I give it to you! (*gives*)
...
Two minutes later.
Pooja: (*to Hande*) You making a pumpkin?
Hande: Yeah, I make it with this one (*holds up cookie cutter*) But you can't get it! Somebody's playing with it! Want heart? (*stands up and points to other cutter on table*)

Pooja looks confused and goes back to playing.

(Video, 6 May 2013)

Although in the final exchange, Pooja was only asking about what Hande was making, by this time, every single one of Hande's interactions had been with peers trying to take something from her and she was not interested in another round. So, rather than answering, she tried

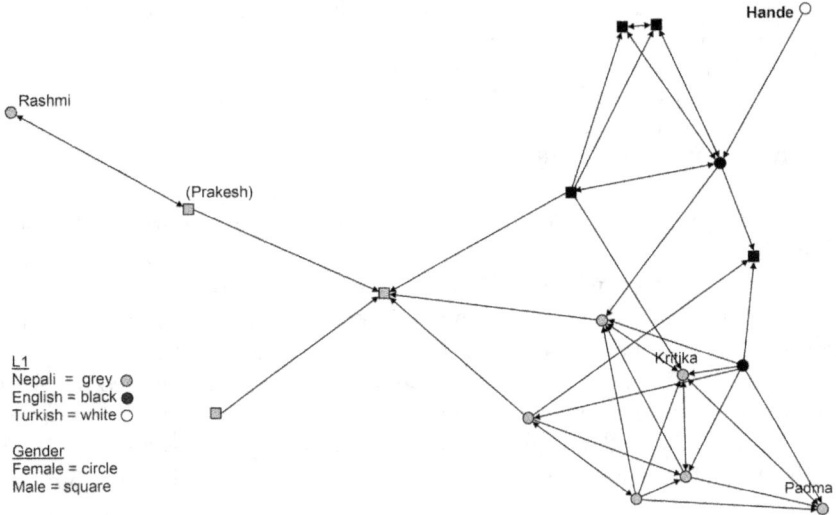

Figure 6.4 Social network map – Hande

to redirect Pooja's attention to another cookie cutter, other than hers. Pooja, confused, ended the conversation and Hande missed out on a positive peer interaction. This example shows how positioning that started as other-imposed could become self-imposed and could sediment into something more lasting.

Over the year, Hande found various ways to enter into play and she did have some enjoyable interactions with a variety of students, but she was never a valued playmate. In student interviews, no one cited her as someone they liked to play with and she cited only one other student, Kelsey, the only kindergarten-bound English-speaking girl in the class, as a friend (see Figure 6.4).

In the teachers' eyes, Hande's identity never quite solidified the way that many other students' identities had. Across the year, she was first the quiet loner, then a too-silly and boisterous squirmer, before finally returning to someone who liked to play on her own, though never retreating back into her former silence. Her positionings, however, were never very positive, except with reference to her artwork. Ellen's comments in June reflect Hande's uncertain social place and Ellen's own uncertainty about Hande's future:

> Uh Hande? Hande did not uh- well, towards the end she was speaking a lot more English I thought, but um she didn't play with the- a lot of kids I didn't think. She kind of was by herself, and again, too, it was like she had a totally different language from everybody. She didn't speak English and she didn't speak Nepali. So she was kinda *(laughing)* like the outsider completely. So she did have- I mean considering.

Again, she was crying a lot, too, and then at the end of the year she was crying [again]. Yeah so I think you know I mean I don't know what's going to happen with her at kindergarten. She really didn't know a lot of the letters. Mom said she was going to put her in some sort of charter school. So I don't even know where she was going. (Ellen, interview, 11 June 2013)

Ellen's comment reflects a classroom social positioning for Hande that, like Rashmi's, was peripheral: 'by herself,' 'the outsider completely.' But unlike Rashmi, who may have been peripheral to her peers but still very much demanded her teachers' attention, Hande's quietness and good behavior meant that she mainly also escaped the attention of her teachers. Ellen had given up for Hande on what she had declared her own top priority for students: knowing their letters. And Ellen's comment reflects how she had resigned herself to not being able to communicate with Hande's mother enough to even know where Hande was going to kindergarten.

Together, the analyses in this chapter paint a picture of each focal student's position within the field of Classroom Three and patterns in how each student participated in Classroom Three's practices. I have shown how four students who looked so similar on paper – in age, gender, socioeconomics, schooling and past English experience – diverged sharply in classroom identity over their first year in school. In the next chapter, I discuss each student's language growth across the same year and address the question, posed in Chapter 1, of whether these different patterns of positioning and participation, by providing different opportunities for learning, would indeed mean different learning outcomes.

Note

(1) Within the context of Classroom Three, naming Kritika together with Kelsey further emphasized Kritika's overall success. Kelsey was considered by both teachers to be the most mature and brightest student in the class. In the fall, for example, Lucia said of Kelsey:

> We couldn't be any happier with Kelsey. She's as sweet as they come and very kind. And she's a little of a ring leader, where she's very cooperative with everybody and everybody kind of clings to her. And of course she so cute. Oh my goodness I do believe that she could be Miss America some day. [...] Hopefully she will continue to grow and to be just as terrific and well-rounded as she can be. (Lucia, Interview, November 16, 2012)

7 Who Learned What? Three Perspectives on Success in Language Learning

In the last chapter, I examined the ways that Kritika, Hande, Padma and Rashmi were positioned within Classroom Three as particular kinds of students, playmates and friends, and how, over time, their patterns of participation shaped (and were shaped by) that positioning. I also showed how they fit into the peer social network of the classroom. This chapter connects students' positioning and participation to their language learning. It turns to the question that drove the project: Would students who are more central to the class, who are positioned in more positive ways, and who therefore can access participation in more interactions, which might provide more opportunities to learn, show more growth in English?

I explore three different answers to this question through three theoretical lenses. First, I examine the perspective of the teachers. While the teachers might not have been able to name a formal theory of language learning or of what counts as language, I showed in Chapter 4 that they drew on their own experiences to engage in theory-building about how second language learning works and what would support it. Here, I examine how Ellen and Lucia brought those theories to bear on assessing students' English-learning outcomes. Second, I examine English learning through the perspective of language as a stable system. This is the theoretical perspective assumed in many studies examining the impact of interaction on language learning, in which language is seen as a dependent variable. Third, I use speech act theory as an approach to examining English learning through the lens of language as social practice, accounting for what students were able to *do* with English, in interactions with peers and teachers, within the social field of Classroom Three. For the first perspective, I draw on teacher interviews. For the second and third, I used the videos I had recorded across the year as language data, pulling each student's English utterances from the transcripts and compiling them together into a language corpus for each student. As I detail below, those corpora served as the basis for analyzing language as both a stable system and as social action.

Perspective 1: The Teachers

Ellen and Lucia did not regularly assess students' English acquisition. In fact, English acquisition was not one of the outcomes their Head Start measured at all.[1] Yet, both teachers had been quietly noting the students' progress, through their lenses of academic and social competence. In interviews at the end of the year, when I asked the teachers, 'Who are the kids that you saw as really successful in how their English developed over the year?' Lucia did not hesitate: 'Kritika. Number one in every which way. Writing her name, following the rules – talk about a successful student, she'll take the cake. Her and Kelsey[2], other world' (Lucia, interview, 11 June 2013).

When I asked Ellen who she thought made the most progress in English, she said that she wished she had a class list in front of her, so together we made a list of the students in the class. Ellen then answered by running her eyes over the list and musing aloud about whether each child would qualify as 'making the most progress':

> I mean Kritika came in knowing a lot. And especially that her mom speaks <u>none</u>, so I am really surprised about her you know. Monal, no. Pooja knew a lot already. Rashmi, <u>NO</u>. Hande, no. Anita, for a little girl, Anita could (*nodding*). Prakesh, no. Dinesh kind of knew some already, he made good- Sreya, no. That should be it right? I don't know, if I had to pick one that made the most progress ... Oh you don't have Padma. I don't know. Padma's ... (2.0) (*sighs*) I guess maybe- I don't know- Dinesh came in knowing a lot so it's hard to say. (4.0) Maybe Kritika (*downward tone*). (Ellen, interview, 11 June 2013)

Ellen's initial inclination was to name Kritika, but she discounted this idea right away, instead crediting Kritika as having begun school with a lot of English (which, as I show below, was not the case). Yet, immediately Ellen also recalled that Kritika's mother did not speak English, making it even less likely, but more impressive to Ellen, that Kritika would have 'come in knowing a lot.' Ellen then progressed through the list of students, either eliminating them as possible contenders or keeping them in the running. She eliminated two focal students, Hande and Rashmi, right away, Rashmi emphatically so. She also realized that we did not have Padma on the list, but she could not settle on whether Padma made good progress or not, sighing before moving on. At the end of this block of speech, Ellen returned to Kritika. The word 'maybe' suggested uncertainty, but her tone implied finality. She paused, then returned to her theory, described in Chapter 4, of language learning depending on exposure to English, both at home and at school:

> I think a factor which is very strange with Kritika is that her mother speaks none, but yet she made a lot of progress in the classroom with it [English]. And then, Monal whose dad speaks excellent English hardly made any. Dinesh, Dinesh's dad speaks excellent English. Maiya's mother and father speak nice English. Sreya::? Mmm, they're so so. Prakesh? Dad's ok, mom is not. So I don't know. I think the ones who are more outgoing, like Kritika and Dinesh, and even Maiya seemed to make more progress. Maybe it's because they spoke to the- you'll have to look back and see: did they speak to the English children more? Did they play with the English children more? You know what I'm saying? Like who did Kelsey [English speaker] play with besides Tommy and Luke and Joey and Caleb [other English speakers]? Like do you see her in the videos playing with- I don't really recall her playing with any of them [the emergent bilingual students]. (2.0) (*looking over list*) So but I mean if I had to pick one I'd say Kritika made the most progress (*sets list down and looks up*). (Ellen, interview, 11 June 2013)

As Ellen worked through her theories of what supported language learning, she maintained her focus on exposure through interaction, moving away from parents as important input providers to peers as potentially the most important. She then ended with the same conclusion, only more certain this time: Kritika made the most progress.

Note that the teachers' conclusions about language growth, in particular Ellen's, very closely track the general social positioning of the focal students in the class and the teachers' own evaluations of the four focal students. Lucia's response also explicitly connects (or conflates) English growth with other skills like name-writing and rule-following, showing how the teachers' perceptions of English growth reflect their learning priorities for students. What the teachers' comments do not reflect, as the next analysis shows, is how much the students learned by more standard measures of language growth, such as vocabulary or utterance complexity.

Perspective 2: Language as Stable System (Use, Vocabulary and Syntax)

To understand growth from the second perspective, of language as a stable system, I divided each student's language corpus into a fall corpus (September–November) and a spring corpus (April–June), so that I could look at growth between those two time periods. I then analyzed each student's corpora for the overall quantity of English they were using, the diversity of the words that they were using (vocabulary), and how grammatically complex their speech was (syntactic complexity). For details about each of these analyses, including why these particular measures were chosen, see Appendix 2.

Surprising outcomes

In examining English learning through this theoretical lens, the assumption that positive positioning means more opportunities to learn means greater acquisition of vocabulary and grammar quickly broke down. Being seen as a good student and playmate and being central to the social network of the class did not have a consistent relationship with language acquisition. Hande – peripheral to the classroom, positioned by the teachers as a loner and by students as an expendable playmate – showed the strongest language growth. Meanwhile, Kritika – the most central to the social network of the class, positioned as a standout student and playmate – showed significantly less growth. Table 7.1 summarizes the results of this analysis, described in the next three sections.

Quantity of English use

The first measures summarized in Table 7.1 – words used in English and turns in English – give a sense for how much English the students were using overall in fall and spring (Table 7.1, Rows 1 and 2). They show that even in the fall, all four students produced many English words per hour: 105 (Kritika), 114 (Padma), 128 (Hande) and 132 (Rashmi). For the three Nepali-speaking girls, English turns made up comparable proportions of their talk (19%, 21%, 17%), with the rest in Nepali. Hande had fewer overall turns at talk than the other three but, because she was the only Turkish speaker in the class, 100% of her turns were in English. By spring, although Kritika and Rashmi each produced a slightly higher proportion of English turns to Nepali turns than in the fall (19% → 25% and 21% → 26%), both were using slightly fewer English words per hour (105 → 98 and 132 → 95). Padma and Hande, on the other hand, showed strong increases in the number of English words they were using per hour, with Padma doubling her fall amount (114 → 237) and Hande more than tripling hers (128 → 449). This meant that in the spring, Padma was using 2½ times as many English words per hour as Kritika and Rashmi and that Hande was using 4 times as many. While Hande's English turns continued to make up 100% of her talk, Padma's English turns now made up 66% of hers (up from 17%).

Vocabulary

The second measure – lexical diversity – illustrates the range of words each student used. In the fall, the three Nepali speakers were recorded using a similar number of *different* English words during each hour that they appeared on camera (24, 27, 27), with Hande using a larger quantity (36) (Table 7.1, Row 3). By spring, all four students showed growth in vocabulary. Kritika's count of different words per hour nearly doubled (24 → 45), and Rashmi showed growth of around 50%

Table 7.1 Students' English use, vocabulary, and complexity in fall and spring (reprinted with permission from Bernstein, 2018)

			Kritika		Rashmi		Padma		Hande	
			Fall	Spring	Fall	Spring	Fall	Spring	Fall	Spring
Use	1	% turns at talk in English)/ hour video	19% (N = 22/118)	25% (N = 29/115)	21% (N = 24/114)	26% (N = 27/105)	17% (N = 20/98)	66% (N = 70/106)	100% (N = 54/54)	100% (N = 60/60)
Vocab	2	# English words/hour	105	98	132	95	114	237	128	449
	3	# different English words/hour	24	45	27	42	27	92	36	116
Complexity	4	Mean utterance length (# wds per AS-unit³)	2.48 (SD=1.00) ex: 'I'm done!'	3.09 (SD=1.57) ex: 'No, it's cupcake!'	2.94 (SD=1.12) ex: 'I'm go here!'	3.22 (SD=1.68) ex: 'Where's my spoon?'	2.37 (SD=.83) ex: 'This no.'	3.16 (SD=1.69) ex: 'I like this girl.'	2.07 (SD=1.44) ex: 'Help me?'	4.54 (SD=1.60) ex: 'I didn't do my picture!'
			Cohen's d: 0.463		Cohen's d: 0.196		Cohen's d: 0.593		Cohen's d: 1.62	
	5	Examples of AS-units	Miss, I'm water! I'm done! Miss, I'm pineapple! Where Padma baby? What your name? Bread! Airplane!!!	Where's the red? It's ball and it's my name. Gimme black, Kelsey! It's circle. My mom's on Saturday. Ewwww, it's gusting. I like pink.	Teacher, I need here in baby! Train! I like apple. I like hungry. I like pumpkin. I'm go here. I'm play here.	You write my name. I want more too! What your name? Where's my spoon? You got a Nepali naam? I done. This cloth is mine!	This no. I'm pineapple! I'm that! I'm bread! Water! Teacher, I'm this! This is hot.	What about cracker? Or jacket! Princess! Don't lie, Miss Katie! My sheet, oopsies! Hey, I'm not go that! And your teeth are white.	Look at this! It's red. Go housekeeping!? Come on. Help me? This a car.	Can I help you? You making it like a tree – big giant tree! Where's the baby doll? I didn't do my picture! Can we do puzzle? Your earrings are so nice.
	6	% AS-units with verbs	17% (N = 6/33)	36% (N = 14/40)	43% (N = 7/16)	50% (N = 16/32)	21% (N = 4/19)	25% (N = 18/76)	25% (N = 7/28)	84% (N = 84/101)

(27 → 42). This meant that while the overall number of English words used by Kritika and Rashmi decreased slightly, the words they did use were more diverse. Yet, in the same time, Padma and Hande each more than tripled their vocabulary (27 → 92 and 36 → 116 different words).

Complexity

The final two measures – mean length of utterance and verb use (Table 7.1, Rows 4-6) – paint a picture of how grammatically sophisticated each student's talk was. In the fall, the four students produced utterances with a mean length (MLU)[3] of between 2.07 words (Hande) and 2.94 words (Rashmi), with Kritika at 2.48 and Padma at 2.37 words. Examples of these utterances are shown in Row 5. The percentage of these utterances that contained verbs ranged from 17% (Kritika) to 43% (Rashmi), with Padma at 21% and Hande at 25%.

Kritika, Rashmi and Padma ended the year with similar mean utterance lengths (3.09, 3.22 and 3.16). For Kritika and Padma, this meant some growth from the fall: about a half word/utterance for Kritika (Cohen's $d = 0.463$, a medium effect size[4]) and one word per utterance for Padma ($d = 0.593$, also a medium effect). For Rashmi, this meant hardly any growth from the fall ($d = 0.196$, a small effect). In terms of verb use, Kritika doubled her proportion of utterances containing verbs (from 17% to 36%), while Padma and Rashmi saw very small growth (from 43% to 50% and from 21% to 25%). On all complexity measures, however, Hande far surpassed the other focal students. Her average utterance length increased from 2.07 to 4.54 words (Cohen's $d = 1.62$, a *very* large effect size), and 84% of her utterances now contained verbs, sometimes more than one.

While Rashmi's growth fit with Ellen's assessment of her, and with the idea that a negative and peripheral position would afford less interaction and practice, the other students defied the teachers' assessments and my own expectations. Kritika showed similar growth to Rashmi in vocabulary, with somewhat stronger growth in utterance complexity. Padma showed medium growth in syntactic complexity but excelled in vocabulary and English use, and Hande excelled on all counts. By these measures, Kritika learned much less than her teachers or I had anticipated and Hande learned much more. In this case then, using students' social and academic competence as proxies for language learning did not result in an accurate assessment of students' English growth in vocabulary and syntax.

Perspective 3: Language as Social Action (The Power To Be Heard and Listened To)

> The competence adequate to produce sentences that are likely to be understood may be quite inadequate to produce sentences that are likely to be listened to...
> (Bourdieu, 1991: 55)

Just as the teachers' analysis did not permit them to see Hande's growth in terms of vocabulary and syntax, an analysis of vocabulary and syntax has its own limitations. While it can account for the words that students were able to produce and the utterances into which those words were combined, it cannot account for the effects of those words or utterances. In order to examine language as a social practice – as utterances produced for a particular audience and valued or obeyed to varying extents – it is necessary to look beyond each speaker's turn to the place of each turn within ongoing discourse.

To understand language growth from a social practice perspective, I used the same student language corpora as those used in the analysis of language as a system. This time, however, I analyzed them for evidence of *effectiveness*, or how often peers and teachers listened to the students, how often peers and teachers understood them, and how often peers and teachers took them seriously when they spoke. Deploying the tripartite framework for speech acts described in Chapter 3 as a heuristic, I examined each utterance for its form, force and effect. In other words, I asked:

(1) Form: Is the form of this utterance a conventional one? (Meaning, in the social field of Classroom Three, was this utterance a recognized or recognizable way of accomplishing a particular act?)
(2) Force: Is there evidence that the utterance was heard by its audience and taken to be a particular speech act?
(3) Effect: Is there evidence in the speaker's reaction that the utterance achieved its desired effects?

Tables 7.2 to 7.5 provide examples of how the same speech act – a request (in these cases, for a marker or playdough) – could unfold quite differently for the four students. These examples also show how I used the three questions above to code students' utterances and to quantify their effectiveness. (For more methodological detail on these analyses, see Appendix 2.)

Table 7.2 April 3, 2013: Kritika's request

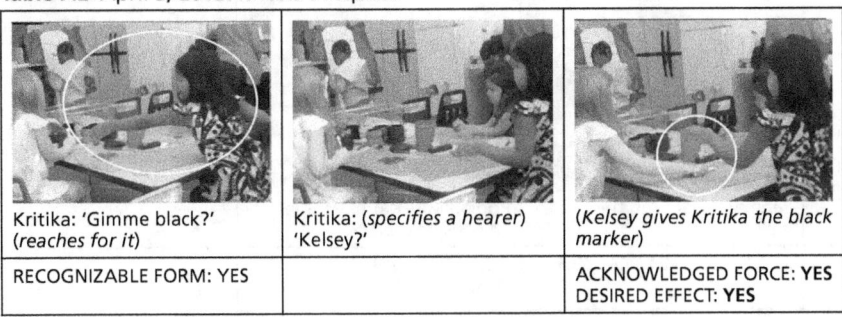

Kritika: 'Gimme black?' (reaches for it)	Kritika: (*specifies a hearer*) 'Kelsey?'	(*Kelsey gives Kritika the black marker*)
RECOGNIZABLE FORM: YES		ACKNOWLEDGED FORCE: YES DESIRED EFFECT: YES

112 (Re)defining Success in Language Learning

Table 7.3 May 6, 2013: Hande's request

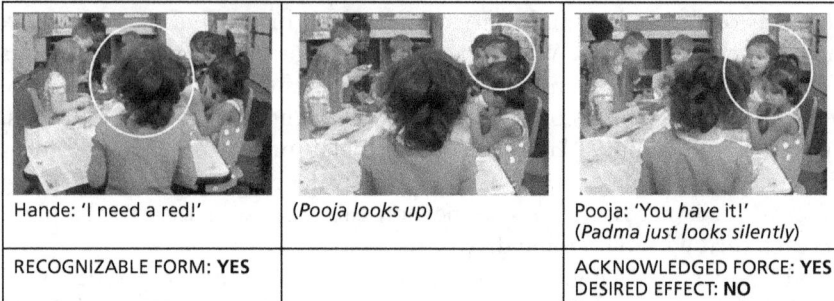

Hande: 'I need a red!'	(*Pooja looks up*)	Pooja: 'You *have* it!' (*Padma just looks silently*)
RECOGNIZABLE FORM: **YES**		ACKNOWLEDGED FORCE: **YES** DESIRED EFFECT: **NO**

Table 7.4 May 6, 2013: Rashmi's request

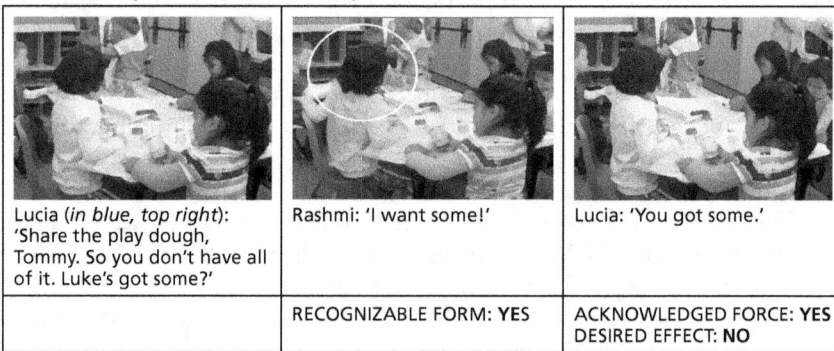

Lucia (*in blue, top right*): 'Share the play dough, Tommy. So you don't have all of it. Luke's got some?'	Rashmi: 'I want some!'	Lucia: 'You got some.'
	RECOGNIZABLE FORM: **YES**	ACKNOWLEDGED FORCE: **YES** DESIRED EFFECT: **NO**

Table 7.5 May 6, 2013: Padma's request (three attempts)

A			
	Padma: 'I want red this one.'	(*no one acknowledges*)	
	RECOGNIZABLE FORM: **YES**	ACKNOWLEDGED FORCE: **NO** DESIRED EFFECT: **NO**	
B			
	Padma: 'I want red this o::::::ne.'	Pooja: 'Miss Katie! Padma wants some red.'	
	RECOGNIZABLE FORM: **YES**	ACKNOWLEDGED FORCE: **YES** DESIRED EFFECT: **NO**	

Who Learned What? Three Perspectives on Success in Language Learning   113

Completing this coding for each speech act allowed me to quantify the percentage of each focal student's utterances that (1) showed conventional form, (2) were heard and acknowledged (force), and (3) were taken seriously and responded to in desired ways (effects). This permitted a comparison of these percentages across students, which I discuss in the next section.

Identifying utterances as particular types of speech acts also allowed a qualitative, discursive comparison of *how* students enacted the same speech act types and the ways that others responded to these acts. Below, I focus on such an analysis for an attempted tattle by both Kritika and Hande. Together, these convergent analyses show that complex syntax and good vocabulary were not enough for a student like Hande to be heard and listened to, while other students, like Kritika, could command attention and action even without language that could be deemed 'correct.'

Quantifying effectiveness

Looking at the children's utterances as speech acts – for whether they took a conventional form, whether they were recognized by others, and whether they were acted upon in desired ways – tells a different story from the analysis of vocabulary/syntax. By completing the process described above for each speech act across the year, it became possible to summarize the percentage of students' speech acts that were successful or not in each of the three elements[5]. These percentages are summarized in Table 7.6 below and represented visually (same data, different presentation) in Figure 7.1.

Table 7.6 and Figure 7.1 show that while Kritika's speech acts were *least* often recognizable or understandable in conventional ways (64%), they were *most* often recognized and responded to in the way she wanted (79%). This discrepancy meant that in a full 15% of Kritika's speech acts, someone was able to read the right intention into her utterances – or to work to figure it out – even when the form was not clear.

Table 7.6 Percentage of students' speech acts that were successful or not in each of the three elements

	Conventional Form	Recognized Force	Desired Effect
Kritika N = 38	64% (23)	79% (27)	79% (27)
Padma N = 42[6]	85% (36)	66% (28)	59% (25)
Rashmi N = 26	96% (25)	57% (15)	53% (14)
Hande N = 61	96% (55)	64% (37)	42% (25)

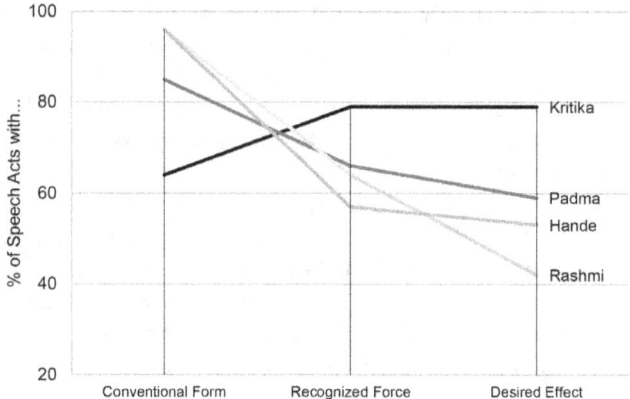

Figure 7.1 Graphical representation of students' speech act data from Table 7.6

Additionally, every single time that Kritika's acts were recognized, they were responded to in the way that she hoped. In the other students' cases, meanwhile, some portion of their speech acts that were recogniza*ble* still went unrecogni*zed* (like Padma's initial request for playdough in Table 7.5). And of the acts that were recognized, another portion of these was ineffective (like Hande's and Rashmi's requests for playdough in Tables 7.3 and 7.4). For Rashmi and Hande, then, the difference between acts that were recognizable (96%) and those that produced a desired social effect (53% and 42%, respectively) was quite large.

From these figures, it is possible to create an effectiveness ratio for each student. This ratio reflects the number of utterances that achieve a desired effect compared to the number of utterances that show conventional form. An effectiveness ratio of 1 would be mean that every utterance with a conventional form was effective, while 0 would mean none were. By this measure, Hande was least effective at 0.45, Rashmi slightly more effective at 0.56, and Padma more so at 0.69. Kritika, however, shows a ratio of 1.17. The next section explores how it was possible for Kritika to achieve an effectiveness ratio greater than 1.

Qualifying effectiveness: Force without form, or Kritika as 'worth understanding'

I was surprised to find that so many of Kritika's utterances were understood and responded to despite not following a conventional form or being, on the surface, recognizable as a particular kind of utterance. When I looked across all of Kritika's effective speech acts to try to understand better how this was possible, I noticed a pattern. In Chapter 5, I showed that peers and teachers listened when Kritika spoke. By looking across her speech acts, I found that not only did they listen, but when Kritika said something that was not clear, they also went to great effort to figure out what she was trying to say. For example, in the following transcript, from May of the school year, Kritika was working one-on-one with Ellen on a drawing of their classroom. Ellen asked Kritika what she had drawn. When Kritika said something that Ellen did not understand (the word 'oven,' referring to the microwave), Ellen asked for clarification no less than seven times. Additionally, Pooja and Padma, who were drawing at the same table, stood up and came over to help.

Ellen:	Okay! Tell me what this stuff is. What's this?
Kritika:	It's circle.
Ellen:	Circle rug? Circle time rug?
Kritika:	Mmm hmm.
Ellen:	(*labels picture with words 'circle time rug'*) What's this?
Kritika:	This is oval [oven].
Ellen:	What is that?
Kritika:	This is oval [oven].
Ellen:	What oval?
Kritika:	(*leans forward, accentuates word*) Ovone [oven].
Ellen:	<u>What</u> is it, honey?
Kritika:	OVONE [oven].
Ellen:	Show me, where?
Pooja:	(*tries to help*) She said, 'Ovone!'
Ellen:	What?
Pooja:	Ovane!
Padma:	Ovan.
Ellen:	The oven! (*turns to Kritika*) The oven?
Padma:	MICRO-OVEN!
Ellen:	The oven … Ohhh! The microwave?
Kritika:	(*nods*)
Ellen:	Oh okay! (*writes*) This is – (*shakes head slightly, chuckles to self*) Okay! Let's write one more thing and you're good.

(Video, 13 May 2013)

In this interaction, Ellen worked for a full minute to understand what Kritika was saying, assuming communicative intent in both her drawing and her speech and working under the assumption Kritika had something of substance to say that needed to be figured out. Kritika's peers also worked to assist her. The participation framework here, thus involved a distribution of the role of speaker across multiple people (Goodwin, 2004, 2006). While Ellen was the addressee, she could not understand Kritika alone and needed Pooja and Padma, ratified but non-addressed hearers, to serve as (re)animators of Kritika's words. Ellen, Pooja and Padma all assumed the importance of what Kritika had to say and were willing to cooperate in order to help her convey it.

Contrast this with Ellen's work on the same activity with the next student, Monal:

Ellen: (*brings Monal over to table*) Monal, you're gonna draw- you're gonna draw- listen- look at me. (*lifts up chin*) You're gonna draw the room. This (*gestures around*) So, I want you to draw the sandbox. Okay? Can you draw the sandbox? Can you draw the SANDBOX?
Monal: (*draws*)
Ellen: That's the sandbox? Okay. (*starts to write*) Wait a minute. Okay? Wait. Now I want you to draw- can you draw the block area? Can you draw the block area?
Monal: (*draws*)
Ellen: K, that's the block area?
Monal: (*nods*)
Ellen: Look, is that the blocks? (*points back*)
Monal: (*looks, nods*)
Ellen: Blocks?
Monal: Yeah.
Ellen: Okay. That's the blocks. (*writes*) Okay what else you want to draw? You wanna draw, um, tables? Draw the table.
Monal: (*draws*)
Ellen: (*laughs*) Okay! Good! Table. (*writes*) How about draw the library? (*slowly*) Draw the library.
Monal: (*makes mark*)
Ellen: Okay, good job! Okay, that's good!

(Video, 13 May 2013)

In this excerpt, Ellen took on both roles in the conversation, providing Monal with what to draw and what to say, assuming that he would otherwise not contribute anything meaningful. Jiang Yan and Zhu Hua (2012), after Auer (1984), refer to this as the 'ascription of incompetence,' in this case to Monal by the teacher. Although in the fall, Kritika might have been one of the 'jabbering' Nepali speakers, by spring Ellen would never speak for Kritika in this way. Instead, the 'oven' example above shows Ellen, as well as Padma and Pooja, ascribe to Kritika competence, importance and, importantly, the assumption of saying something worth understanding.

Qualifying effectiveness: Comparing across speech acts

A closer look at a tattle carried out by Kritika and then one from Hande illustrates the quantitative patterns shown above as well as the pattern of ascribing competence to Kritika. It also illustrates how the opposite ascription undermines Hande's speech act.

Tattling is a speech act particular to young children and prevalent in school contexts. It involves recruiting an authority figure, often a teacher, to intervene in the restoration of the classroom moral order on behalf of a student, who lacks the language or the authority to do so on her own (Cekaite, 2012). In the first example, from late spring, Kritika and a group of other Nepali-speaking girls were playing together in the playground. Three-year-old Sreya left the bouncy, spring-rider motorcycle she had been on to go look at what another student was doing in the dirt, and, when she returned a minute or two later, Anita, another three-year-old, was riding the motorcycle. Sreya pushed Anita off and re-mounted it. Anita protested but, largely unphased, brushed herself off and went to play somewhere else. Kritika, having witnessed this, ran to tell Lucia. When she had Lucia's attention she said breathlessly, 'Anita Sreya hit!' meaning that Sreya hit Anita (Field notes, 6 May 2013). Lucia thanked Kritika and responded by calling Sreya over for a talk.

Although from a grammatical perspective, Kritika's tattle was somewhat ambiguous, and although Anita had now crossed the playground and was playing happily on the monkey bars, Kritika's tattle was quite effective in bringing Lucia into the desired participation framework, 'tattling,' and into the correct role, as restorer of order. This example shows how a speech act which might not be conventionally 'correct' or recognizable out of context could still be understood and taken up when carried out by the right person in the right context. It also shows Kritika being positioned as a reliable witness and authoritative source of information. (That Lucia also knew right away who had done the hitting in this grammatical construction also speaks to the respective classroom identities of Anita and Sreya, but that is another story!)

A tattle from Hande, which occurred one week before Kritika's tattle, illustrates the opposite: that a well-formed tattle and clear evidence of the transgression are not necessarily enough for the teacher to take action. One afternoon at snack time, Hande watched as Tommy took all the orange slices from the bowl at the center of the table, squeezed each one onto his plate, poured the plate full of juice into his milk, and then soaked his napkin in the cup. As he began squeezing the milk-juice from his napkin onto his plate and then slurping it up from there, Hande called to the teachers:

Hande:	(*pointing*) Look she did her paper this! Tommy this her paper did this! She did her paper all this! Tommy did all milk. Miss Lucia! Miss Lucia!
Lucia:	(*comes closer*)
Hande:	No more in here liquid! She's there. All mixed up. And she's eating. Tommy all milk. She drink it. Now she drink it! No more orange!
Lucia:	Alright thanks, Hande.
Tommy:	(*interrupts*) No, I'm NOT a girl. I a boy!
Lucia:	Tommy, finish your snack.
Tommy:	She called me a girl!

Lucia:	She gets mixed up, that's all. It's okay.
Tommy:	(*to Hande*) <u>You</u> called me girl. (*to Lucia*) <u>She</u> did. She did that to me. (*crossing arms across chest*)
Hande:	I called you a boy.
Lucia:	(*to Tommy*) Alright sweetheart, want to eat some of your bread and jelly? (Audio recording and field notes, 15 April 2014; Reproduced with permission from Bernstein, 2016a)

Hande began her tattle in a conventional way, by flagging down a teacher and explaining the transgression. Yet, Lucia thanked Hande without investigating and when Tommy loudly objected that Hande called him a girl, Lucia shifted her focus to assuring Tommy that, 'She gets mixed up' and 'It's okay,' without intervening in Tommy's orange monopoly and mess. When Tommy persisted, Lucia called him 'sweetheart' and directed him to his bread and jelly.

While Hande's tattle was much more complex and information-rich than Kritika's – and was supported by immediately visible evidence – Hande was not positioned as a reliable source. Instead, she was positioned as 'mixed-up,' with Lucia focusing on Hande's pronoun error rather than on the content of Hande's claim. Hande, did not, therefore succeed in bringing Lucia into her participation framework of 'tattling,' in which Lucia would set the classroom moral order straight by making Tommy clean his mess and perhaps leave the table, while refilling the bowl of oranges so that Hande could have her snack. Instead, Lucia was recruited into Tommy's competing framework, 'counter-tattle,' in which Hande had committed the offense of calling him by the wrong pronoun, and Lucia focused her attention on restoring order there.

Discussion: Speech Acts and Participant Frames

Bourdieu (1991) wrote that felicity conditions – the conditions that make a speech action function (Austin, 1975) – are essentially social conditions. One mechanism by which social positioning can translate into successful linguistic practice, or felicitous speech acts, is through participant frameworks. Speech acts have particular participant frames that are a condition for their success. For instance, for a student to successfully request more milk at lunch, say, she has to be recognized as speaker and a legitimate potential receiver of milk. Meanwhile, someone who *has* milk has to take up the position of hearer and of milk provider. The most direct way to accomplish bringing this framework into being would be for the student who wants milk to address a person with milk (whether teacher or another student near a milk carton). But if the intended hearer doesn't hear, and an unaddressed overhearer with milk access does hear, she may still pass the milk. They key is therefore to evoke, for someone capable of helping, the speech event frame for 'request' and to provoke the potential helper to participate in the appropriate participation framework. A successful speech act therefore involves getting someone to hear, then listen, then recognize the frame, then participate in it.

In the Request examples above (Tables 7.2–7.5), Padma was not even able to get anyone to listen to her first attempt at a request. In her second attempt, her friend Pooja heard her, but rather than taking up the role of an addressee who could give Padma playdough, she instead took the role of animator (amplifier) of Padma's request. This was not Padma's desired outcome, however, nor did it help secure playdough. Hande and Rashmi were both able to get someone to listen and to recognize the event frame, but neither hearer was the right kind of addressee (in that neither was willing to help). Only in Kritika's case did she enlist the right person (the one with the marker) into the right role (addressee) in the right frame (request) and then have the addressee accommodate the request. While Kritika's social position in the classroom community of practice may have made it easier to get someone to listen and eventually to participate, there were other things that Kritika did that helped here, too. For instance, she chose an addressee who could fill the role in her speech event frame, and she used that addressee's name in her request to make this clear. She also looked at Kelsey and reached her arm toward her, first to ask for the marker and then to receive it.

In the tattling examples above, Kritika and Hande both attempted to create an event framework for tattling, in which an offended speaker reports on an absent or silent third party's deviant behavior to an authority figure addressee, who listens, who possibly asks the third party to answer to the tattle, and who intervenes or punishes the third party. In Kritika's case, that is indeed how the tattle went. In Hande's case, the third party (Tommy) did not remain silent but managed to hijack the speech event, take the role of offended speaker, and force Hande to answer to his claim of offense. Lucia never had time to intervene in Hande's tattle before being drawn in as addressee and arbiter in Tommy's. Thus, successful linguistic practice in Classroom Three was less about linguistic tools and more about having both the symbolic capital (Bourdieu, 1991) as well as the symbolic competence (Kramsch, 2006, 2016; Kramsch & Whiteside, 2008) across many modes to bring about the correct participant frameworks.

Notes

(1) One of the reviewers pointed out the necessity of making clear that this is not national Head Start policy. Many Head Starts do monitor progress in language development. While this Head Start *did* attend to the social uses of language by all students – things like, 'Student is able to use oral language to ask for things she needs' – these measures were not specific to English learners and were focused on function rather than form.
(2) Kelsey was the second most-cited friend in interviews with students and certainly the teachers' favorite English-speaking student. She was mature, focused, gentle with the younger children, always smiling, creative and clever.

(3) To be more specific, I looked at mean length of AS-unit. An AS-unit, or Analysis of Speech Unit (Foster et al., 2000) is 'a single speaker's utterance, consisting of an independent clause or a sub clausal unit, together with any subordinate clause(s) associated with either' (365). For example, Padma had a turn at talk: 'This is hot and this is hot and this is hot and this is hot and this is hot.' The longest AS-unit in this turn would be 4 words long ('and this is hot'), because clauses coordinated by 'and' count as separate AS-units. If Padma had said: 'This is hot, but this is cold,' the whole turn would be one AS-unit (7 words), because clauses subordinated by 'but' are part of the AS-unit. The AS-unit is an alternative to a T-unit, but more suited for spoken language as it counts sub-clausal units, not just independent clauses. Intonation and pauses help to define boundary markers. Thus, 'train,' 'I?,' and 'this no' all qualify as AS-units, although they would not qualify as T-units.
(4) As suggested by Cohen (1988), $d = 0.2$ is typically considered to represent a small effect, $d = 0.5$ is a medium effect, and $d = 0.8$ is large.
(5) While Austin and Searle both came to see all utterances as speech acts, including 'reporting,' 'stating,' 'wondering aloud,' and 'describing,' I excluded those speech acts in this analysis because of the difficulty in determining what might count as success, since not all statements demand responses (where all requests or invitations or (legitimate) questions do). For the purposes of analysis, I therefore only include speech acts that were directed at others and required a response.
(6) An astute reader may notice that Padma had many more turns than this according to Table 7.1. Turns in which Padma was involved in language play with the researcher were not counted here, as this was a speech event that no other student participated in and that Padma never participated in with anyone else, meaning that there were no established practices outside our interactions to help me understand what felicitous language play would be in this classroom. I would therefore say that all of her language play acts were felicitous, since she and I were making it up as we went. Were I to include these, therefore, Padma would look much more successful in classroom practice than she was outside this play.

8 Beyond English: Multimodal, Multilingual Repertoires at Work

This chapter builds on the findings of the previous chapter. It addresses the questions of how Kritika came to be seen as a competent English speaker, despite her comparatively moderate growth in vocabulary and syntax, and what made her so successful at being listened to and taken seriously.

In Chapter 2, I introduced the notion of communicative repertoires as a way to think about the resources that speakers bring to interactions, resources that extend beyond a single language system (like English or Spanish or Nepali) and beyond a single mode (like oral language or gesture). I also introduced the idea of translingual practice as the natural outcome of speakers with a multilingual habitus interacting in a multilingual field, or more specifically, a multilingual field that aligns with their multilingual repertoires.

So, what was it about the relationship between Kritika's repertoire and the field of Classroom Three that helped Kritika succeed as a communicator? And why, when considered mono-modally (looking at just vocabulary and grammar) and monolingually (looking at just English), did Kritika not look particularly successful?

The Linguistic and Social Field of Classroom Three: Conditions Right for Kritika's Repertoire

In Chapters 3 and 4, I wrote about Ellen and Lucia's language policymaking in the classroom, describing how the two teachers saw English as a top priority for students and how Ellen resisted incorporating any Nepali or Turkish into the classroom. Yet, I also described how, despite reminders to speak English in the class, the classroom remained a place where Nepali was spoken regularly by the majority of students. Table 7.1 provided evidence of this: even at the end of the year, 34% of Padma's turns at talk and 75% of Rashmi's and Kritika's took place in Nepali.

Chapter 6 illustrated that Kritika was quick to learn the rules of the classroom and to incorporate school practices for how to sit and walk and play and eat into her own way of doing things. She was also highly verbal in Nepali, able to engage in complex stories and play. In a different social field – one without her many Nepali peers or one without teachers whose policies permitted Nepali to flourish, albeit in unsanctioned ways – Kritika would not have been able to showcase these practices or abilities. In Classroom Three, however, because she could use the Nepali in her repertoire, she was able to make friends quickly; as her peers' reactions showed and my translator confirmed, Kritika was eloquent, funny and imaginative in Nepali. These interactions, in turn, helped non-Nepali speakers see that Kritika was a responsive and competent playmate and was worth inviting into their interactions. Because Nepali was a valid classroom language – if not for official classroom business, then at least for play – Kritika sidestepped the language learner double bind (Tabors, 2008) of having to prove her friend-worthiness in a language she could not yet use well.

In Chapter 6, I also introduced Kritika as a social resource for other students. Across the year, Nepali-speaking peers who could not, or would not, ask for help from teachers instead called on Kritika to settle disputes and to intervene on their behalf. Even in late spring, videos show Padma and Anita yelling across the room to Kritika for help with a conflict or with a tattle. Because these interactions were spoken ones, this meant that Kritika served not just as a social resource but also a linguistic one. (Recall, for example, in Chapter 6 when Rashmi and Prakesh asked Kritika to intervene on their behalf to evict Hande from the sand table). In other situations, students relied on Kritika as a spokesperson to the teachers. At lunch one day, when Rashmi had spilled her milk onto her snack plate, students at the table gasped and pointed. When no teachers appeared, the students looked to Kritika. Kritika then was the one to call out: 'Miss Lucia! Miss Ellen, look!' which brought Ellen to the table with paper towels (Video, 6 May 2013).

The teachers, too, needed language help at times. At the start of the year, faced with many students with whom they did not share a language, they drew on Dinesh, the only Nepali speaker who also spoke English, for help. At circle times in early fall, when they could not understand a student's response, they looked to Dinesh, and on a few occasions, when a student was hurt and the teachers had not seen what happened, they asked Dinesh to come talk with the crying child. Yet, by November, while the teachers continued to draw on Dinesh in order to understand other students, they also began to use Kritika as an intermediary, but for the opposite situation – when they needed students to understand and listen to *them*. The following examples illustrate this role:

(1) At morning circle time, during talk about the weather, Maiya leaves her place and crawls up to the teacher to get a closer look. Kritika appears tempted to join her as she begins to move forward onto her knees. Rather than reprimand both girls, Lucia says: 'Kritika, show Maiya what to do' (Video, 3 December 2012).

(2) During free play time, Lucia approaches the housekeeping area.
Lucia: 'Shhh. Boys and girls, we're getting too loud. Kritika! Kritika! Tell everybody quiet. Go around and tell everybody quiet for me' (Video, 17 December 2012).
(3) Kritika and Maiya are at the sand table.
Lucia: 'Kritika and Maiya be careful with the sand. Kritika, tell Maiya. Careful. Don't touch your face' (Video, 19 November 2012).

As García wrote: 'There is no simpler translanguaging than what takes place in translations' (García *et al.*, 2011: 46). Yet, while Dinesh-the-translator was simply a linguistic resource, Kritika-the-translator served a dual purpose: she could convey the teachers' messages to other students, as well as use her social capital and authority to make sure that the students followed through. Thinking about participant roles and production formats is helpful here. In these interactions, the teachers were asking Kritika to act as their mouthpiece. In Goffman's (1981) terms, while the teachers were authors (composers of the words) and principals (the ones whose viewpoint the words expressed), Kritika was the animator (mouthpiece) or, better still, the amplifier for them. The many occasions on which Kritika enforced the rules without having been asked to, showed that she was willing to take on this role of animator (and even co-principal, though not author) of the rules. It also showed that her peers accepted her role. The examples of her peers asking her to intervene for them illustrate that they also asked her to animate and lend authority to their words, too.

Being a successful amplifier of the teachers' words was not a participant role available to all students, as it required a certain social status as well as the institutional backing of the teachers. Yet, like her role as a competent playmate and friend, Kritika's role as an authority figure was also made possible by both her own translingual competence and its alignment with the social field of the classroom, which allowed and, at times, demanded, Nepali as the language of interaction.

Repertoires Beyond Words: Kritika as Semiotically Resourceful

In addition to allowing Kritika to use the Nepali in her repertoire, Classroom Three's social field also allowed Kritika to showcase other embodied elements of her repertoire. Andersen (2017) has argued that multimodal representations, such as gesture, are indeed forms of translanguaging. In her classroom interactions, Kritika deftly translanguaged across modes as well. The following interaction (Table 8.1), from 14 January, illustrates how Kritika used intonation, body position, gaze, and facial expression, in addition to language to convey authority in settling a dispute.

124 (Re)defining Success in Language Learning

Table 8.1 Kritika as authority figure and dispute settler

1:53 (*I'm sitting in the housekeeping corner, holding a baby doll, wearing a toy stethoscope, and taking field notes. Padma places her baby doll with the one in my lap and walks away*)

2:01 (*Pooja also gives me a doll to hold*)

2:55 (*Pooja returns. She and I talk about why I have so many babies. Rashmi presents us with her baby and adds her to my lap*)

3:02 (*We talk about what the babies' names are*)

3:18 (*I invite Padma into the conversation, pointing to the baby she had given me in frame 1:53*) '**Padma, what's your baby's name?**'

3:24 (*Padma points at the baby in question*) '**This the- this the- this the Pooja's baby.**' (*denies ownership, implying ownership of another baby*)

3:30 (*Pooja corrects her*)
'**MY baby- MY baby's name is Pooja.**'
(*simultaneously pulling Padma away from it*)

3:35 (*Padma leans in, putting her hands on Pooja's doll*) '**MY baby's name is Joni!**' (*louder voice*)

(*Continued on next page*)

Table 8.1 Kritika as authority figure and dispute settler (Continued)

 3:40 (Padma and Pooja both pull on the doll, Padma switches to Nepali) **'NO! Pooja! Yo mero nani ho!'** 'NO! Pooja! It's my doll!'	 3:48 **'Ya hera na::::.. Yo mero nani ho:::::'** 'Come o::::n ...this is my ba::::by!' (Pooja whines as Padma pulls the baby away and turns her back to Pooja)
 4:10 (Pooja makes another plea in English) **'My ba:::::by!'** (Kritika notices the conflict)	 4:13 (Padma pulls the baby to her chest)
 4:15 (Pooja sees Kritika watching and appeals to her) **'Yo mero nani ho.'** 'It's my baby!'	 4:16 (Kritika dives in and seperates Padma from Pooja and her doll)
 4:18 **'Timro nani yo!'** 'That's your doll!' (pointing)	 4:20 **'Maile dekh- maile dekhirako thye'** 'I saw – I was noticing it!'

(Continued on next page)

126 (Re)defining Success in Language Learning

Table 8.1 Kritika as authority figure and dispute settler (Continued)

 4:21 *'Aghi tyaha rakheki'* 'Earlier you put it'	 4:23 *'thiyau!'* 'right there!'
 4:24 *'Kina khoseko usko nani?'* 'Why did you snatch her doll?'	 4:26 *'Malai yesto nani manpardaina kalo! Malai YESTO!'* 'I don't like the black baby! (*in researcher's arms*) I like THIS!' (*Pooja's baby*)
 4:27' *Ma bokidinchu ullai, ma bokidinchu!'* 'I will hold her, I will hold!' (*Padma says and reaches for baby*)	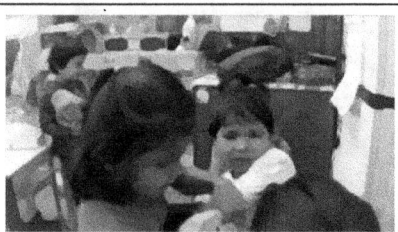 4:28 (*Kritika pushes Padma back from Pooja with the baby*)
 4:28 (*Kritika then steps forward*)	 4:30 (*She positions herself physically between Pooja (with the baby) and Padma*)

On this morning, I had been sitting on the floor, taking field notes and watching the students play in the housekeeping area. In frame 3:18, I point to Padma's baby and ask what her name is, but in frame 3:24, Padma insists that Pooja's doll is hers. At 3:30 a fight breaks out over the doll. At 4:10, Kritika happens by and notices the fight, and at 4:16, she intervenes.

While this interaction illustrates Kritika's role as an authority figure and dispute settler, it also highlights the many embodied elements of her repertoire that Kritika skillfully deployed. In frame 4:18, she grabs Padma's arm, bends to her level, and points in order to draw Padma's gaze to her abandoned baby. In 4:20 and 4:21, the forward lean of her torso with her arms slightly akimbo suggest anger as well as authority. In 4:21 and 4:24, Kritika's head leans forward and her gaze is directly at Padma. As she says the words 'there' (4:23) and 'her' (4:24), she jabs her finger in the direction of the doll with pointed finger and straight arm, in the manner of a prosecutor directing the jury's attention to the accused. In addition, the elements of Kritika's repertoire that are not possible to convey here – her volume, her intonation – all pointed toward the same message: 'You are at fault here.' As I watched this interaction, unconsciously holding the unwanted doll protectively to my chest, the only word I recognized was *nani* (doll), but Kritika's cues made very clear exactly what kind of interaction was happening. I could also see in frames 4:20-4:24, from Padma's body positioning (slumped forward), head positioning (hanging) and facial expression (pouting mouth, eyes looking up from under her wrinkled brow), that the participation framework was clear to Padma as well.

What made Kritika's scolding so effective – and so recognizable as scolding, even by a non-Nepali-speaking observer – was her coordination of multiple semiotic means: words, intonation, facial expression, body position and gesture. The alignment of multiple modes to produce the same meaning, what Royce (2007) called 'intersemiotic complementarity,' amplified Kritika's linguistic output, as well as made her speech act understandable even to a hearer who could not understand her words. The layering of complementary repertoire elements provided a wealth of contextualization cues that helped to orient and recruit Padma into the participation framework of 'being scolded,' allowing Kritika to carry out the speech act of 'scolding.' Additionally, acts like these contributed over time to securing Kritika's position in the classroom as a someone with the authority and capacity to scold.

Kritika's resourcefulness at simultaneously deploying multiple repertoire elements from different modalities was not limited to moments of authority. In the following interaction (Table 8.2) (reprinted with permission from Bernstein, 2016a), Kritika uses a carefully timed gesture to engage in conversational repair, clarifying a misunderstanding, which she had not been able to do through words alone. In this

128 (Re)defining Success in Language Learning

interaction, from the morning of 8 April 2013, Kritika, Rashmi and Pooja were working at the art table. Miss Lucia was preparing lunch off-camera, at the counter just to the right of the table. When Lucia asked what the children were talking about, Kritika answered but Lucia did not understand what Kritika was saying. Kritika worked to clarify:

Table 8.2 Kritika engages in conversational repair

 Kritika (left) is with Rashmi (center) and Pooja (right) at the art table.	 25:39 Pooja picks up a drawing of the sun (see inset) that Kritika made earlier. Kritika objects loudly.
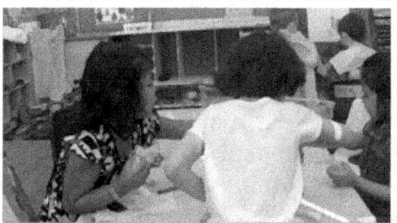 25:40 Kritika says something in Nepali as she reaches for the drawing.	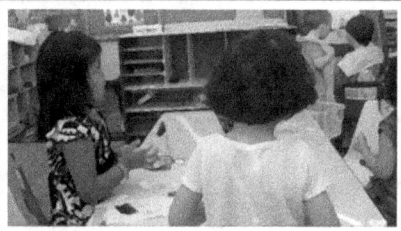 25:42 Teacher Lucia overhears and asks, 'What does that mean Kritika?'
 25:43 Kritika answers, 'Sun,' but her pronunciation (/sɒn/) is closer to the 'o' in 'song' than the 'u' in 'sun' (/sən/)	25:44 Lucia, off camera: 'Huh? Song?'
 25:46 Trying to emphasize the final, Kritika produces something more like /sɒnnɪ/	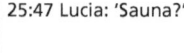 25:47 Lucia: 'Sauna?'

(Continued on next page)

Table 8.2 Kritika engages in conversational repair (Continued)

25:48 Kritika repeats 'sun,' but now coordinates with a gesture pointing up, so that her gesture begins with /s/ and reaches its highest point when she says /n/	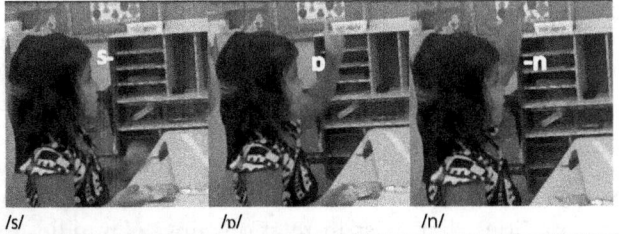 /s/ /ʊ/ /n/
 25:48 As she brings her hands back together, she repeats the word once more	25:49 Lucia: 'Ohhh, sun! How do you say "sun" in Nepali?' (without waiting for the answer, starts singing the children's song, 'Mister Sun')

This interaction further highlights that Kritika was seen as worth understanding, even when it took some work: Lucia engaged her in a multi-turn clarification sequence, while a passing student (far left, 25:48) stopped to listen as well, and Pooja watched closely, following Kritika's gesture with her gaze (she can be seen looking at the location of the gesture's apex in 25:48). This example also highlights Kritika's sophisticated use of gesture, pointing to up in order to indicate that she was saying 'sun.' To do so, Kritika made the on-the-fly decision that Lucia would know that the sun was in the sky and that it would not confuse Lucia that the ceiling is in the way. Kritika also perfectly coordinated her gesture with her speech, reaching the gesture's apex just as she hit the 'n' in 'sun.' In this example, Kritika again utilized multiple repertoire elements, including words, intonation, timing, gesture and gaze (always holding Miss Lucia's) to achieve shared meaning.

Affordances: Kritika's Repertoire and the Classroom Three Field of Practice

As discussed in Chapter 3, Ellen often expressed concern that she was not seeing as much interaction as she would have liked between the Nepali- and English-speaking students in Classroom Three. She worried that having so many Nepali speakers in the class might hinder the students' English growth. At the same time, at the end of the year, she acknowledged that having many speakers of the same L1 must have been comforting to students in what could have otherwise been a scary, new setting. In interviews with parents of the Nepali-speaking students, the parents echoed the insight that Nepali could have been beneficial in some ways and costly in others. They debated whether it might not be better to have only one or two Nepali peers with their children, so that the children would not feel, as Monal's father put it, 'linguistic suffocation,' but so that they might also have more chances to use English.

The comments of the teachers and parents illustrate an idea proposed by Gibson (1977): that a given object or environment does not provide fixed opportunities or constraints but, rather, *affordances*, or potentialities that exist in relationships. A puddle, for example, affords a child something to splash in, a water strider a surface to walk on, and a pigeon something to drink, while it might not even be noticed by the driver of a car. From the perspective of affordances, an object or environment is never inherently beneficial or detrimental, but can offer different things to different users. It is therefore impossible to ask, 'What did the language ecology of Classroom Three afford?' without asking, 'For whom?'

For Kritika, for instance, the classroom language ecology afforded immediate friendships, as well as the chance to quickly showcase her competence and to develop her authority among peers. These immediate opportunities were what allowed Kritika to position herself, and to be positioned, as someone worth listening to and taking seriously. They also led Ellen to think Kritika had 'come in knowing a lot' of English (Chapter 7), and these opportunities, presented across the year, led the teachers to see Kritika as a competent social actor and interlocutor. As Ellen told me:

> Kritika would come up and you could ask her a que:::stion, ta:::lk to her, carry on a little conversatio:::n. As short as it might be, you could carry on a conversation with her. I could <u>not</u> carry on a conversation with Monal or Rashmi really. I could carry on a conversation with Dinesh, to an extent. The others not. Maybe one or two- a quick question, 'Yes,' 'No,' you know, one-word answer, two-word answer, that would be about it. But Kritika you could <u>ask</u> her, you know. You might not understand everything she said but (*shrugs*). (Interview, 11 June 2013)

While Ellen and Lucia did not have any formal tools or district support for assessing the students' English, comments like these show that they were always thinking about it. Without formal assessments, the teachers drew on their own experiences to generate theories about language, tying students' English learning to other kinds of classroom competences that they knew more about, such as social/emotional development and academic skill. Recall Ellen's supplications for the children to speak English for the sake of the students going to kindergarten, and Lucia's linking of English to pro-social behaviors like sharing. These links to other kinds of competence thus became the tools that teachers used to assess students' linguistic progress. And, because the classroom conditions, in relationship with Kritika's particular repertoire, allowed her to shine in those domains, Ellen and Lucia came to see her as a competent English speaker, as well.

Importantly, limiting the analysis of the classroom social field to the languages spoken there, or limiting an analysis of Kritika's repertoire to Nepali and English, would not be sufficient to explain Kritika's positioning in the classroom. Padma and Rashmi also spoke Nepali and English and were part of the same social field of Classroom Three, but the environment did not have the same affordances for them nor did they experience the same positioning. It is only by looking at *all* the practices of Classroom Three – the intersection of language, academic knowledge, rules, behaviors, expected ways of sitting, eating and playing – as they aligned with *all* the elements of Kritika's repertoire – her language, her academic knowledge, her interest and inclination to both follow and enforce rules, her gestures, her movements, and ways of sitting, eating and playing – that the story of Kritika's effectiveness and her positioning as a competent speaker becomes clear.

9 The Edge Has its Advantages: Participation and Learning on the Periphery

As Chapters 6 and 7 showed, Classroom Three provided Hande, Kritika, Rashmi, and Padma with very different social experiences and language learning outcomes. This chapter explores exactly how the classroom language ecology and social field of Classroom Three interacted with Hande's repertoire in ways that led to her growth in vocabulary and syntax, while not providing Kritika with the same affordances. It also shows how a peripheral position in the classroom social network may have afforded opportunities to both Hande and Padma, while Kritika's central position may have offered constraints.

Because of Hande's language profile and her two-week-late arrival to the class, Hande did not start the year with easy opportunities to make friends. In fact, she experienced what all the Nepali-speaking parents wanted to avoid for their children: to be the only speaker of her language in a new setting. Recall Ellen's comment from Chapter 6:

> Uh Hande? Hande did not uh- well, towards the end she was speaking a lot more English I thought, but um she didn't play with the- a lot of kids I didn't think. She kind of was by herself, and again, too, it was like she had a totally different language from everybody. She didn't speak English and she didn't speak Nepali. So she was kinda (*laughing*) like the outsider completely. So she did have- I mean considering. Again, she was crying a lot, too, and then at the end of the year she was crying [again]. Yeah so I think you know I mean I don't know what's going to happen with her at kindergarten. She really didn't know a lot of the letters. Mom said she was going to put her in some sort of charter school. So I don't even know where she was going. (Ellen, interview, 11 June 2013)

Hande cried a lot at the start of the year, and although she showed interest in others and she carefully deployed strategies for non-verbal social engagement (recall her delicately helping with the sand tower in Chapter 6), these interactions were silent and, therefore, difficult to see without careful observation. It took her much, much longer than it did for any of the Nepali speakers to have enough language skill in one of the two classroom languages to showcase for the teachers the pro-social behaviors that indicated adaptation to school and readiness for kindergarten. In her comment above, Ellen links all of these things: Hande's linguistic isolation, Hande's loner status, her crying, her lack of knowledge of key kindergarten skills like the alphabet and, finally, Ellen's not knowing 'what's going to happen with her at kindergarten.' The classroom social field, therefore, that aligned so neatly with Kritika's repertoire and afforded ample opportunities for her to showcase her social prowess, did not provide the same affordances for Hande, whose communicative repertoire differed markedly from Kritika's.

But the story does not end there, of course. From a different perspective, the affordances also look different. While the number of Nepali speakers in the class meant that Kritika could demonstrate her competence and fulfill her social needs in Nepali, this may have, as the teachers and parents suspected, afforded fewer opportunities to practice English. And although Hande, who began school speaking a language different from everyone else, had to work for interactions and work to maintain them, she had to use English for all of it. While this afforded Hande a much harder year socially, her vocabulary and syntax also grew significantly during that time.

In this chapter, I re-visit Hande's surprising learning outcomes and explain why they might not be so surprising after all. To do so, I briefly review social network analysis theory, and through that lens, I examine how Hande's place in the classroom network may have supported her successful acquisition of English vocabulary and syntax, without comparable success in rallying her peers or teachers to action on her behalf.

Social Network Theory: The Affordances of Centrality and Peripherality

This study set out to understand the relationship between positioning, participation and language learning outcomes. The hypothesis, based on past research on identity, interaction and language learning (see Chapter 1), was that students who were more positively positioned and more central to the classroom network would have the opportunity to participate in more and more varied interactions. Given the importance of interactions for input in English and chances to practice speaking, the students with more access to English-speaking interactions would show the strongest English growth.

In some ways, this hypothesis is supported by prior research using social network analysis (SNA). As Borgatti et al. (2013) stated, 'A generic hypothesis of network theory is that an actor's position in a network determines in part the constraints and opportunities that he or she will encounter, and therefore identifying that position is important for predicting actor outcomes such as performance, behavior or beliefs' (p. 1). SNA studies of individual outcomes have indeed found that being well connected to people who possess desired skills or knowledge has a positive influence on the development of those skills or knowledge: from institutional knowledge (Zappa-Hollman & Duff, 2015) to literacy skills (Gremmen *et al.*, 2017; Kiuru *et al.*, 2017) to English language skills (Carhill–Poza, 2015; Elreda *et al.*, 2016). Additionally, being well connected as a resource *for others* also can be positive. In online classes, for example, those with a high out-degree centrality – those, who are sources of information and resources for others – have shown the strongest individual learning outcomes (Reychav *et al.*, 2018; Russo & Koesten, 2005). In studies that focus on whole network properties and outcomes, connectedness also matters. Denser networks, or networks with a greater degree of closure, in which people are all connected to one another, are better for enforcing norms – in behavior, in language use, in beliefs – which in turn can produce higher degrees of conformity and trust (Coleman, 1988; Gal, 1979; Maroulis & Gomez, 2008; Milroy, 1987). (For more on how network density is determined, see Appendix 2.)

Yet, while conformity can be positive when a network is made up of, say, high-achieving peers (Gremmen *et al.*, 2017; Kiuru *et al.*, 2017), a highly dense network composed of low-achieving peers would instead enforce those norms for a student who is part of that network (Haynie, 2001; Maroulis & Gomez, 2008). Additionally, being centrally well connected within a dense network can constrain access to new ideas or new possibilities for action. A looser network, with many 'structural holes' (Burt, 1992), can provide opportunities for people on the periphery of tight groups to bridge holes between groups. Through their weak ties to multiple groups, people on the periphery may have more access to diverse ideas, as well as the greatest freedom of action, since they are less obligated or less constrained to answer to any of the groups to which they are loosely affiliated (Burt, 1992, 2001, 2004). Additionally, peripheral individuals might bring ideas or practices from one group to another, fostering innovation (Friedkin, 1980; Granovetter, 1973). Social network analysis aligns well, then, with the idea of affordance: It is not possible to determine in the abstract if peripherality or centrality is empowering or disempowering, positive or negative. The affordances of a given position can only be understood in the context of an actual network or community and in examining a particular kind of knowledge, skill or resource. Neither density nor looseness (characteristics of networks), and neither centrality nor peripherality (characteristics of actors), are inherently positive or negative.

Although Bourdieu did not use the same spatial metaphors in his theory of practice, these concepts can be helpful for understanding habitus and practice, as well. Bourdieu developed his theory of practice through study in the late 1950s and early 1960's of the Kabyle people in Algeria, a dense network with relatively high degrees of closure, in which norms were stable and conformity was high. His notions of habitus and field came out of that work, as did the idea of social reproduction – that, when habitus and field are closely aligned and groups are stable, practices will also remain stable from generation to generation. Yet, practices are not *always* stable: sometimes they change through dramatic events (locusts ruin the crops one year and actors must react); sometimes they change through large shifts in actors (a missionary arrives); and sometimes they change through small improvisations (recall that habitus do not determine action, only shape it). Although Bourdieu did not provide a theory of *who* might improvise, it is not difficult to imagine that those on the periphery of a group, who are both less invested in the group norms and less constrained by them, might be most likely to engage in improvisation. Chances of improvisation might also increase in a less closed social group, in which peripheral actors might participate in multiple social fields.

What the Focal Students' Positions Afforded

My hunch going into this study – that a central social place and being positioned as competent and authoritative would benefit English learning and that peripherality and negative positioning would constrain it – held true only in Rashmi's case. In Rashmi's case, her way of remaining on the edge of everyone else's play, her preference to play only with Prakesh, and her air of being in her own world, did in fact mean that she missed opportunities for English practice (e.g. when she did not realize she was being invited into play by Joy and Joey – see Chapter 6). Yet for the other three students, the question of whether centrality was positive and peripherality negative was more complex.

For Kritika, centrality and a positioning as authoritative and competent came with obligations. Students and teachers came to call on her for assistance in negotiations and conflict resolutions. This meant that several times a day each day that I visited, someone yelled across the room to her for her help. Sometimes these conversations involved her using English, but most often she carried out her assistance or direction in Nepali. Additionally, as a central player in the social world of the Nepali-speaking girls, Kritika was almost always involved in play with these students. I hardly ever saw Kritika playing alone and, when she did, it was not long before she was joined by Padma or Anita or Maiya. This popularity made her a welcome playmate in the eyes of the English speakers, yet she rarely joined the English-speaking children's play precisely because of her popularity with the dense cluster of girls who spoke Nepali.

Being seen as a competent student and authority figure may have constrained Kritika in other ways. Across the year, for instance, Kritika was the only emergent bilingual student whom I ever saw become upset about not being understood. The following example (in Table 9.1)

Table 9.1 Kritika is upset at being misunderstood

9:18	9:20	9:21
(*Kritika hands picture to Lucia*)	(*Starts to walk away*)	Lucia: 'Kritika, what is it?' (*Kritika turns back*)
9:27	9:29	9:30
Kritika: 'It's ball (*points*) and it's my name (*points*).'	Lucia: 'It's balls?'	Kritika: (*Points; Kelsey now also looking*)
9:31	9:37	9:41
Lucia: 'Ball. Ok. (*writes*) Ok, what else?'	Kritika: 'It's my name B ("beh").'	Lucia: 'Huh? Say that again.' (*Kelsey looks to Kritika too; Maiya looking at page.*)
9:42	9:43	9:45
Kritika: 'It's my name B ("beh")' (*points*).	(*Everyone at the table now looks to where Kritika pointed.*)	Lucia: 'Big?' (*Kelsey and Lucia look at Kritika expectantly.*)
9:46	9:47	9:49
Kritika: 'Be::::::ee. A-B!'	Lucia: 'A B?'	Kelsey (*tries to help*): 'She says, "A-B."'

(*Continued on next page*)

Table 9.1 Kritika is upset at being misunderstood (Continued)

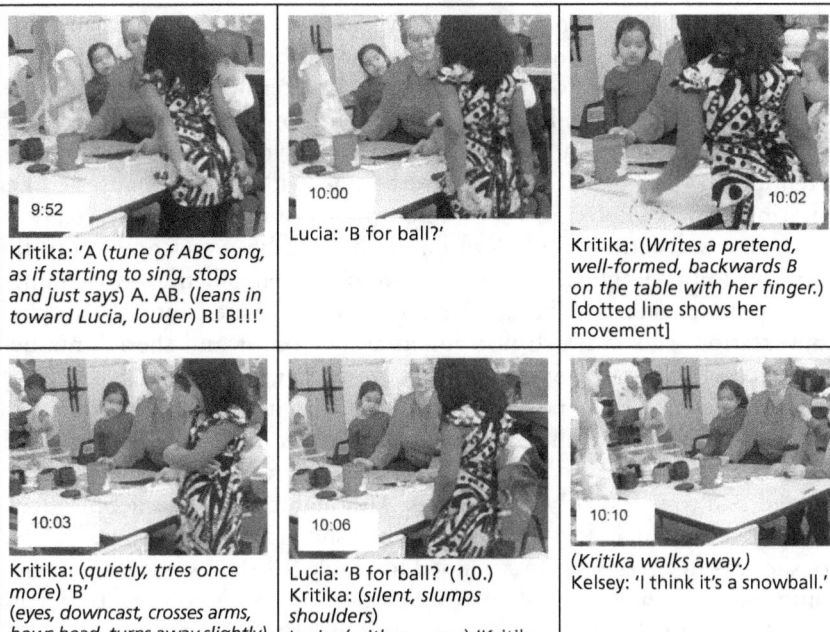

9:52 — Kritika: 'A (*tune of ABC song, as if starting to sing, stops and just says*) A. AB. (*leans in toward Lucia, louder*) B! B!!!'	10:00 — Lucia: 'B for ball?'	10:02 — Kritika: (*Writes a pretend, well-formed, backwards B on the table with her finger.*) [dotted line shows her movement]
10:03 — Kritika: (*quietly, tries once more*) 'B' (*eyes, downcast, crosses arms, bows head, turns away slightly*)	10:06 — Lucia: 'B for ball?' (1.0.) Kritika: (*silent, slumps shoulders*) Lucia: (*with concern*) 'Kritika, you're doing so good.'	10:10 — (*Kritika walks away.*) Kelsey: 'I think it's a snowball.'

illustrates such a situation. In this interaction, Lucia came to the art table to ask what the students had drawn. When Kritika answered, Lucia did not immediately understand. As on other occasions though, Lucia worked very hard to try to understand Kritika, as did the other children. Yet, despite Kritika's repetition and effort, Lucia still did not understand, and Kritika left, visibly upset.

In this example, it is clear that teachers and peers presumed that Kritika had something legitimate to say and that they would collaboratively go to great lengths to try to understand. Yet, Kritika was not able to make herself understood here, and although Lucia tried to reassure her, in the end, Kritika became upset and left the table. Why was Kritika the only student whom I ever saw react this way to Lucia's lack of understanding? Perhaps it was because being misunderstood was a more common experience for other students, rendering it more routine and thus more tolerable. Or perhaps it was because being misunderstood was not a threat to their social positions. Kritika, seen as knowing and able, might have sought to avoid or minimize situations in which she would be positioned as 'not knowing' or 'not able.' Working to keep up her identity as competent and an authority, in turn may have hindered her actual learning of English words and structures (Rymes & Pash, 2001).

Meanwhile, Padma and Hande were not constantly in demand. For Hande, this meant being able to play alone uninterrupted, even when surrounded by peers. In one video, Hande drew at the busy art table without being spoken to for 34 minutes – an eternity in preschool time. In a theory of language learning that depends on interaction, this would be wasted time. Yet, a closer look at these videos shows her paying attention to the English talk around her, as evidenced by pauses in her coloring and her looking up at interesting points in the conversation. In the same situation, while Kritika might have been welcomed into the conversation in English, she might also have been called away or joined by Nepali speakers. Although Hande was not invited into the English conversation, she was also not pulled away from it and she maintained her place as a tolerated bystander and overhearer (Goffman, 1981).

Hande's peripheral positioning combined with her lack of authority offered another possibility as well: semi-private rehearsal and practice. When Kritika spoke, people tried to figure out what she meant; Hande instead had to work to be listened to. Although this was sometimes frustrating for Hande, it also meant that when she did *not* want to be listened to, she was free to speak un-attended to. Table 9.2 shows one such opportunity, when Hande was able to carry out an entire conversation with herself without the other student at the table ever looking up (Video, 15 April 2013). In instances like these, Hande was able to practice English in a private way that was not available to Kritika, the public figure.

Table 9.2 Hande in conversation with herself

Padma, too, was given certain possibilities by her social identity. When Padma wandered away from playing with the other Nepali-speaking girls, no one came to join her where she went and no one needed her social help. While Hande used her social freedom to listen and practice on her own, Padma used it to spend time with me (the researcher). I have notebooks filled with Padma's 'field notes' from free play time and more than a dozen recordings of meals where I found myself last at the table with Padma, as she delayed finishing her food in order to extend our time together. On the rare occasion that Kritika came to sit by me or write in my notebook with me, videos show other students flocking to us. Padma and I, in contrast, spent a lot of time chatting alone. The following transcript provides an example of one such conversation. While typical in length and setting, the content – which involves extended play at translation between English and Nepali – provides a striking example of how Padma's interactions with me provided different language opportunities from those that interactions with teachers or peers might provide.

Snack Table – Only Padma left, Katie (the researcher) next to Padma

Padma:	(*silent, then smiles*) (*points to her cup*) 'Kolfani,' 'glass.' Eh, English eh, Nepali eh '*kolfani*' and (*laughs, covers her mouth with her hand and shrugs shoulders*)
Katie:	(*understanding that Padma is translating, laughs*) I like that game. What about 'orange?' (*points to Padma's plate*) English, 'orange'; Nepali...?
Padma:	(*giggles*) Um (*looks off toward windows*) (4.0) English, 'orange'; and Nepali eh '*sundala*'! (*smiles and crinkles her nose*)
Katie:	(*not sure if it is made up. Later I find that it is accurate*) That's a long word! How bou:::t? (*looking around for a word I know*)
Padma:	How bout 'water'? (2.0) English, 'water'; and Nepali, ['*paani*']
Katie:	['*paani*!']
Padma:	(*smiles*)
Katie:	English, 'friend'; Nepali, '*saati*'!
Padma:	(*nodding, smiling*) Yeah! (*looks around*) English, 'trash' and Nepali- eh- uh- Nepali- Nepali (1.0) 'trash can'!
Katie:	(*laughs*) No::::::. Nepali, 'trash can'? (*laughing*) What else?
Pooja:	(*calls from carpet*) Miss Katie, look! (*holds up paper*)
Katie:	Oh wow!
Pooja:	My name!
Lucia:	Did you see how she wrote her name? Look!
Katie:	Beautiful! (*reads*) P-J-A!
Pooja:	No, P-O-O-J-A (*coming closer to show*)
Katie:	Nice!
Padma:	(*pulls on Katie's sleeve*) What about 'cracker?'
Katie:	(*inhales excitedly, points to Pooja's paper*) English, 'name'; Nepali, '*naam*'!

Padma:	*(laughs)* Yes!
	[brief interaction with Lucia about whether Padma is still eating]
Padma:	How bou:::t 'eyes'. *(points to hers)* mmmm English, 'eyes', Nepali::. Nepali::: (3.0) I don't know
Katie:	I don't know either
Padma:	'Eyes', I don't know.
Katie:	What's 'hair'? *(touches head)* D'you know 'hair'?
Padma:	*(Nods emphatically)* Nepali- English, 'hair', Nepali '*kapaal*'.
Katie:	Oh, ok. What else?
Padma:	*(sees Katie's water bottle on table)* Bottle! English, *(glances at cup)* 'kap' and Nepali 'bottle' *(giggles, crinkles nose)*
Katie:	How bout (5.0) hmm I don't know that many words
Padma:	*(looks at art hanging from ceiling)* 'Kite'!
Katie:	'Kite'? I don't know 'kite' in Nepali, do you?
Padma:	*(Shakes head)*
Katie:	No?
Padma:	Uhhh 'tea'. 'Tea'. I know 'tea' and I know 'orange'. English, 'orange'; Nepali, '*sundala*'!
Katie:	*(inhales, sits up)* Ooh, I know another one. English, 'cold' *(rubs arms)*, Nepali=
Padma:	='Hot'!
Katie:	*(laughs)* no::: Is it '*chiso*'?
Padma:	*(nods, smiling)* Yeah!

(Video, 6 May 2013)

In this example, Padma and I played with language in a way that was only made possible by our extended and largely uninterrupted time together and mutual interest in each other's languages. Looking back at these kinds of interactions, it is hard to imagine that our conversations did not contribute in some way to Padma's vocabulary growth (which was double that of Kritika and Rashmi, and approaching Hande's growth – see Table 7.1).

Taken together, this chapter and Chapter 8 illustrate how the same social conditions that enabled Kritika to be a very effective language user in the social practice of the classroom may have constrained her growth in language-as-a-system. Meanwhile, the social positioning that made Hande and Padma less socially effective with their language allowed them a freedom to (over)hear and to play with language in ways that Kritika could not have, and this may have contributed to their language-as-a-system growth. Additionally, because so many theories of language learning prize face-to-face interaction as the ideal participation framework, Hande's story raises questions about the kinds of social interaction and participation necessary for language learning. These implications for research and for theory are discussed in the next, concluding chapter.

10 Concluding Thoughts: Success Stories

This book has explored the question of how the classroom social positioning of young emergent bilinguals might contribute to their participation in interaction, and therefore to their English learning outcomes. I have shown how the social field of Classroom Three was shaped by teachers' beliefs as well as by the children themselves, and how that context in turn informed the ways that the four focal students negotiated positions and participation in interactions across the year. This study has also shown that the students' positions and ways of participating shaped their learning in complex and unexpected ways. In particular, Kritika's and Hande's outcomes challenge an assumption made by my own study's research questions and design: that an identity as competent and authoritative, and a central place in the class, are inherently beneficial, providing more opportunities for interaction, more opportunities for language learning, and therefore, more learning. This chapter presents some implications of this study's findings, for theory, for research methods and for teaching and learning.

Participation in Language Learning: Quiet Learners and Productive Silence

First, Hande's case and her ways of participating in social interactions raise questions about interaction and language learning. In Chapter 1, I introduced the idea that interaction is an important condition for children's learning language (e.g. Palermo *et al.*, 2014). In Chapter 2, I presented a sociocultural explanation for the importance of interaction in learning: that all learning is social and the use of any new tool, even language, occurs first on a social plane, in interaction with others, before being internalized. Hande's participation, however, brings into question what that initial use on the social plane, in interaction, must entail. For instance, Swain (1997) found that the most important element of language learning interactions was negotiation of meaning, and Swain and others who draw on sociocultural theory in L2 learning all discuss interactions as spaces for co-construction of knowledge (Donato, 1994, 2000; Lantolf, 2000, 2013; Lantolf & Thorne, 2006, 2007). Hande's interactions, however, frequently did not involve cooperation or coordination with other speakers at all. Instead, Hande was often on the sidelines of peer interaction, in the participant role of a tolerated overhearer: listening, looking at the speaker, laughing at the right times, but never being drawn in as a speaker or addressee. Yet, paradoxically, videos show Hande engaging in the kinds of private rehearsals of speech that many sociocultural researchers view as originating in social interactions with others.

This apparent paradox, however, may not be a paradox at all but, rather, a product of the belief that learning should be noisy and collaborative. This belief shapes foreign language classrooms, where teachers design classes around peer interaction, crafting activities and grade structures to encourage participation in conversation (Sato & Ballinger, 2016). It shapes bilingual schools, which aim for a balance of Spanish and English or Mandarin and English speakers, so that learners of both languages can interact with model speakers throughout the day (Lindholm-Leary, 2012). And the belief that learning must be collaborative undergirds the many strategies that new teachers learn to encourage peer interaction – think-pair-share, jigsaw readings, fishbowl discussions, participation points. Yet, as early as 1988, Saville-Troike cautioned:

> [T]he now-dominant conception of language learning as critically involving social/interpersonal interaction has left potentially important non-interactive phenomena generally out of researchers' awareness. Further, there has been a tendency in the second language learning field to equate overt production with active learning and lack of overt production with passivity and disengagement. (Saville-Troike, 1988: 568)

Saville-Troike demonstrated that, on the contrary, some children learn a second language primarily through private speech, such as repetition, recall and rehearsal. She showed that these strategies, too, served as productive approaches to language learning.

In the years since Saville-Troike's study, despite periodic arguments for more attention to silence (e.g. Jaworski, 1992), researchers and teachers continue to equate verbal interaction with learning (Bernales, 2016; Ellwood & Nakane, 2009; Rosheim, 2018). Rosheim, for instance, described one teacher's surprise at her student's strong performance on a screening assessment, 'because the student was so quiet' (Rosheim, 2018: 663). Schultz (2009), in a book called *Rethinking Classroom Participation*, wrote that most US-based educators continue to understand participation as giving verbal responses at appropriate times, such as when called on or as part of small group discussions. Shultz argued that this definition, however, implies that silence equates with non-participation, and that, for many teachers, non-participation is assumed to indicate a lack of learning, understanding or preparation.

Because of these assumptions, 'silence can be a sorting mechanism for success and failure' (Schultz, 2009: 6). Shultz also pointed out that, in educational research, silence has most often been studied as something done to students: silencing is akin to marginalizing, disenfranchising or excluding. Yet, Schultz's classroom research showed that silence can mean many things – including resistance, protection, thoughtfulness, strategic timing, or holding space for others – and that all of these are kinds of participation.

Indeed, researchers who have studied silent members of groups in classrooms have shown that they, too, are learning. Fernández Dobao (2016) studied vocabulary learning during group collaborative writing tasks in a Spanish-as-a-foreign-language classroom. She examined students' participation in language-related episodes, or collaborative dialogue in which students negotiated meaning (Swain & Lapkin, 2001). She first identified roles within the conversations – trigger, contributor, solver or observer – and then analyzed language learning outcomes by role. She found that while initiators of language negotiations, or 'triggers,' learned the most, 'observers,' the silent participants, learned nearly as much and, in fact, more than contributors or solvers. Fernández Dobao concluded that 'silent observers, although apparently passive, were in fact active participants in the interaction' (Fernández Dobao, 2016: 46). Her conclusion mirrors the findings of Ellis *et al.* (1994), who studied learning outcomes of negotiations about meaning during high school English classes in Japan and found no advantage to active participation over simply listening.

By defining participation exclusively as synchronous talk with peers, studies of language learning, including this one, may have limited how we investigate students' paths to language. Hande, through active listening and later self-talk, was successful at mediating her learning in ways that Kritika, who engaged in the kinds of interactions traditionally valued in Second Language Acquisition, was not. By expanding our notion of interaction to include participant roles like overhearers and eavesdroppers, and by considering responses across time and space as potentially part of the same interaction, we may better understand learners like Hande.

A Case for Submersion Education?

In addition to the questions that Hande's case raises about how interaction supports language learning, this study also prompts questions about what kinds of social fields best support language learning. A mounting body of evidence shows that experience in a language – the quality and quantity of time that a person spends engaging in that language – best predicts language learning success (de Carli *et al.*, 2015; Gibson *et al.*, 2014; Sheng *et al.*, 2013; Unsworth,

2016; Unsworth *et al.*, 2014). One possible interpretation of this study's findings, therefore, is that the teachers (and some parents) were right: Hande, the only student who was completely linguistically isolated in the class, learned the most English grammar and vocabulary, because she *had to*. In order to make friends and participate, English was her only option. By this logic, the classroom language ecology would have had the opposite affordances for the Nepali speakers: While having many Nepali speakers in the class supported Kritika's social success and all of the Nepali speakers' social comfort, perhaps it hindered their language learning.

Wray, in a meta-synthesis of the use of formulaic language in L2 learning, supports this argument:

> In children of primary school age, the degree of success in language learning seems to depend in part on their social alliances with peers. Most helpful will be if their friends do not speak the learner's L1, are talkative, are committed to mutual social integration, and engage in patterns of play which naturally incorporate (second) language use. [...] Even in very young children, the L1 can hinder the process of L2 acquisition if it is perceived as being a legitimate medium of communication in the L2 setting. Thus, best L2 learning is obtained when the child is forced to engage with the L2 for meeting basic needs. (Wray, 2002: 148)

In the cases of Kritika, Hande, Rashmi and Padma, when language outcomes are examined in terms of syntax and vocabulary, this theory seems plausible. Yet, when taken as a whole, this study raises further questions. For instance, why wasn't anyone able to see Hande's very impressive growth? And what would have helped them see it? Would it have been visible if she had been able to show her knowledge from the start, in Turkish? If teachers had been expecting success, would they have seen success?

Double Opportunity, Double Obligation: A Different Explanation – and a Better Question

Kritika's case provides some insight here. In some ways, Kritika experienced (some of) the benefits of bilingual education: in the unofficially multilingual space of Classroom Three, she was able to use Nepali to avoid the double bind of language learning in school – needing language to make friends and participate in interactions, but needing friends and interactions to learn English. Because she could showcase her social competences right away in Nepali with her Nepali-speaking peers, Kritika also got to showcase her competence right away to her teachers and English-speaking peers. Even if they couldn't understand her words, seeing Kritika's interactional competence, her compliance, and her subteaching, primed the teachers to see competence when they looked at Kritika, and primed her peers to see authority. This positioning by teachers and peers in turn supported Kritika's success at using English to accomplish social action. Thus, calling the classroom conditions right for Hande's language learning and wrong for Kritika's is both an oversimplification and a red herring.

Another, more complex interpretation might lie in the nature of peer interaction itself. Blum-Kulka *et al.* (2004) called peer interaction a 'double opportunity space,' in that it provides chances for language-learning as well as the construction of peer social worlds. Yet, the other side of the double-opportunity coin is that interaction also provides double obligations: it is not possible to simply use an interaction for language learning without that interaction also shaping peer relations and social positioning. Interaction therefore obligates simultaneous management of both language-learning *and* peer social worlds. And these two obligations can sometimes be in contradiction with one another. As Blum-Kulka and Gorbatt put it, in addition to being keys to language learning, 'peers pose a serious challenge; what's at stake is not just communicating, but rather finding ways to avoid being ridiculed, to change one's social status within the group, and to move from periphery to center' (Blum-Kulka & Gorbatt, 2014: 179).

Philp and Duchesne (2008) illustrate this tension in their study of peer interaction and language learning with the case of one first-grade student, Yessara, learning English in Australia. They show that for Yessara, peer interaction and language learning had a synergistic relationship: social skills helped Yessara participate in interactions that supported language learning; language learning then amounted to a further resource to support Yessara's social relationships. However, while the authors documented Yessara seeking help from teachers and taking linguistics risks in her conversations with them, they found that Yessara limited the help she was willing to receive from peers. Additionally, when she interacted with peers, she took few linguistic risks, limiting her output to language in which she felt confident. Philp and Duchesne therefore argued that Yessara's social goals – of establishing friends and establishing a social positioning as competent – were 'at cross-purposes' with linguistic goals, and for Yessara, social goals took precedence. Yessara skillfully managed interactions so that they would support her positioning as a competent peer and interlocutor, even at the expense of language learning.

The students in Hawkins' (2005) study, kindergartners Anton and William, introduced in Chapter 1, demonstrated similar skill. Each took an active role in managing his positioning as a good playmate or a good workmate, in part by choosing to participate only in conversations that would make him look successful. Neither boy attempted to gain access to other conversations, in which he might look less successful.

This selective participation in turn shaped, and in some ways limited, their learning opportunities. Rymes and Pash (2001), too, found that Rene, a student from Costa Rica learning English in first grade in the United States, similarly prioritized managing his identity. They described how, when Rene arrived at the school, he carefully copied his peers' behavior and their responses to teachers' questions. Having soon established a social identity as a competent student, Rene avoided grappling with content or showing a lack of understanding, as those actions would have 'blown his cover.' Rymes and Pash argued, therefore, that Rene's performance of competence at learning compromised his actual learning. The strategy of displaying competence was also taken by Nok, a seven-year-old student in Cekaite's (2017) study, who was learning Swedish as a new language in school. Nok attended closely to classroom procedures and routines and aligned her actions with the 'institutional agenda.' She used minimal, formulaic language, but focused on inserting those snippets of language into conversation at just the right times to produce interactionally relevant contributions. Through these procedural displays (Bloome *et al.*, 1989)– knowing how and when to respond using the minimal language she knew – Nok was able to 'pass' as a competent language learner. Yet, at the end of the school year, she was still using those strategies, rather than developing complex language.

In many ways, these cases parallel Kritika's. Kritika, too, was a keen observer and quickly mastered classroom routines. Kritika's teachers and peers used her skill in those routines to position her as competent and authoritative early on, and Kritika positioned herself that way as well, through her self-initiated subteaching and her teacher-sanctioned role as interpreter. Kritika also got upset at *not* being understood or seen as competent and was not comforted in being positioned as 'working hard to learn,' even when Lucia framed that struggle to learn as positive: 'doing so good.' Hande's case tells the opposite story, but also supports the idea that language-learning goals and social goals may have been at odds in Classroom Three. While Hande's language grew exponentially when measured as a stable system, this ability to produce grammatically correct and conventionally recognizable speech acts did not help her socially, neither to secure a desirable social position nor to produce desired effects in real interactions with peers.

These cases then – of Nok, Rene, Anton, William, Yessara, Kritika and Hande – seem to contradict the studies reviewed in Chapter 1. They raise the question: So, which is it? Is it that being positioned as competent – as a speaker, student, playmate, peer – facilitates learning, in that it allows students entry into interactions, which are crucial for language acquisition? Or is it that being positioned as competent hinders learning, in that looking competent and actually learning can be at odds with one another (where true learning requires at times demonstrating *not* knowing or *not* understanding)? Or could it be both and neither? Are looking competent and becoming more competent both kinds of success that are sometimes at odds, that sometimes align, and that always require a balancing act?

Looking across studies, including this one, the answer seems to be: it depends. 'It depends,' first, on what is meant by language learning. If language learning means gaining the capacity to use language to rally others into social action, then looking competent and learning language aligned well in this study. But if language learning means acquiring words and grammar, the answer is different. 'It depends,' too, on which child, in which context, with which repertoire is being studied. In Wong Fillmore's (1976) study, social goals and linguistic goals were not at odds for Nora, the most successful language learner. In fact, Nora's primary goal of establishing social relationships with English speakers was what drove her learning: as Wong Fillmore put it, Nora 'not only wanted to be around English speakers, she wanted to be *like* them, and, therefore, she adopted their way of talking' (Wong Fillmore, 1976: 227). At the same time, Nora showed a combination of lack of inhibition, in whom she was willing to interact with, in the content of her interactions, and in the use of novel forms. Nora did not seem to worry about the risk of looking incompetent. To account for all of these cases, a better version of the question that drove this study might be: For which learners, with which repertoires, in which types of classrooms, and as measured by which definition of language, does being positioned as competent and authoritative support language learning? Answering *that* question is only possible in a study that is explicitly designed to layer an investigation of positioning and participation with an investigation of outcomes.

A Call for Layering – and Another Question

In studies of positioning and participation that do not examine outcomes, the only indicators of learning may be teachers' perceptions, which as Toohey (2000) and Willett (1995) deftly illustrated, are never based on students' linguistic skill alone but are tied to social skill, temperament, physical appearance, academic skill, race, class and so on. This is not to say that teachers' perceptions of competence are wrong. As this study has shown, the teachers were skilled evaluators of students' social effectiveness in language. I also do not mean to imply that teachers' perceptions do not have real consequences. In Toohey and Willett's work, teachers' perceptions drove placement decisions for students for the entire subsequent school year. But, in Toohey and Willett's studies, as well as in this one, teachers' perceptions were flatly contradicted by measures of students' progress in acquiring language-as-a-stable-system (measured in this study as part of the research itself and in Toohey's and Willett's studies by a school language exam).

So, while no single study can produce a generalizable answer to the question posed above ('for which learners, with which repertoires ... etc.'), looking across studies can point to patterns in those answers. And what this study *does* produce is the suggestion of a slightly different research agenda from that presented by the studies in Chapter 1: Rather than examining how students negotiate positions and participation (with outcomes implied) or how certain kinds of participation lead to particular outcomes, we might ask how students negotiate the double-opportunity/double-obligation of peer interaction, constructing their peer social world and their place in it *while* learning a new language.

Toward Aligning Linguistic and Social Aims

Beyond asking how children themselves negotiate that double-opportunity/double-obligation, we might also ask how different kinds of classrooms facilitate that negotiation. What was it about Classroom Three that might have put linguistic and social aims at 'cross purposes?' And what kind of classroom might instead support alignment between linguistic and social aims?

In Chapter 2, I discussed the metaphor of context as rope: a rope is constituted by its strands at the same time that the strands get their meaning by being part of the rope. 'That which surrounds' is therefore never prior to that which it surrounds. I now realize that I should have been more specific. While it is true that any one rope (a token) does not exist outside its strands, the category of ropes and the idea of ropes (type) exist before and after the life of any specific rope. Similarly, while Classroom Three (the token) was brought about precisely as a result of the presence of Kritika, Rashmi, Hande and Padma's families in the neighborhood, the field of classrooms (types) – along with the subfield of preschool classrooms, and the institution called Head Start (also types) – long preceded these particular students. So, although teachers need students in order to be teachers, they do not need any one particular group of students. The teachers in Classroom Three were teachers before Classroom Three existed, and their histories and the institutional histories of preschool and schooling entered the classroom through their individual and institutional habitus. Thus, it might not be as easy for the strands to redefine the rope as the original metaphor may have made it seem.

And when the stability offered by the institutions of school and Head Start and by the teachers' habitus met the variability in the field created by the students' linguistic and cultural backgrounds, it produced tensions as well as contradictory practices for Ellen and Lucia. Both teachers spoke about the emergent bilinguals in the class as the single most defining element in the story of their year, and they told me – and I observed – all the ways that they adapted to assist their emergent bilingual students. Yet, both teachers at other times insisted that their teaching was exactly the same as it would have been had the class been made up of only English speakers. Lucia nearly scolded me when I asked if teaching so many emergent bilinguals presented any challenges or opportunities, saying, 'No. (2.0) <u>Sorry</u>. (3.0) You know, children are children. Boy, girl, big, small, race, creed, language, outspoken, sad' (Lucia, interview, 16 November 2012). Ellen likewise told me:

> I still planned what I would have planned whether I had all Americans or not. 'Cause I just I thought, 'Well, they'll eventually learn it. This is stuff they have to learn so even if they get a smidgen of it, even if they learn the letter B and Q this year, ok, that's two more letters they know.' No, I don't think having non-English speaking [students] affected how I planned. (Ellen, interview, 11 June 2013)

The teachers' inability to see, or perhaps unwillingness to say, that they adapted their teaching for their emergent bilingual students might have come from their belief, formed long ago in their family immigration narratives, that equality comes about through erasure of difference. This might have been the same belief that prevented them from making other adaptations to support their emergent bilingual students, like learning about and inviting the families' languages and traditions into the classroom. For instance, on the day that the Nepali students all showed up with rice on their foreheads, teachers chose to ignore it rather than ask about the occasion. And the teachers never asked why Hande did not eat pork or the Nepali speakers, beef. Just as Ellen felt that posting signs in Nepali or using the iPad to translate would have done students a disservice, the teachers felt that discussing language and culture or inviting home practices into the classroom would have meant highlighting difference and that this would have done students a disservice as well.

In making these decisions, the teachers unintentionally created a context in which language learning, while all around them, was meant to be invisible. Across the year, the teachers' comments to the children about language consisted of just two types: first, reminders to speak English, and second, explanations of students' social missteps as products of language learning. For example, recall Lucia's comments to Joey when Maiya, a younger Nepali speaker, grabbed his toy: 'She doesn't speak English too good yet, so we're gonna help her. Say, "Here Maiya, let's share."' Or recall when Tommy hijacked Hande's tattle about the oranges and Lucia attempted to calm Tommy down by explaining that Hande just 'gets mixed up, that's all.' While the reminders to speak English socialized students to see Nepali as less valuable in the classroom, the second type of comments may have instead socialized students to see a lack of English or a lack of correct English as linked to social failure.

This socialization stands in sharp contrast to what I have seen many dual language classrooms, where every child and all teachers are positioned as language learners, where talk about languages and language learning permeates, and where taking playful, translingual risks is something the teachers explicitly model (Axelrod, 2017; Gort & Pontier, 2013). Through these practices, language learning and multilingual identities become normal and valued, rather than invisible or undesirable (García-Mateus & Palmer, 2017; Sayer, 2011). Importantly, when taking linguistic risks is commonplace and is something that teachers both do and praise, taking linguistic risks no longer means taking social risks.

Although the Classroom Three teachers' language policymaking permitted an unofficial, multilingual underlife to flourish – which shaped Kritika's year in some positive ways – a multilingual underlife is not the same thing as an officially multilingual classroom. First, a multilingual underlife does not make visible and valuable the process of language learning or being multilingual. Second, while the multilingual underlife permitted Kritika to display her social skill and her procedural knowledge – her ability to 'do school' – Nepali did not help her or any of the other students show academic or content knowledge. The day that the teacher asked children at circle time to identify a picture of a butterfly and Kritika yelled '*Putali*!', or the day that Rashmi repeated '*Saati*! *Saati*!', as Ellen read a book about friendship, are just two examples of the kinds of missed opportunities that filled my videos. In some ways, my being in the classroom that year helped teachers see a tiny slice of this knowledge. When I brought in transcripts of extended free play in Nepali with English translations, Ellen and Lucia were always surprised and impressed with the richness of the children's play narratives. Yet, their surprise would have been unnecessary had the classroom been one where students could show their skills and knowledge in both languages right away.

Finally, an unofficial multilingual underlife does not help students access content while they are still learning English. More than half a century of work has focused on the challenge of developing strong early literacy skills in all English-speaking children, across parental income and education levels (Flesch, 1955; Snow *et al.*, 1998). The English-speaking children in Classroom Three had the advantage of doing this already difficult work in a language they already knew. The emergent bilingual students in the class, however, did not benefit from learning concepts of print, letter names, and sounds in a language they already knew, but had to learn language and literacy at the same time. Thus, although as Wray (2002) pointed out, being tossed in and forced to swim in 'submersion' learning (García & Kleifgen, 2010; Wright, 2010) may be best for short-term gains, when children's outcomes are compared over the long term, bilingual programs do a better job of getting students to academic English proficiency (while maintaining their home language), and they are the only programs that succeed in erasing the achievement gaps in the United States between students who are identified as language learners and those who are not (Collier & Thomas, 2017; Steele *et al.*, 2017).

This is not to say that only bilingual classrooms can normalize language learning, value multilingualism and support linguistic risk-taking. Gillanders (2007) studied a teacher who could not speak her students' L1 (Spanish) but who made attempts to learn Spanish and to use it in the classroom. By making visible her own process of learning Spanish and asking students for help, she elevated the status of Spanish and Spanish expertise in the class, resulting in positive effects on peer relationships and interaction. These findings are supported by decades of work on culturally responsive teaching, which has shown positive outcomes for students when teachers express curiosity about and learn about their students' cultural, linguistic and social practices and draw upon these as a classroom resource (Gay, 2018; Moll *et al.*, 1992; Souto-Manning, 2013). In Classroom Three, engaging with linguistic and cultural differences, rather than only tolerating them, may have supported students' learning and risk-taking.

Supporting Teachers, Preventing Harm

Yet (small) changes did occur in Classroom Three. Ellen came into the year thinking that parent language was what was holding the emergent bilingual students back, and she was able to revise her theory to think about classroom social dynamics. While a person's habitus may change reluctantly, changes can occur, particularly when the field shifts and people experience a mismatch between habitus and field: suddenly old practices do not quite work and things that are usually invisible come to light (Bourdieu, 1977). In the fall of this study, Ellen and Lucia entered a field that they thought was the same as others that they had been in, but, by the nature of the participants – Kritika, Rashmi, Hande and Padma, but also Pooja, Sreya, Anita, Dinesh, Prakesh, Monal and Maiya – it was different in important ways. Yet, when this disruption occurred, creating potential for change, the teachers were not offered, and did not seek, any alternative narratives or practices. They thus fell back on (slightly adapted) old ones. And, as discussed above, these old practices may have served to limit what their students were able or willing to learn.

Additionally, those old practices have the potential to do real damage. For instance, anyone who has raised a multilingual child in the United States is likely not surprised by the teachers' suggestion that parents should use English at home. Despite decades of evidence that fluent and complex use of a first language bootstraps children's learning of a second language (Bialystok, 2012; Cárdenas-Hagan *et al.*, 2007; Cummins, 1979, 2008; Goodrich *et al.*, 2013), the advice to parents to switch to English is common, coming from well-meaning teachers as well as other professionals such as pediatricians (King & Mackey, 2009; Rodriguez, 1983; Tabors, 2008). This advice can lead children to stop developing their family language and to replace it with English, which can have serious consequences, such as breakdowns in family communication and intergenerational conflict (Wong Fillmore, 1991b, 1996, 2000).

I recently had the chance to speak to a group of applied linguistics PhD students about my research. As I talked about a collaboration with students in my university's bilingual Speech Language Pathology training program, a student raised his hand and expressed shock that bilingual speech therapy was a possibility. I casually assured him that it was and remarked that language delay and disability do not preclude bilingualism. To my surprise, the student began to cry. He told the story of how his eldest child's teachers and pediatrician told him to speak only English with his son, who had autism, and how he and his wife took their advice. And when he had more children, he wanted to avoid speaking with them in a language his eldest did not know, so he spoke to them only in English, too. Now, nearly two decades after the birth of his eldest, he described how painful it is to have children who are completely cut off from grandparents, cousins, aunts and uncles. His story highlights the damage that well-meaning professionals can do when they advise parents to stop using home languages. Similarly, while neither Ellen and Lucia's actions, nor their advice, was ever intended to do anything but help, they, too, had the potential to damage. One of the few times I contradicted Ellen and Lucia that year was to advise parents in interviews that speaking Nepali and Turkish at home was right, that their children would learn English, and that the real risk in the United States would be that the children would come home insisting on speaking English (Tuominen, 1999).

Throughout the year, Ellen and Lucia made sense of their new students the best way they were able to, given the resources available to them, and in light of their own experiences. But what would have happened if there had been some district support? What if teachers had been introduced to ideas about multilingualism, shown how it does not hinder English, and given practices to support growth in multiple languages? What if teachers were introduced to the principles of culturally responsive teaching, walked through why talking about difference is appropriate and beneficial, and given tools to support talk about languages, clothes, and rice on foreheads? What if they played Nepali music or asked to hear Hande's voice in Turkish? How would it have changed the year for the children, for the parents and for Ellen and Lucia?

All across the United States, in places where multiple languages are the norm, as well as in places that long seemed immune to new immigration, there are teachers like Ellen and Lucia. In many of these places, preschool teachers are not required to learn about multilingual language development or engage in any special preparation for working with students whose language and culture differ from theirs. When teachers are left to their own devices, for better or for worse, they – we – fall back on our habitus. This can mean that very caring teachers, who truly love their students, can end up teaching in ways that may not help their students grow as much as they could. In the push to support all students, helping them get read for kindergarten through expanded preschool programs, we should not forget that supporting students means supporting their teachers as well.

Success in Language Learning

One of the findings of this study was that assessing language learning in three different ways produced three different versions of success. In her spring interview, Ellen told me that, overall, the students had not learned as much English as she would have liked:

> To me, I think that (1.0) being that there was just so many, they fell back on their language and they didn't have to, you know, try that hard to learn English. But if you are the only one, you're either going to sink or swim. (Ellen, interview, 11 June 2013)

Yet, Ellen did not think of Hande in this discussion of sinking and swimming, and she never viewed Hande as having an advantage. What counted for Ellen and Lucia was what students could accomplish socially and academically through language, as part of ongoing social practice in the classroom. As such, Hande's quiet learning went unnoticed. At the same time, Kritika's slower acquisition of syntax and vocabulary also went unnoticed. The teachers understood Kritika's ability to write the alphabet, to count to 20 and to draw people with arms and legs, as indicators of language ability. For them, Kritika – the listener, the helper and the subteacher, who was never rowdy, never running in school, never throwing sand or water or food – was a socially, academically and linguistically competent student. The teachers, lacking a way to understand language as extracted from what students could do with it, were unable to see language in the decontextualized, systematic way that would have permitted them to see Hande's acquisition or Kritika's needs. Only when I applied tools of analysis – recording, transcription, building a corpus, sorting and counting – was I able to see how Hande excelled but also how Padma could manipulate language for fun, and even how Rashmi used language in unexpected ways. I was also able to see not *just* that Kritika was successful, but exactly *how* she was successful.

These findings are a reminder, then, that the tools, including the definitions, that we use to look at language matter a great deal. The definition of language that we choose, the slice of language that we focus on and the ways we amass data points, all shape what counts as success and who looks successful. In this study, examining language as vocabulary and syntax made Hande look successful, while examining language for its social effects made Kritika seem to have had more success. Neither of these is wrong; each only tells a partial story.

Although Ellen and Lucia's assessment methods (or lack thereof) may have been unfair to Hande, the district language assessment that the students would be given before kindergarten would likely not showcase Kritika's skill. And while Ellen and Lucia could be given tools to help them assess language in ways that would allow them to see Hande's progress, their instinct to understand language as socially embedded should be fostered as well. Teachers should be supported in seeing language in both ways.

Yet, Padma and Rashmi's cases provoke the question: What *other* ways of defining language could there be and who would be made to look successful by them? What if I were to judge success by ability to engage in metalinguistic talk and language play? In that case, Padma would emerge as more successful than anyone. Or what about an evaluation of linguistic resiliency, or the ability to persist in creating a multilingual classroom in the face of adults who say, 'We only speak English here'? In that case, all the Nepali speakers would be deemed to have shown remarkable success. While children, and particularly children as young as three and four, are not typically considered policymakers in language policy literature, the children in Classroom Three shaped their classroom policies in significant ways (see also Boyd & Huss, 2017; Henderson & Palmer, 2015; McCarty *et al.*, 2009).

And what might Rashmi's version of success be? What did she learn? When I say that I do not know, it implies a failure not on her part but on mine. I simply have yet to find the right lens for her. Teachers – and researchers – must be able to understand and assess language in multiple ways, and thus hold multiple definitions of success. As the stories of the children in Classroom Three make clear, success in language learning does not – and should not – mean one thing.

Appendix 1: Details about Conflicts that Brought Classroom Three Families to the United States and their Experiences with Resettlement

Becoming Refugees: What Happened in Bhutan

Most of the families in Classroom Three who had arrived in the United States as refugees were from Bhutan, a tiny South Asian country that lies between India and China, near Nepal. They were part of an ethnic Nepali population that had been in Bhutan since the 1890's, when the government of Bhutan gave permission to settlers from Nepal to come and live in the largely unpopulated southern, sub-tropical region, in order to clear the forests and begin farming there (BCAP: About us, n.d.; Mishra, 2013; Pulla, 2016). The ethnic Nepali population grew, both through further immigration from Nepal and through local births. Meanwhile, the southern area of Bhutan remained relatively separated from the north. In the South, the population – known as Lhotshampa, or 'Southerners' – was Hindu, ethnic Nepali, and spoke Nepali. In the north, the ruling Drupka population was Buddhist, Bhutanese, and spoke the national language, Dzongkha.

Through porous borders, the southern Lhotshampa population continued to grow. In the 1950s, in an effort toward modernization and unification, the king in the north declared a two-pronged plan: infrastructure development to better connect the north and south and a closing of the borders to new immigration. At the same time, the Citizenship Act of 1958 granted citizenship to any Nepali people who could show that they had been in Bhutan for 10 years or more (BCAP: About us, n.d.; Hutt, 2005) Yet, in order to build infrastructure, particularly in the South, more laborers were needed and thus the immigration regulations were not enforced. The Nepali-speaking Lhotshampa population continued to grow, showing almost no signs of assimilation into the larger Bhutanese society and maintaining their own language and cultural practices, despite cash payments offered for intermarriage (BCAP: About us, n.d.).

In the 1980s, as the Lhotshampa population threatened to surpass the ethnic Bhutanese population, the government began to see the Lhotshampa as a risk to national order. A 1985 Citizenship Act attempted to enforce the 1958 rules (Bhutan Citizenship Act 1985, n.d.). In a 1988 census, residents who could not prove that they had been in Bhutan prior to 1958 were labeled 'non-nationals.' The same year, the government's 'One Nation, One People' policy, aimed at preserving a national culture, banned the Nepali language in schools and legalized fines for wearing Nepali dress in public, even for citizens (BCAP: About us, n.d.; Hutt, 2005; Mishra, 2013; Pulla, 2016). Protests broke out among Lhotshampa and 20,000 people marched against the government. Between 2000 and 12,000 southerners fled Bhutan during this time. Ethnic clashes continued into the early 1990s, with violent encounters between organizations supporting Lhotshampa rights in Bhutan and the Bhutanese government. Schools and government offices were closed in the South, and the government carried out violent raids on southern villages. Many people were arrested, injured, kidnapped and killed. Many southerners fled Bhutan throughout the early 1990s and many more were forced to sign Voluntary Migration Documents before being expelled (Mishra, 2013). The property of those who fled or were expelled was confiscated, destroyed or redistributed (Pulla, 2016), effectively erasing the 100-year presence of the Lhotshampa in Bhutan.

In total, this ethnic cleansing produced 112,523 refugees (United Nations High Commissioner for Refugees, 2005). Some settled in India but most were forced to continue on to Nepal (Mishra, 2013). These refugees first settled along the Mai River, where hunger, lack of clean water, and sickness were rampant. In 1992, the United Nations stepped in and built several refugee camps. Although Nepal and Bhutan engaged in bilateral talks beginning in 1993, the Bhutanese government continued to deny that any of the refugees were Bhutanese citizens, effectively preventing repatriation. Meanwhile, Nepal denied the refugees the possibility of becoming citizens, preventing local integration. The Bhutanese Nepalis lived in limbo in the camps for nearly two decades, establishing villages, schools, stores and lives (In the camps, n.d.). In 2006, when it finally became clear that repatriation was not a viable option, the United States and several other countries agreed to take in the Lhotshampa as refugees. The UNHCR began the resettlement process in 2007. While many Lhotshampa initially resisted, worrying that they would miss out on a chance to return to Bhutan, eventually more than 100,000 refugees were resettled in other countries (Shrestha, 2015), with 85,000 in the United States. This is how the families in my study ended up in River City.

From the parents' perspectives

All the parents in Classroom Three were young – from 5 to 14 years old – when they left Bhutan. While the youngest could hardly remember the conflict, the oldest recalled:

> I studied Nepali up to Class 5 in Bhutan and after that the government banned the language and the language was no longer in practice in the academic field, in the schools, or in the education institutions. Later, I went to one of the schools in northern part once the schools in the south were closed. (Monal's father, interview, 30 January 2013)

Another mother recounted: 'We were forced to wear Bhutanese dress, we were forced to cut our hair, and then we were forced to leave Nepali culture, so that's why we left Bhutan' (Anita's mother, interview, 30 January 2013). The one grandmother who participated in an interview was 30 when her family left, and she remembered more about life before. She recalled:

> When I lived there, everything was fine, everything was normal, but then we had to leave and we had to leave everything, our belongings. I had an orange farm and a spices farm. I had all my properties, land, and animals and house and I had to leave it all. So I'm feeling not good. (Padma's grandmother, interview, 30 January 2013)

Once in Nepal, all the parents/grandparents lived in refugee camps for between 18 and 19 years (Interviews, 28 and 30 January 2013.) When they were finally resettled to the United States in 2007 and 2008, two of the parents were placed in River City, the location they had requested in order to join family. The others were placed in cities like Boise, Idaho or St Louis, Missouri and later chose to move to River City, primarily for jobs. Prakesh's father told me: 'I heard that we get lot of job opportunities here. That's why we moved here' (Interview, 28 January 2013). Other parents echoed his sentiment: 'In Idaho there was no work; here we have work. There were lots of problem [in Bhutan], but here you can work as you wish' (Pooja's mother, interview, 30 January 2013). Anita's mother told me: 'It's convenient for kids. There is the school bus nearby our home and also there are jobs. Everybody's working' (Interview, 30 January 2013). Padma's grandmother told me: 'My children, they can work here, they can pay bills. My husband also works' (Interview, 28 January 2013). Several parents also mentioned having family and community in River City. One father, when asked what was good about River City, said: 'Mmmmm a big community. I'm in a similar community,' meaning a community of people similar to himself in terms of history, language and culture (Monal's father, interview, 28 January 2013.) All the Nepali preschool students in the study, born after their parents had arrived in the United States, were born into a large and vibrant Nepali-speaking community.

Becoming Refugees: What happened in Uzbekistan

Although they spoke Turkish, Hande's family was not from Turkey, as the teachers originally thought, but were part of an ethnically Turkish population referred to as Meskhetian or Ahiska Turks, a group of people who originated in Georgia, speak a dialect of Turkish, and are Muslim. In the 1950s, Stalin evicted the Meskhetian population, along with several other ethnic minorities, from Georgia, for the official (and invented) reason that they had collaborated with Hitler (Aydingün *et al.*, 2006). They settled across Kyrgyzstan, Kazakhstan and Uzbekistan. In 1989, however, during rising nationalism and tensions around modernization in Uzbekistan, interethnic violence directed toward the Meskhetian Turks broke out, with mobs throwing stones and burning houses. More than 100 people were killed. As a result, the Soviet army helped to evacuate 17,000 Meskhetian Turks, and many more fled on their own (Aydingün *et al.*, 2006). They settled in surrounding countries, including Russia. While most regions of Russia granted the Meskhetian Turks citizenship, the Krasnodar region, where Hande's parents' families had settled, did not. The region refused to give them *propiska*, a document that registered their residences and let them move around the country. This refusal made them stateless in the eyes of Soviet (and eventually Russian) law, and it effectively prevented them from getting birth certificates, enrolling in school, working, receiving medical care and marrying (Koriouchkina, 2010; Swerdlow, 2006).

Keeping the Meskhetian Turks in Krasnodar from working amounted to what Aydingün *et al.* called a 'soft ethnic cleansing,' because it effectively starved them out of the region (Aydingün *et al.*, 2006: 9). This was combined with official raids for proper 'guest registration' documents, as well as unofficial and more violent raids by vigilante, neo-Cossack groups dedicated to maintaining local ethnic purity. Then, in 2002, a law was enacted that prevented Meskhetian Turks from cultivating land, leaving them with no way to produce food or make money (Swerdlow, 2006). After hunger strikes by local Meskhetian Turks, world human rights organizations took notice and began to try to broker repatriation to Georgia. In 2006, with still no durable solution in sight, the United States opened its doors for Meskhetian Turks to come as refugees. Hande's mother and father were among those chosen to resettle in River City.

From Hande's mother's perspective

Hande's mother explained that she was born in Uzbekistan and left for Russia in 1989, when she was eight. She lived in Russia until

2006, when she and her family came to the United States as refugees because they could not go to their first choice, Turkey (Hande's mother, interview, 19 February 2013). Hande's mother described the situation in Russia:

> A lot of us couldn't get citizenship, Russian citizenship. They worked in the fields, couldn't get a real job. They were making crafts and trying to make a living, by farming and- it started in 1989 and up to the year when we moved, it was like that for us. We couldn't work. And the children who were born there, they couldn't get the family name from their father because their father was nobody in the country. (Hande's mother, interview, 19 February 2013)

Hande's mother and father were both born in Uzbekistan and had lived near one another in Russia, but they did not meet until they were in River City. There, they married and had children. Hande was their eldest. Like many of the other parents, Hande's mother was happy with the job opportunities in River City. Her husband had worked in a factory for several years and had saved enough money to purchase a pizza shop with his brothers. They lived in an apartment with her sister, her husband's brothers, and their families – 17 people in all – so Hande and her younger sister were immersed in Turkish. Hande's parents both spoke Russian as well but did not want to teach it to their children yet, reserving it for now as a secret language to use between themselves in front of the children.

Appendix 2: Detailed Methodological Information

Methods Details for Chapters 3 and 4

The data for Chapters 3 and 4 come from several sources. First, I used field notes and video transcripts from across my year in Classroom Three to understand teachers' language policies, through an analysis of all instances of teacher talk about language (e.g. commenting on language use, directing students to use language in particular ways, etc.). Through these analyses, I sought to understand teachers' language management approaches as well as their underlying beliefs about language and language learning.

In addition to examining classroom practices, I conducted and audio recorded four teacher interviews, one in November with each teacher and another in June. In the fall interview, I spoke with teachers about five general topics: their backgrounds and paths to becoming teachers in Classroom Three, their experiences with language and language learning, how they think about language and language learning in their classroom, their views on the class as a whole and on each student in particular, and their goals for the year. In the spring interview, I revisited the same topics, but from a retrospective approach, asking how students changed and grew, how language learning went, what helped or didn't help students learn English, and what advice they would give new teachers in their position next year.

Finally, I drew on parent interviews, carried out in January of the school year. In total, parents of nine children chose to participate. Of these nine, three spoke English at home, five spoke Nepali, and one spoke Turkish (although she was bilingual in Russian and suggested I find a Russian interpreter instead, since River City has a substantial Russian-speaking community). This sample of parents represented a variety of languages that was roughly proportionate to the class as a whole. Table A2.1 summarizes the students whose parents participated in an interview, as well as their home language and the language in which their parent's interview was conducted. All interviews in English took place one on one, while those in Nepali or Russian occurred through interpreters (or, in one case, in English with an interpreter present). Both the Nepali and Russian interpreters were women in their late

Table A2.1 Students whose parents participated in an interview

Student	Home Language	Parent who participated in interview	Interview Language
Luke	English	Mother	English
Joey	English	Mother	English
Tommy	English	Mother	English
Hande	Turkish	Mother	Russian
Monal	Nepali	Father	English/Nepali
Prakesh	Nepali	Father	Nepali
Anita	Nepali	Mother*	Nepali
Pooja	Nepali	Mother*	Nepali
Padma	Nepali	Grandmother	Nepali

*These two mothers were friends and chose to do their interview together.

20s/early 30s, who were referred by friends or colleagues. The Nepali interpreter had grown up in Nepal, moved to River City for college, and was now interpreting full time for courts as well as two local resettlement agencies. The Russian speaker had grown up in River City and was a part-time Russian teacher and full-time student. In selecting the interpreters, I was careful to make sure that neither might have been from a group involved in the persecution of the families before they had moved to the United States.

Parent interviews addressed parents' educational and linguistic histories, US arrival stories, feelings about living in River City, motives/goals for sending student to school, and feelings about the school. I also posed a series of hypothetical language situations – having bilingual teachers or a bilingual classroom, having more languages represented in the classroom, having a different balance of speakers in the classroom – to gain a better understanding of parents' beliefs about language learning. These interviews were audio recorded and, at the end of the interview, I gave parents a picture book to take home (in English, English/Nepali, or English/Turkish, based on their home language).

Methods Details for Chapter 6

Analysis of positioning

To examine students' positioning in Classroom Three, I primarily drew on teacher interview data, field notes and transcripts from video data. My primary method of analysis was a back and forth between microanalysis of interaction (Bloome *et al.*, 2008; Erickson, 1992) and coding. Through close interaction analysis, I was able to tease apart how students were positioned in interactions in which they were participants, as well as in interviews (in which they were not participants). From those microanalyses, I created codes for types of positions. I was then able to recognize these position types in discourse analyses of other interactions. I started with general, descriptive codes, like 'sloppy,' 'wild,' 'quiet,' 'good friend,' and, through multiple rounds of coding, found that most of the positioning happening in the classroom boiled down to students being competent (or not) and authoritative (or not) within four domains: social/play; classroom rules/procedures; academic; and linguistic. Through these iterative cycles of discourse analysis and coding, I found that being positioned as competent within a certain domain was necessary but not sufficient for being positioned as authoritative in that domain. I also saw that competence/authority from one domain often 'bootstrapped' other domains. Using these codes, I was able to trace students' positioning as more and less competent/authoritative across the year and to tell each focal student's story. I supplemented this analysis with data from teacher interviews, in which teachers talked about individual students, as well as with data from classroom interactions between teachers and students.

Social network analysis

In addition to this qualitative and discursive data, I also used student interviews as a way to quantify, as well as visually map, students' positions, using social network analysis (Borgatti *et al.*, 2013; Friedkin & Thomas, 1997). Social network analysis (SNA) is a theoretical framework for thinking about how members of social networks can influence each other in various ways, like providing support, information, or in this case, linguistic input. SNA uses quantitative data to map relationships among groups of people and to understand how those relationships affect the spread of resources. Because of this study's presumption that peer interaction, particularly with English speakers, is important for English learning, social network mapping provides a visual and numeric representation of how connected students are within the classroom peer network. As Borgatti *et al.* stated: 'A generic hypothesis of network theory is that an actor's position in a network determines in part the constraints and opportunities that he or she will encounter, and therefore identifying that position is important for predicting actor outcomes such as performance, behavior or beliefs' (Borgatti *et al.*, 2013: 1). In this case, the network is one preK class and the outcome in question is English learning.

In order to build a social network map of the class, I interviewed students at the end of the school year using a procedure in which I laid out pictures of their classmates in random order and asked each student to pick out whom she liked to play with (see Figure A2.1). After noting the student's choices, I replaced those photos and, to make sure

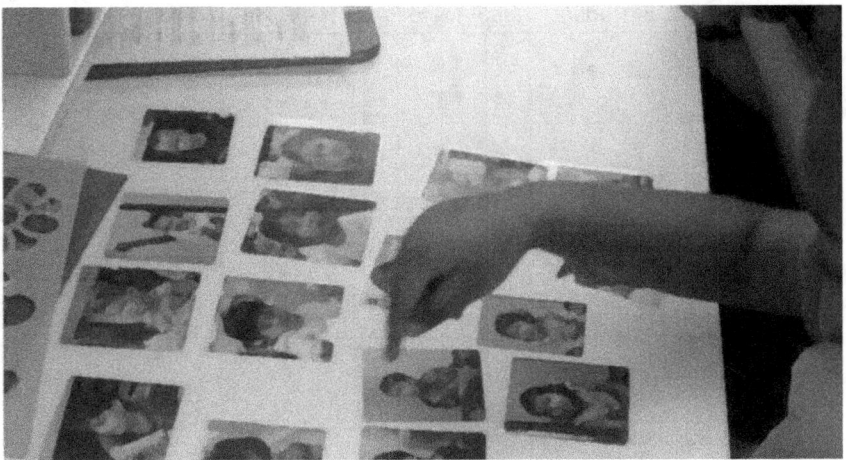

Figure A2.1 Building the social network map of the class

the students were not picking at random, asked whom they did *not* like to play with. The 'like to play with' interview data were entered into a matrix, with each student's name across the top and side (see Table A2.2). Within the matrix, a 1 was used to represent 'like to play with,' while a 0 represents an absence of 'liking to play with.' In a *non-directed* relationship, like kinship, in which relationships are always reciprocal, each person's column and row would be the same. But in a *directed* relationship, such as whom a student likes to play with, where the answers might not always be reciprocal, the columns and rows can differ. Thus, the 1s in Kelsey's *row* show that Kelsey reported liking to play with Luke, Joey, Caleb, Tommy and Pooja. The 1's in Kelsey *column* show that Luke, Joey, Caleb and Hande reported liking to play with her.

This matrix is a useful way to organize data, but it can also be used to calculate mathematical descriptors about the structure of a network and of an individual's place within it. For instance, one important network-level descriptor is cohesion, or density. In the densest network possible, all actors would be connected to each other. I would expect such network density if, in spring of a school year, I asked the students, 'Show me who you know in your class.' If I asked them, however, to show me whose house they had visited, I would expect a much less dense network. Network density is measured by the proportion of the number of actual relationships in a network to the number of possible relationships (1 = most dense, 0 = no relationships at all). Density is important for understanding things like flows of information or spread of diseases, as these move faster in more tightly-connected networks than in loose ones.

The relationship matrix also provides a way to quantitatively describe an actor's role within the network. One key actor-level measure

Table A2.2 Matrix of students' responses to 'Show me who you like to play with'

	Kelsey	Luke	Joey	Joy	Caleb	Tommy	Anita	Pooja	Padma	Kritika	Rashmi	Sreya	Maiya	Dinesh	Prakesh	Monal	Hande
Kelsey		1	1	0	1	1	0	1	0	0	0	0	0	0	0	0	0
Luke	1		1	0	0	0	0	0	0	0	0	0	0	0	0	0	0
Joey	1	1		0	0	0	0	0	0	0	0	0	0	0	0	0	0
Joy	0	0	0		0	1	1	1	1	1	0	0	1	0	0	0	0
Caleb	1	1	1	0		0	0	0	0	1	0	0	0	1	0	0	0
Tommy	0	0	0	0	0		0	0	0	0	0	0	0	0	0	0	0
Anita	0	0	0	0	0	0		1	1	1	0	0	0	0	0	0	0
Pooja	0	0	0	0	0	0	0		0	1	0	0	0	1	0	0	0
Padma	0	0	0	0	0	0	0	0		1	0	0	0	0	0	0	0
Kritika	0	0	0	0	0	0	1	1	1		0	0	0	0	0	0	0
Rashmi	0	0	0	0	0	0	0	0	0	0		0	0	0	1	0	0
Sreya	0	0	0	0	0	0	1	1	1	1			1	0	0	0	0
Maiya	0	0	0	0	0	1	1	0	0	0	0	1		1	0	0	0
Dinesh	0	0	0	0	0	0	0	0	0	0	0	0	0		0	0	0
Prakesh	0	0	0	0	0	0	0	0	0	0	1	0	0	1		0	0
Monal	0	0	0	0	0	0	0	0	0	0	0	0	0	1	0		0
Hande	1	0	0	0	0	0	0	0	0	0	0	0	0	0	0	0	

is centrality, or how central to a network a node is. There are a few kinds of centrality. In-degree centrality measures how many inbound connections an actor has, or for instance, how many people report a given actor as a friend or resource or mentor. This measure is important in a study like mine where being named as a playmate is an indicator of the number and range of the people a student interacts with. Out-degree centrality instead measures how many outbound connections an actor has, or how many others the actor herself reports liking, playing with, etc. In a study of, say, who borrows money from whom, the ratio of in-degree to out-degree centrality could be an important indicator of the flow of money; in a classroom study of who students turn to for help with school work, the two kinds of centrality might indicate which students are viewed as resources and which are not. Finally, betweenness centrality measures how many second-degree connections between actors would disappear if an actor were not present. This is an important kind of centrality when examining how key each actor is to the spread of something like advice or disease through a network.

Importantly, these measures can be used to predict outcomes. SNA researchers can test hypotheses about the relationship between the structure of a network or the location of an actor within it (independent variable) and particular outcomes (dependent variable). For instance, in a study of disease spread, the density of a network might predict speed of transmission. In a study of academic success, a person's connections to other academically successful people might predict that person's own success. In my study, the hypothesis was that a student's centrality in the classroom would predict better language-learning outcomes.

While the matrix provides a way to quantify network data, it is less helpful for visualizing patterns. By importing matrix data into SNA software, such as UCINET's Netdraw (Borgatti *et al.*, 2002), it becomes possible to create a map of a network, which can provide information at a glance about the network and individuals' positions within it (Figure A.2.2). In this network map, all the students are represented by *nodes*. The ties, or lines, represent students' answers to the question: 'Who do you like to play with?' Ties with one arrow head indicate a non-reciprocal answer, while ties with two arrow heads are reciprocal. For instance, Rashmi and her cousin, Prakesh, each reported liking to play with the other, so her node is connected to his with a two-headed arrow. Meanwhile, Hande reported liking to play with Kelsey, but Kelsey did not say that she liked to play with Hande, so the arrow connecting them points from Hande to Kelsey, indicating that their relationship is directed rather than reciprocal.

Social network maps make it possible to see visually what measures like in-degree centrality and betweenness centrality describe numerically.

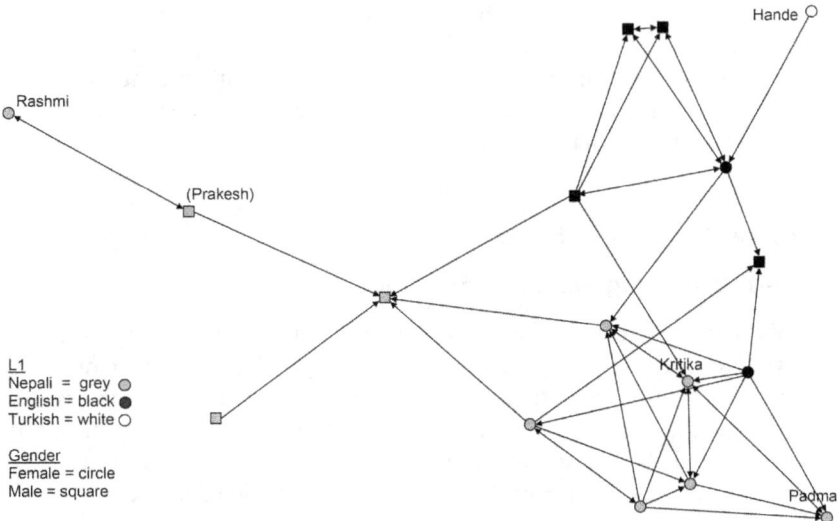

Figure A2.2 Classroom Three social network map

In the case of the Classroom Three network, for example, it is possible to see that Kritika has many arrows leading to her node (high in-degree centrality) or that Dinesh links Prakesh and Monal to the rest of the class and were he not present, the second-degree connections between Prakesh, Monal, Caleb, Maiya and Pooja would all disappear (high betweenness centrality).

In addition to showing the presence, absence and direction of relationships, social network maps can give other information as well. The color, size and shape of nodes can represent actor-level *attributes,* or variables. In the Classroom Three map in Figure A2.2, for example, node color represents the attribute 'first language,' while node shape represents 'gender.' Visualizing attributes can help to make patterns visible. For instance, in the Classroom Three map, it is easy to see that class friendship groups mainly split along language lines. It is also clear that, among the Nepali speakers, friendships follow gender lines, with the exception of Rashmi. Finally, although measures of density can help to describe the whole network, network maps make it possible to easily identify pockets of density *within* the network. SNA researchers describe small, maximally-dense pockets in which all actors are connected to all other actors as *cliques*. In Classroom Three, for example, Kelsey, Luke, Caleb and Joey are part of a four-person clique in which all four are connected to each other.

Since social network analysts have found that reported data are not always reliable (Bernard & Killworth, 1977; Killworth & Bernard, 1976), I also used UCINET to create maps from counts of actual interactions between student dyads in videos from the last three months of school. Because there is no way for me to normalize these counts (I would have to know the number of interactions between each pair that *could have taken place* but I did not), the measures from this mapping were not valid representations of relationship strength, but the close resemblance of this map to the map of reported friendship did confirm that students' reports of whom they like to play with were accurate representations of whom they actually played with.

Methods Details for Chapter 7

Analyzing language as a stable system

While there are many ways to assess language growth, I wanted to understand growth in terms of the language that the students were actually using. So instead of eliciting language through an assessment tool, I used the video I had recorded across the year as data, pulling each student's English utterances from the transcripts and compiling them together into a corpus for each student. I then divided each corpus into a fall corpus (September – November) and a spring corpus (April-June), so that I could look at growth between those two time periods.

I analyzed each student's fall and spring corpus for several measures: the overall quantity of English they were using, how diverse the words that they were using were (vocabulary), and how grammatically complex their speech was (syntactic complexity). To measure overall quantity, I calculated the percentage of their conversational turns that were in English, as well as totaled the number of English words that each student used, per hour of video. (I counted 'per hour of video' so that differences in on-screen time would not make one student look like she was speaking more than another when really she just happened to be on camera more.) To measure vocabulary, I used a web-based lexical complexity analyzer (Ai, 2014; see also Ai & Lu, 2010; Lu, 2012) to count all the unique words that each student used. To measure syntactic complexity, I calculated average words per utterance, or Mean Length of Utterance (MLU), a standard, if basic, measure of complexity (Bulté & Housen, 2012; Dubasik & Wilcox, 2013; Norris & Ortega, 2009). While other measures have been proposed, such as amount of coordination or subordination, or even systems that specifically measure the developmental level of child speech (D-level scale, Lu, 2009), none of these measures was sensitive enough for my students' levels of language use. For example, even according to the D-level scale, which is meant for children, all the focal students would be at level 0, even at the end of the year. Lastly, I counted the number of AS-units containing verbs (Dubasik & Wilcox, 2013). (See Note 3 at the end of Chapter 7 for a definition of AS-unit.)

Analyzing language as social effectiveness

In order to understand how effective an utterance was as a speech act, I first examined each utterance in the corpus without going back to read it in its original context. Based on the utterance alone, I labeled each utterance as the speech act that, I, a year-long participant in the social field of Classroom Three, thought the speaker was trying to accomplish (request, protest, question, tattle, invitation to play, etc.). I then examined each utterance back in its context (both transcript and video) and by looking at the context – ongoing activity and participation framework, eye gaze, gesture, body position, and intonation of both speaker and hearers, as well as reactions of both – I was able to see, in all cases but one, what the speaker likely hoped to accomplish with her utterance. Particularly strong evidence for this intention came in the speaker's reaction to the hearers' response. Four-year-olds are rarely stoic in the face of success or disappointment, and students showed these reactions through their facial expressions (smiling versus pouting with brows furrowed), body position (back to play or sitting relaxed, versus slumped down or arms crossed with back turned to interlocutor), or even sometimes their words. For example, when I read the utterance, 'Miss, I'm water!' I categorized it as a request (to the teacher). In this preK, the

Nepali-speaking emergent bilingual students used the format 'I'm X' to mean 'I want X,' particularly early on in the year[1]. They also called both teachers 'Miss' at first, before learning to call them by their names. When I analyzed this utterance back in context, I found that it had been produced by Padma on 29 October 2012 to Miss Ellen. Having pushed her milk carton away, Padma was sitting at the snack table, holding her empty water cup above her head, when she said: 'Miss, I'm water.' This confirmed for me that her utterance was indeed a request. Miss Ellen, passing by, shook her head at Padma and said: 'Milk milk milk. Drink your milk. Gotta have your strong bones and milk!' Padma set her cup back down and, pouting, poked at the peaches on her plate. I therefore answered the three questions about effectiveness in the following way:

(1) **Form**: Is the form of this utterance a conventional one? (In other words, in this social field, was this utterance a recognized or recognizable way of accomplishing a particular speech act?) **YES.**
(2) **Force**: Is there evidence that the utterance was heard by its audience and taken to be a particular speech act? **YES.**
(3) **Effect**: Is there evidence in the speaker's reaction that the utterance achieved its desired effects? **NO.**

Note

(1) I think this was an approximation of how some English-speaking children pronounced, 'I want water' as something close to 'Unna water!'

References

Ai, H. (2014) Lexical complexity analyzer. Retrieved 3 March 2014 from http://aihaiyang.com/software/synlex/lexical/.
Ai, H. and Lu, X. (2010) A web-based system for automatic measurement of lexical complexity. Presented at the 27th Annual Symposium of the Computer-Assisted Language Consortium (CALICO-10), 8 June. Amherst: MA.
America's Most Affordable Cities (2013) *Forbes Magazine*. Retrieved 21 August 2013 from https://www.forbes.com/pictures/emeg45effdi/introduction/#3cb62f1b2e27.
Andersen, K.N. (2017) Translanguaging pedagogy in multilingual early childhood classes. A video ethnography in Luxembourg. *Translation and Translanguaging in Multilingual Contexts* 3 (2), 167–183. doi:10.1075/ttmc.
Auer, P. (1984) *Bilingual Conversation*. Amsterdam: John Benjamins Publishing.
Auerbach, E.R. (1993) Reexamining English only in the ESL classroom. *TESOL Quarterly* 27 (1), 9–32. https://doi.org/10.2307/3586949.
Austin, J.L. (1975) *How To Do Things with Words*. Cambridge, MA: Harvard University Press.
Axelrod, Y. (2017) 'Ganchulinas' and 'Rainbowli' colors: Young multilingual children play with language in Head Start classroom. *Early Childhood Education Journal* 45 (1), 103–110.
Axelrod, Y. and Cole, M.W. (2018) 'The pumpkins are coming ... vienen las calabazas ... that sounds funny': Translanguaging practices of young emergent bilinguals. *Journal of Early Childhood Literacy* 18 (1), 129–153. https://doi.org/10.1177/1468798418754938.
Aydingün, A., Harding, Ç.B., Hoover, M., Kuznetsov, I. and Swerdlow, S. (2006) *Meskhetian Turks: An Introduction to their History, Culture and Resettlement Experiences* (Culture Profile). Washington, DC: Center for Applied Linguistics.
Baker, C. (2001) *Foundations of Bilingual Education and Bilingualism* (3rd edn). Clevedon: Multilingual Matters.
BCAP: About us. (n.d) Retrieved 1 October 2017 from http://www.bcap.us/about-us/.
Bernales, C. (2016) Conflicting pathways to participation in the FL classroom: L2 speech production vs. L2 thought processes. *Foreign Language Annals* 49 (2), 367–383. https://doi.org/10.1111/flan.12200.
Bernard, H.R. and Killworth, P.D. (1977) Informant accuracy in social network data II. *Human Communication Research* 4 (1), 3–18. https://doi.org/10.1111/j.1468-2958.1977.tb00591.x.
Bernard, H.R., Killworth, P.D. and Sailer, L. (1982) Informant accuracy in social-network data V. An experimental attempt to predict actual communication from recall data. *Social Science Research* 11 (1), 30–66. https://doi.org/10.1016/0049-089X(82)90006-0.
Bernstein, K.A. (2016a) 'Misunderstanding' and (mis)interpretation as strategic tools in intercultural interaction between preschool children. *Applied Linguistics Review* 7 (4), 471–494. http://dx.doi.org/10.1515/applirev-2016-0021.
Bernstein, K.A. (2016b) Writing their way into talk: Emergent bilinguals' emergent literacy practices as pathways to peer interaction and oral language growth. *Journal of Early Childhood Literacy* 17 (4), 485–521. http://dx.doi.org/10.1177/1468798416638138.
Bernstein, K.A. (2018) The perks of being peripheral: English learning and participation in a preschool classroom network of practice. *TESOL Quarterly* 52 (4), 798–844. doi.org/10.1002/tesq.428.

Bernstein, K.A. (2019) Accountability and ethics-in-practice in complex, multi-participant studies. In D. Warriner and M. Bigelow (eds) *Critical Reflections on Research Methods: Power and Equity in Complex Multilingual Contexts* (pp. 123–138). Bristol: Multilingual Matters.

Bhutan Citizenship Act, 1985 (n.d.) Retrieved 12 September 2014, from http://www.refworld.org/cgi-bin/texis/vtx/rwmain?docid=3ae6b4d838.

Bialystok, E. (2012) The impact of bilingualism on language and literacy development. In T.K. Bhatia and W.C. Ritchie (eds) *The Handbook of Bilingualism and Multilingualism* (pp. 624–648). Malden, MA: Wiley-Blackwell.

Bialystok, E. and Hakuta, K. (1999) Confounded age: Linguistic and cognitive factors in age differences for second language acquisition. In D. Birdsong (ed.) *Second Language Acquisition and the Critical Period Hypothesis* (pp. 161–181). Mahwah, NJ: Lawrence Erlbaum.

Bloome, D., Carter, S., Christian, B., Madrid, S., Otto, S., Shuart-Faris, N. and Smith, M. (2008) *On Discourse Analysis in Classrooms: Approaches to Language and Literacy Research.* New York, NY: Teachers College Press.

Bloome, D., Puro, P. and Theodorou, E. (1989) Procedural display and classroom lessons. *Curriculum Inquiry* 19 (3), 265–291. https://doi.org/10.2307/1179417.

Blum-Kulka, S. (1997) *Dinner Talk: Cultural Patterns of Sociability and Socialization in Family Discourse.* Mahwah, NJ: Lawrence Erlbaum Associates.

Blum-Kulka, S. and Gorbatt, N. (2014) 'Say princess': The challenges and affordances of young Hebrew L2 novices' interaction with their peers. In A. Cekaite, S. Blum-Kulka, V. Grøver and E. Teubal (eds) *Children's Peer Talk: Learning from Each Other* (pp. 169–193). Cambridge: Cambridge University Press.

Blum-Kulka, S., Huck-Taglicht, D. and Avni, H. (2004) The social and discursive spectrum of peer talk. *Discourse Studies* 6 (3), 307–328.

Borgatti, S.P., Everett, M. and Freeman, L. (2002) *Ucinet for Windows.* Cambridge, MA: Analytic Technologies. https://sites.google.com/site/ucinetsoftware/home.

Borgatti, S.P., Everett, M.G. and Johnson, J. (2013) *Analyzing Social Networks.* London: Sage.

Bourdieu, P. (1977) *Outline of a Theory of Practice.* Cambridge, MA: Cambridge University Press.

Bourdieu, P. (1990) *The Logic of Practice.* Palo Alto, CA: Stanford University Press.

Bourdieu, P. (1991) *Language and Symbolic Power.* Cambridge, MA: Harvard University Press.

Boyd, S. and Huss, L. (2017) Young children as language policy-makers: Studies of interaction in preschools in Finland and Sweden. *Multilingua* 36 (4), 359–373.

Bronfenbrenner, U. (1979) *The Ecology of Human Development: Experiments by Nature and Design.* Cambridge, MA: Harvard University Press.

Bulté, B. and Housen, A. (2012) Defining and operationalising L2 complexity. In A. Housen, F. Kuiken and I. Vedder (eds) *Dimensions of L2 Performance and Proficiency: Complexity, Accuracy and Fluency in SLA* (pp. 21–46). Philadelphia, PA: John Benjamins Publishing.

Burdelski, M. (2011) Language socialization and politeness routines. In A. Duranti, E. Ochs and B.B. Schieffelin (eds) *The Handbook of Language Socialization* (pp. 275–295). Malden, MA: Wiley-Blackwell. https://doi.org/10.1002/9781444342901.ch12.

Burt, R. (1992) *Structural Holes.* Cambridge, MA: Harvard University Press.

Burt, R.S. (2001) Structural holes versus network closure as social capital. In N. Lin, K.S. Cook and R. Burt (eds) *Social Capital: Theory and Research* (pp. 31–56). Hawthorne, NY: Aldine de Gruyter.

Burt, R.S. (2004) Structural holes and good ideas. *American Journal of Sociology* 110, 349–399.

Caldas, S.J. (2012) Language policy in the family. In B. Spolsky (ed.) *The Cambridge Handbook of Language Policy* (pp. 351–383). Cambridge: Cambridge University Press. https://doi.org/10.1017/CBO9780511979026.022.

Cárdenas-Hagan, E., Carlson, C.D. and Pollard-Durodola, S.D. (2007) The cross-linguistic transfer of early literacy skills: The role of initial L1 and L2 skills and language of instruction. *Language, Speech, and Hearing Services in Schools* 38 (3), 249–259. https://doi.org/10.1044/0161-1461(2007/026).

Carhill–Poza, A. (2015) Opportunities and outcomes: The role of peers in developing the oral academic English proficiency of adolescent English learners. *The Modern Language Journal* 99 (4), 678–695. https://doi.org/10.1111/modl.12271.

Cekaite, A. (2012) Tattling and dispute resolution: Moral order, emotions and embodiment in the teacher-mediated disputes of young second language learners. In M. Theobald and S. Danby (eds) *Disputes in Everyday Life: Social and Moral Orders of Children and Young People* (vol. 15, pp. 165–191). Bingley: Emerald Group Publishing Limited.

Cekaite, A. (2017) What makes a child a good language learner? Interactional competence, identity, and immersion in a Swedish classroom. *Annual Review of Applied Linguistics* 37, 45–61. https://doi.org/10.1017/S0267190517000046.

Cekaite, A. and Evaldsson, A.-C. (2017) Language policies in play: Learning ecologies in multilingual preschool interactions among peers and teachers. *Multilingua* 36 (4), 451–475. https://doi.org/10.1515/multi-2016-0020.

Center for Applied Linguistics (Cultural Orientation Resource Center) (2012a) *Welcome to the United States: A Guidebook for Refugees (English Version)*. Washington, DC: Center for Applied Linguistics.

Center for Applied Linguistics (Cultural Orientation Resource Center) (2012b) *Welcome to the United States: Refugee Guide to Resettlment DVD (English Version)*. Washington, DC: Center for Applied Linguistics.

Chesterfield, K.B., Chesterfield, R.A. and Chavez, R. (1982) Peer interaction, language proficiency, and language preference in bilingual preschool classrooms. *Hispanic Journal of Behavioral Sciences* 4 (4), 467–486. https://doi.org/10.1177/07399863820044004.

Clarke, P. (1999) Investigating second language acquisition in preschools: A longitudinal study of four Vietnamese-speaking children's acquisition of English in a bilingual preschool. *International Journal of Early Years Education* 7 (1), 17–24.

Cohen, J. (1988) *Statistical Power Analysis for the Behavioral Sciences* (2nd edn). Hillsdale, NJ: Routledge.

Cole, M. (1998) Putting culture in the middle. In M. Cole *Cultural Psychology: A Once and Future Discipline* (pp. 116–145). Cambridge, MA: Harvard University Press.

Coleman, J.S. (1988) Social capital in the creation of human capital. *American Journal of Sociology* 94, S95–S120.

Collier, V.P. and Thomas, W.P. (2017) Validating the power of bilingual schooling: Thirty-two years of large-scale, longitudinal research. *Annual Review of Applied Linguistics* 37, 203–217. https://doi.org/10.1017/S0267190517000034.

Copp Mökkönen, A. (2012) Social organization through teacher-talk: Subteaching, socialization and the normative use of language in a multilingual primary class. *Linguistics and Education* 23 (3), 310–322. https://doi.org/10.1016/j.linged.2012.06.001.

Corsaro, W. (1985) *Friendship and Peer Culture in the Early Years*. New York, NY: Ablex Publishing.

Cummins, J. (1979) Cognitive/academic language proficiency, linguistic interdependence, the optimum age question and some other matters. *Working Papers on Bilingualism Toronto* (19), 197–202.

Cummins, J. (2008) Teaching for transfer: Challenging the two solitudes assumption in bilingual education. In N. Hornberger (ed.) *Encyclopedia of Language and Education* (pp. 1528–1538). New York, NY: Springer.

Curdt-Christiansen, X.L. (2009) Invisible and visible language planning: Ideological factors in the family language policy of Chinese immigrant families in Quebec. *Language Policy* 8 (4), 351–375. https://doi.org/10.1007/s10993-009-9146-7.

Curtiss, S. (1977) *Genie: A Psycholinguistic Study of a Modern-day 'Wild Child.'* New York, NY: Academic Press.

Davies, B. and Harré, R. (1990) Positioning: The discursive production of selves. *Journal for the Theory of Social Behaviour* 20 (1), 43–63.

Day, E. (2002) *Identity and the Young English Language Learner*. Clevedon: Multilingual Matters.

De Carli, F., Dessi, B., Mariani, M., Girtler, N., Greco, A., Rodriguez, G., Salmon, L. and Morelli, M. (2015) Language use affects proficiency in Italian–Spanish bilinguals irrespective of age of second language acquisition. *Bilingualism: Language and Cognition* 18 (2), 324–339.

De Houwer, A. (1999) Environmental factors in early bilingual development: The role of parental beliefs and attitudes. In G. Extra and L. Verhoeven (eds) *Bilingualism and Migration* (pp. 75–96). New York, NY: Mouton de Gruyter.

De Houwer, A. (2007) Parental language input patterns and children's bilingual use. *Applied Psycholinguistics* 28 (3), 411–424. https://doi.org/10.1017/S0142716407070221.

Demographics and Arrival Statistics. (n.d.) Retrieved 21 August 2017, from http://www.refugeesinpa.org/aboutus/demoandarrivalstats/index.htm.

Dewey, D.P., Ring, S., Gardner, D. and Belnap, R.K. (2013) Social network formation and development during study abroad in the Middle East. *System* 41, 269–282. https://doi.org/10.1016/j.system.2013.02.004.

DLIFLC.edu – Languages at DLI (n.d.) Retrieved 22 August 2017, from https://www.dliflc.edu/home/about/languages-at-dliflc/.

Donato, R. (1994) Collective scaffolding in second language learning. In J. Lantolf and G. Appel (eds) *Vygotskian Approaches to Second Language Research*. Westport, CT: Ablex Publishing.

Donato, R. (2000) Sociocultural contributions to understanding the foreign language classroom. In J.P. Lantolf (ed.) *Sociocultural Theory and Second Language Learning* (pp. 27–50). Oxford & New York: Oxford University Press.

Dörnyei, Z. (2003) Attitudes, orientations, and motivations in language learning: Advances in theory, research, and applications. *Language Learning* 53 (1), 3–32.

Douglas Fir Group. (2016) A transdisciplinary framework for SLA in a multilingual world. *The Modern Language Journal* 100 (S1), 19–47. https://doi.org/10.1111/modl.12301.

Dubasik, V.L. and Wilcox, M.J. (2013) Spanish and early English development in young dual language learners: A preliminary study. *Speech, Language and Hearing* 16 (3), 163–175.

Ellis, R. (2008) *The Study of Second Language Acquisition* (2nd edn). Oxford & New York: Oxford University Press.

Ellis, R., Tanaka, Y. and Yamazaki, A. (1994) Classroom interaction, comprehension, and the acquisition of L2 word meanings. *Language Learning* 44 (3), 449–491. https://doi.org/10.1111/j.1467-1770.1994.tb01114.x.

Ellwood, C. and Nakane, I. (2009) Privileging of speech in EAP and mainstream university classrooms: A critical evaluation of participation. *TESOL Quarterly* 43 (2), 203–230. https://doi.org/10.1002/j.1545-7249.2009.tb00165.x.

Elreda, L.M., Kibler, A., Futch Ehrlich, V.A. and Johnson, H. (2016) Learning in linguistically diverse middle school classrooms: The role of the classroom peer network. Evanston, IL: Society for Research on Educational Effectiveness.

Engeström, Y. (1991) Non scholae sed vitae discimus: Toward overcoming the encapsulation of school learning. *Learning and Instruction* 1 (3), 243–259.

Erickson, F. (1992) Ethnographic microanalysis of interaction. In M.D. LeCompte, W.I. Milroy and J. Preissle (eds) *The Handbook of Qualitative Research in Education* (pp. 201–225). New York, NY: Academic Press.

Erickson, F. and Shultz, J.J. (1982) *The Counselor As Gatekeeper: Social Interaction in Interviews*. New York, NY: Academic Press.

Ervin-Tripp, S. (1981) Social process in first- and second-language learning. *Annals of the New York Academy of Sciences* 379 (1), 33–47.

Ervin-Tripp, S. (1986) Activity types and the structure of talk in second language learning. In W. Corsaro, J. Cook-Gumperz and J. Streek (eds) *Children's Language and Children's Worlds* (volume 1, pp. 327–358). Berlin: Mouton de Gruyter.

Ervin-Tripp, S. (1991) Play in language development. In B. Scales, M.C. Almy, A. Nicolopoulou and S. Ervin-Tripp (eds) *Play and the Social Context of Development in Early Care and Education* (pp. 84–98). New York, NY: Teachers College Press.

Fernández Dobao, A. (2016) Peer interaction and learning: A focus on the silent learner. In M. Sato and S. Ballinger (eds) *Peer Interaction and Second Language Learning: Pedagogical Potential and Research Agenda* (pp. 33–61). Amsterdam & Philadelphia: John Benjamins Publishing.

Flesch, R. (1955) *Why Johnny Can't Read*. New York, NY: Harper & Row.

Foster, P., Tonkyn, A. and Wigglesworth, G. (2000) Measuring spoken language: A unit for all reasons. *Applied Linguistics* 21 (3), 354–375. https://doi.org/10.1093/applin/21.3.354.

Frey, W.H. (2000) The new urban demographics: Race space & boomer aging. *The Brookings Review* 18 (3), 20–23.

Friedkin, N. (1980) A test of structural features of Granovetter's strength of weak ties theory. *Social Networks* 2 (4), 411–422. https://doi.org/10.1016/0378-8733(80)90006-4.

Friedkin, N.E. and Thomas, S.L. (1997) Social positions in schooling. *Sociology of Education* 70 (4), 239–255.

Gal, S. (1979) *Language Shift: Social Determinants of Linguistic Change in Bilingual Austria*. San Francisco, CA: Academic Press, 1979.

Gal, S. (1989) Language and political economy. *Annual Review of Anthropology* 18, 345–367.

García, O. (2009) *Bilingual Education in the 21st Century: A Global Perspective*. Malden, MA: Wiley-Blackwell.

García, O. and Kleifgen, J.A. (2010) *Educating Emergent Bilinguals: Policies, Programs, and Practices for English Language Learners*. New York, NY: Teachers College Press.

García, O. and Li Wei (2014) *Translanguaging: Language, Bilingualism and Education*. New York: Palgrave Macmillan.

García, O. with Makar, C., Starcevic, M. and Terry, A. (2011) The translanguaging of Latino kindergartners. In J. Rothman and K. Potowski (eds) *Bilingual Youth: Spanish in English Speaking Societies* (pp. 33–55). Amsterdam: John Benjamins Publishing.

García-Mateus, S. and Palmer, D. (2017) Translanguaging pedagogies for positive identities in two-way dual language bilingual education. *Journal of Language, Identity & Education* 16 (4), 245–255. https://doi.org/10.1080/15348458.2017.1329016.

Gay, G. (2018) *Culturally Responsive Teaching: Theory, Research, and Practice* (3rd edn). New York, NY: Teachers College Press.

Genesee, F. (1994) *Educating Second Language Children: The Whole Child, the Whole Curriculum, the Whole Community*. Cambridge: Cambridge University Press.

Genishi, C. and Dyson, A.H. (2009) *Children, Language, and Literacy: Diverse Learners in Diverse Times*. New York, NY: Teachers College Press.

Giarratani, F., Singh, V.P. and Briem, C. (2003) Dynamics of growth and restructuring in the Pittsburgh metropolitan region. In U. Hilpert (ed.) *Regionalisation of Globalised Innovation: Locations for Advanced Industrial Development and Disparities in Participation* (pp. 135–150). New York, NY: Routledge.

Gibson, J.J. (1977) The concept of affordances. In R. Shaw and J. Bransford (eds) *Perceiving, Acting, and Knowing: Toward an Ecological Psychology* (pp. 67–82). Mahwah, NJ: Lawrence Erlbaum.

Gibson, T.A., Peña, E.D. and Bedore, L.M. (2014) The relation between language experience and receptive-expressive semantic gaps in bilingual children. *International Journal of Bilingual Education and Bilingualism* 17 (1), 90–110. https://doi.org/10.1080/1367005 0.2012.743960.

Gillanders, C. (2007) An English-speaking prekindergarten teacher for young Latino children: Implications of the teacher–child relationship on second language learning. *Early Childhood Education Journal* 35 (1), 47–54. https://doi.org/10.1007/s10643-007-0163-x.

Goffman, E. (1961) *Asylums: Essays on the Social Situation of Mental Patients and Other Inmates*. Garden City, NY: Anchor Books.

Goffman, E. (1981) Footing. In E. Goffman *Forms of Talk* (pp. 124–159). Philadelphia, PA: University of Pennsylvania Press.

Gogonas, N. and Kirsch, C. (2018) 'In this country my children are learning two of the most important languages in Europe': Ideologies of language as a commodity among Greek migrant families in Luxembourg. *International Journal of Bilingual Education and Bilingualism* 21 (4), 426–438. https://doi.org/10.1080/13670050.2016.1181602.

Goodrich, J.M., Lonigan, C.J. and Farver, J.M. (2013) Do early literacy skills in children's first language promote development of skills in their second language? An experimental evaluation of transfer. *Journal of Educational Psychology* 105 (2), 414–426. https://doi.org/10.1037/a0031780.

Goodwin, C. (1981) *Conversational Organization: Interaction between Speakers and Hearers*. New York, NY: Academic Press.

Goodwin, C. (2000) Gesture, aphasia and interaction. In D. McNeill (ed.) *Language and Gesture: Window into Thought and Action* (pp. 84–98). Cambridge: Cambridge University Press.

Goodwin, C. (2004) A competent speaker who can't speak: The social life of aphasia. *Journal of Linguistic Anthropology* 14 (2), 151–170. https://doi.org/10.1525/jlin.2004.14.2.151.

Goodwin, C. (2006) Interactive footing. In E. Holt and R. Clift (eds) *Reporting Talk: Reported Speech in Interaction*. Cambridge: Cambridge University Press. Retrieved from http://dx.doi.org/10.1017/CBO9780511486654.003.

Goodwin, C. and Goodwin, M.H. (2005) Participation. In A. Duranti (ed.) *A Companion to Linguistic Anthropology* (pp. 222–244). Oxford: Blackwell.

Goodwin, M.H. and Kyratzis, A. (2007) Children socializing children: Practices for negotiating the social order among peers. *Research on Language and Social Interaction* 40 (4), 279–289. https://doi.org/10.1080/08351810701471260.

Gort, M. and Pontier, R.W. (2013) Exploring bilingual pedagogies in dual language preschool classrooms. *Language and Education* 27 (3), 223–245. http://dx.doi.org/10.1080/09500782.2012.697468.

Government of the United States of America. (2016) The United States of America [Country Chapter]. In United Nations High Commissioner for Refugees (ed.) *UNHCR Resettlment Handbook*. Geneva, Switzerland: UNHCR.

Granovetter, M.S. (1973) The strength of weak ties. *American Journal of Sociology* 78 (6), 1360–1380. https://doi.org/10.1016/B978-0-12-442450-0.50025-0.

Grant, T. (2013) Pittsburgh area ranks high for affordable housing. *Pittsburgh Post-Gazette*. 14 November. Retrieved from http://www.post-gazette.com/local/region/2013/11/15/City-given-high-marks-for-affordable-housing-Pittsburgh-area-ranks-high-for-affordable-housing/stories/201311150100.

Green, J.L. and Stewart, A. (2012) Linguistic perspectives in qualitative research in education: A brief history. In S. Delamont (ed.) *Handbook of Qualitative Research in Education* (pp. 61–81). Northampton, MA: Edgar Elgar.

Gremmen, M.C., Dijkstra, J.K., Steglich, C. and Veenstra, R. (2017) First selection, then influence: Developmental differences in friendship dynamics regarding academic achievement. *Developmental Psychology* 53 (7), 1356–1370.

Grøver Aukrust, V. (2004) Explanatory discourse in young second language learners' peer play. *Discourse Studies* 6 (3), 393–412. https://doi.org/10.1177/1461445604044296.

Gumperz, J.J. (1958) Dialect differences and social stratification in a north Indian village. *American Anthropologist* 60 (4), 668–681.

Gumperz, J.J. (1964) Linguistic and social interaction in two communities. *American Anthropologist* 66 (6), 137–154.

Gumperz, J. (1965) Language. *Biennial Review of Anthropology* 4, 84–120.

Gumperz, J.J. (1979) Conversational analysis of interethnic communication. Presented at the SEAMEO Regional Language Centre Seminar on Acquisition of Bilingual Ability and Patterns of Bilingualism, Singapore.

Gumperz, J.J. (1982) *Discourse Strategies*. Cambridge: Cambridge University Press.
Gumperz, J.J. (1992) Contextualization and understanding. In A. Duranti and C. Goodwin (eds) *Rethinking Context: Language as an Interactive Phenomenon* (pp. 229–252). Cambridge: Cambridge University Press.
Hall, M., Singer, A., Jong, G.F.D. and Graefe, D.R. (2011) *The Geography of Immigrant Skills: Educational Profiles of Metropolitan Areas*. Washington, DC: Brookings Institution. Retrieved 21 August 2017, from http://www.brookings.edu/research/papers/2011/06/immigrants-singer.
Hanks, W. (2006) Context, Communicative. In K. Brown (ed.) *Encyclopedia of Language and Linguistics* (2nd edn) (pp. 115–128). Oxford: Elsevier Science.
Hatch, E. (1978) Discourse analysis and second language acquisition. In E. Hatch (ed.) *Second Language Acquisition: A Book of Readings* (2nd edn) (pp. 383–400). Rowley, MA: Newbury House Publishers.
Hawkins, M. (2005) Becoming a student: Identity work and academic literacies in early schooling. *TESOL Quarterly* 39 (1), 59–82. http://dx.doi.org/10.2307/3588452.
Haynie, D.L. (2001) Delinquent peers revisited: Does network structure matter? *American Journal of Sociology* 106, 1013–1057.
Heath, S.B. (1983) *Ways with Words: Language, Life and Work in Communities and Classrooms*. Cambridge: Cambridge University Press.
Hélot, C. (2010) 'Tu sais bien parler maîtresse!': Negotiating languages other than French in the primary school classroom in France. In K. Menken and O. García (eds) *Negotiating Language Policies in Schools: Educators as Policymakers* (pp. 52–71). New York, NY: Routledge.
Henderson, K.I. and Palmer, D.K. (2015) Teacher and student language practices and ideologies in a third-grade two-way dual language program implementation. *International Multilingual Research Journal* 9 (2), 75–92.
Hill, J.H. and Hill, K.C. (1986) *Speaking Mexicano: Dynamics of Syncretic Language in Central Mexico*. Tuscon, AZ: University of Arizona Press.
Holland, D., Lachicotte, W. Jr, Skinner, D. and Cain, C. (2001) *Identity and Agency in Cultural Worlds*. President and Fellows of Harvard College. Cambridge, MA: Harvard University Press.
Holland, D. and Lave, J. (2001) History in person: An introduction. In D. Holland and J. Lave (eds) *History in Person: Enduring Struggles, Contentious Practice, Intimate Identities* (pp. 3–33). Santa Fe, NM: School of American Research.
Howard, E.R., Lindholm-Leary, K.J., Rogers, D., Medina, N.O.J., Kennedy, B., Sugarman, J. and Christian, D. (2018) *Guiding Principles for Dual Language Education* (3rd edn). Washington, DC: Center for Applied Linguistics.
Hutt, M. (2005) The Bhutanese refugees: Between verification, repatriation and royal realpolitik. *Journal of Peace and Democracy in South Asia* 1 (1), 44–55.
'In the Camps' (n.d.) Retrieved from http://bhutaneserefugees.com/in-camps/.
Irvine, J. (1989) When talk isn't cheap: Language and political economy. *American Ethnologist* 16, 248–267.
Isaacson, M.P. (2014) Pittsburgh's response to deindustrialization: Renaissance, renewal and recovery, 1946–1999. CUNY Graduate Center Dissertations and Theses, 2014-Present. Retrieved from http://works.gc.cuny.edu/etd/230.
Isaacson, M.P. (2015) Fantasy meets reality: The Pittsburgh renaissance and urban utopias. *Journal of Urban History* 41 (1), 13–19. https://doi.org/10.1177/0096144214551729.
Jaworski, A. (1992) *The Power of Silence: Social and Pragmatic Perspectives*. London: Sage.
Jiang Yan and Zhu Hua (2012) Communicating in a lingua franca: Children's interaction in an international summer camp. *Sociolinguistic Studies* 4 (3). https://doi.org/10.1558/sols.v4i3.535.
Johnson, C.J. (2010) Implementational and ideological spaces in bilingual education language policy. *International Journal of Bilingual Education and Bilingualism* 13 (1), 61–79.

Kamarck, E., Hudak, J. and Stenglein, C. (2017) *Immigration by the Numbers*. Washington, DC: Brookings Institution. Retrieved 21 August 2017, from https://www.brookings.edu/interactives/immigration-by-the-numbers/.

Kanno, Y. (1999) Comments on Kelleen Toohey's '"Breaking them up, taking them away": ESL students in grade 1': The use of the community-of-practice perspective in language minority research. *TESOL Quarterly* 33 (1), 126–132. https://doi.org/10.2307/3588195.

Killworth, P.D. and Bernard, H.R. (1976) Informant accuracy in social network data *Human Organization* 35 (3), 269–286.

King, K.A., Fogle, L. and Logan-Terry, A. (2008) Family language policy. *Language and Linguistics Compass* 2 (5), 907–922. https://doi.org/10.1111/j.1749-818X.2008.00076.x.

King, K. and Mackey, A. (2009) *The Bilingual Edge: The Ultimate Guide to Why, When, and How*. New York, NY: Harper Collins.

King, K.A. and Mackey, A. (2016) Research methodology in second language studies: Trends, concerns, and new directions. *The Modern Language Journal* 100(S1), 209–227. https://doi.org/10.1111/modl.12309.

Kirsch, C. (2012) Ideologies, struggles and contradictions: An account of mothers raising their children bilingually in Luxembourgish and English in Great Britain. *International Journal of Bilingual Education and Bilingualism* 15 (1), 95–112. https://doi.org/10.1080/13670050.2011.607229.

Kirsch, C. (2017) Young children capitalising on their entire language repertoire for language learning at school. *Language, Culture and Curriculum* 31 (1), 39–55.

Kiuru, N., DeLay, D., Laursen, B., Burk, W. J., Lerkkanen, M.-K., Poikkeus, A.-M. and Nurmi, J.-E. (2017) Peer selection and influence on children's reading skills in early primary grades: A social network approach. *Reading and Writing* 30 (7), 1473–1500. https://doi.org/10.1007/s11145-017-9733-5.

Koriouchkina, L. (2010) Meskhetian Turks and the regime of citizenship in Russia. *Ethnology: An International Journal of Cultural and Social Anthropology* 48 (1), 39–52.

Kramsch, C. (2003) Identity, role, and voice in cross-cultural (mis)communication. In J. House, G. Kasper and S. Ross (eds) *Misunderstanding in Social Life: Discourse Approaches to Problematic Talk* (pp. 129–153). New York, NY: Routledge.

Kramsch, C. (2006) From communicative competence to symbolic competence. *The Modern Language Journal* 90 (2), 249–252. https://doi.org/10.1111/j.1540-4781.2006.00395_3.x.

Kramsch, C. (2012) Subjectivity. In C. Chapelle (ed.) *Encyclopedia of Applied Linguistics*. Oxford: Blackwell. https://doi.org/10.1002/9781405198431.wbeal1122.

Kramsch, C. (2016) The multiple faces of symbolic power. *Applied Linguistics Review* 7 (4), 517–529. https://doi.org/10.1515/applirev-2016-0023.

Kramsch, C. and Whiteside, A. (2008) Language ecology in multilingual settings. Towards a theory of symbolic competence. *Applied Linguistics* 29 (4), 645–671. https://doi.org/10.1093/applin/amn022.

Krashen, S. (1977) Some issues relating to the Monitor Model. In H. Brown, C. Yorio and R. Crymes (eds) *On TESOL '77* (pp. 144–158). Washington, DC: Teachers of English to Speakers of Other Languages.

Krashen, S.D., Long, M.A. and Scarcella, R.C. (1979) Age, rate and eventual attainment in second language acquisition. *TESOL Quarterly* 13 (4), 573–582. https://doi.org/10.2307/3586451.

Kroskrity, P. (2004) Language ideology. In A. Duranti (ed.) *Companion to Linguistic Anthropology* (pp. 496–517). Oxford: Blackwell.

Lantolf, J. (ed.) (2000) *Sociocultural Theory and Second Language Learning*. New York, NY: Oxford University Press.

Lantolf, J. (2013) Sociocultural theory: A dialectical approach to L2 research. In S.M. Gass and A. Mackey (eds) *The Routledge Handbook of Second Language Acquisition* (pp. 57–72). New York, NY: Routledge.

Lantolf, J.P. and Thorne, S.L. (2006) *Sociocultural Theory and the Genesis of Second Language Development*. Oxford: Oxford University Press.

Lantolf, J.P. and Thorne, S.L. (2007) Sociocultural theory and second language learning. In B. VanPatten and J. Williams (eds) *Theories in Second Language Acquisition* (pp. 201–224). New York & London: Routledge.
Larson, J. and Gatto, L.A. (2004) Tactical underlife: Understanding student's perceptions. *Journal of Early Childhood Literacy* 4 (1), 11–41.
Lave, J. and Wenger, E. (1991) *Situated Learning: Legitimate Peripheral Participation*. Cambridge: Cambridge University Press.
Leander, K.M. (2002) Locating Latanya: The situated production of identity artifacts in classroom interaction. *Research in the Teaching of English* 37 (2), 198–250.
Lindholm-Leary, K. (2012) Success and challenges in dual language education. *Theory Into Practice* 51 (4), 256–262. https://doi.org/10.1080/00405841.2012.726053.
Long, M.H. (1981) Input, interaction, and second-language acquisition. *Annals of the New York Academy of Sciences* 379 (1), 259–278. https://doi.org/10.1111/j.1749-6632.1981.tb42014.x.
Long, S. (1997) Friends as teachers: The impact of peer interaction on the acquisition of a new language. In E. Gregory (ed.) *One Child, Many Worlds: Early Learning in Multicultural Communities*. London: Routledge.
Long S. (2004) Making a place for peer interaction: Mexican American kindergartners learning language and literacy. In E. Gregory, S. Long and D. Volk (eds) *Many Pathways to Literacy: Young Children Learning with Siblings, Grandparents, Peers and Communities* (pp. 93–104). London & New York: Routledge-Falmer.
Lu, X. (2009) Automatic measurement of syntactic complexity in child language acquisition. *International Journal of Corpus Linguistics* 14 (1), 3–28.
Lu, X. (2012) The relationship of lexical richness to the quality of ESL learners' oral narratives. *The Modern Language Journal* 96 (2), 190–208.
Mackey, A. and Goo, J. (2007) Interaction research in SLA: A meta-analysis and research synthesis. In A. Mackey (ed.) *Conversational Interaction in Second Language Acquisition: A Collection of Empirical Studies* (pp. 407–453). Oxford: Oxford University Press.
Mackey, A. and Oliver, R. (2002) Interactional feedback and children's L2 development. *System* 30 (4), 459–477. https://doi.org/10.1016/S0346-251X(02)00049-0.
Mackey, A. and Silver, R.E. (2005) Interactional tasks and English L2 learning by immigrant children in Singapore. *System* 33 (2), 239–260. https://doi.org/10.1016/j.system.2005.01.005.
Marinova-Todd, S.H., Marshall, D.B. and Snow, C.E. (2000) Three misconceptions about age and L2 learning. *TESOL Quarterly* 34 (1), 9–34. https://doi.org/10.2307/3588095.
Maroulis, S. and Gomez, L.M. (2008) Does 'connectedness' matter? Evidence from a social network analysis within a small-school reform. *The Teachers College Record* 110 (9), 1901–1929.
McCarty, T.L. (2011) Entry into conversation: Introducing ethnography and language policy. In T.L. McCarty (ed.) *Ethnography and Language Policy* (pp. 1–28). New York, NY: Routledge.
McCarty, T.L., Romero-Little, M.E., Warhol, L. and Zepeda, O. (2009) Indigenous youth as language policy makers. *Journal of Language, Identity, and Education* 8 (5), 291–306.
Menken K. and García O. (eds) (2010a) *Negotiating Language Policies in Schools: Educators as Policymakers*. New York, NY: Routledge.
Menken, K. and García, O. (2010b) Introduction. In K. Menken and O. García (eds) *Negotiating Language Policies in Schools: Educators as Policymakers* (pp. 1–10). New York, NY: Routledge.
Michaels, S. (1981) 'Sharing time': Children's narrative styles and differential access to literacy. *Language in Society* 10 (03), 423–442. https://doi.org/10.1017/S0047404500008861.
Milroy, L. (1987) *Language and Social Networks* (2nd edn). Oxford: Basil Blackwell.
Mishra, V. (2013) Bhutan is no Shangri-La. *The New York Times*. Retrieved from http://www.nytimes.com/2013/06/29/opinion/bhutan-is-no-shangri-la.html.

Moll, L.C., Amanti, C., Neff, D. and Gonzalez, N. (1992) Funds of knowledge for teaching: Using a qualitative approach to connect homes and classrooms. *Theory into Practice* 31 (2), 132–141.

Nassaji, H. (2016) Anniversary article Interactional feedback in second language teaching and learning: A synthesis and analysis of current research. *Language Teaching Research* 20 (4), 535–562. https://doi.org/10.1177/1362168816644940.

Norris, J.M. and Ortega, L. (2009) Towards an organic approach to investigating CAF in instructed SLA: The case of complexity. *Applied Linguistics* 30 (4), 555–578.

Norton Peirce, B. (1995) Social identity, investment, and language learning. *TESOL Quarterly* 29 (1), 9–31.

Ochs, E. and Schieffelin, B. (1984) Language acquisition and socialization: Three developmental stories. In B. Blount (ed.) *Language, Culture, and Society: A Book of Readings*. Long Grove, IL: Waveland Press.

Otheguy, R. (2016) Foreword. In O. García and T. Kleyn (eds) *Translanguaging with Multilingual Students: Learning from Classroom Moments* (pp. ix–xii). New York, NY: Routledge.

Palermo, F. and Mikulski, A.M. (2014) The role of positive peer interactions and English exposure in Spanish-speaking preschoolers' English vocabulary and letter-word skills. *Early Childhood Research Quarterly* 29 (4), 625–635. https://doi.org/10.1016/j.ecresq.2014.07.006.

Palermo, F., Mikulski, A.M., Fabes, R.A., Hanish, L.D., Martin, C.L. and Stargel, L.E. (2014) English exposure in the home and classroom: Predictions to Spanish-speaking preschoolers' English vocabulary skills. *Applied Psycholinguistics* 35 (06), 1163–1187. https://doi.org/10.1017/S0142716412000732.

Peck, S. (1980) Language play in child second language acquisition. In D. Larsen-Freeman (ed.) *Discourse Analysis in Second Language Research* (pp. 154–164). Rowley, MA: Newbury House Publishing.

Pettit, S.K. (2011) Teachers' beliefs about English language learners in the mainstream classroom: A review of the literature. *International Multilingual Research Journal* 5 (2), 123–147. https://doi.org/10.1080/19313152.2011.594357.

Philp, J. and Duchesne, S. (2008) When the gate opens: The interaction between social and linguistic goals in child second language development. In J. Philp, R. Oliver and A. Mackey (eds) *Second Language Acquisition and the Younger Learner: Child's Play?* (pp. 83–103). Amsterdam: John Benjamins Publishing.

Piker, R.A. (2013) Understanding influences of play on second language learning: A microethnographic view in one Head Start preschool classroom. *Journal of Early Childhood Research* 11 (2), 184–200.

Pinter, A. (2007) Some benefits of peer–peer interaction: 10-year-old children practising with a communication task. *Language Teaching Research* 11 (2), 189–207. https://doi.org/10.1177/1362168807074604.

Portolés, L. and Martí, O. (2017) Translanguaging as a teaching resource in early language learning of English as an additional language (EAL). *Bellaterra Journal of Teaching & Learning Language & Literature* 10 (1), 61–77. https://doi.org/321507.

Pulla, V. (ed.) (2016) *The Lhotsampa People of Bhutan: Resilience and Survival*. New York, NY: Palgrave Macmillan.

Ramanathan, V. (2005) Rethinking language planning and policy from the ground up: Refashioning institutional realities and human lives. *Current Issues in Language Planning* 6 (2), 89–101. https://doi.org/10.1080/14664200508668275.

Razfar, A. and Rumenapp, J.C. (2012) Language ideologies in English learner classrooms: Critical reflections and the role of explicit awareness. *Language Awareness* 21 (4), 347–368.

Reychav, I., Raban, D.R. and McHaney, R. (2018) Centrality measures and academic achievement in computerized classroom social networks: An empirical investigation. *Journal of Educational Computing Research* 56 (4), 589–618. https://doi.org/10.1177/0735633117715749.

Rodriguez, R. (1983) *Hunger of Memory: The Education of Richard Rodriguez.* Toronto & New York: Bantam.

Rogoff, B. (2003) *The Cultural Nature of Human Development.* Oxford: Oxford University Press.

Rosheim, K.C. (2018) A cautionary tale about using the word shy: An action research study of how three quiet learners demonstrated participation beyond speech. *Journal of Adolescent & Adult Literacy* 61 (6), 663–670. https://doi.org/10.1002/jaal.729.

Roth, M. (2014) Pittsburgh's economy has gained from high-skilled immigrants. *Pittsburgh Post-Gazette.* Retrieved from http://www.post-gazette.com/local/city/2014/05/18/Pittsburgh-s-economy-has-gained-from-high-skilled-immigrants/stories/201405180099.

Royce, T. (2007) Intersemiotic complementarity: A framework for multimodal discourse analysis. In T.D. Royce and W.L. Bowcher (eds) *New Directions in the Analysis of Multimodal Discourse* (pp. 63–109). Mahwah, NJ: Lawrence Erlbaum.

Russell, J. and Spada, N. (2006) The effectiveness of corrective feedback for the acquisition of L2 grammar: A meta-analysis of the research. In J.M. Norris and L. Ortega (eds) *Synthesizing Research on Language Learning and Teaching* (pp. 133–164). Amsterdam & Philadelphia: John Benjamins Publishing.

Russo, T.C. and Koesten J. (2005) Prestige, centrality, and learning: A social network analysis of an online class. *Communication Education* 54 (3), 254–261. DOI: 10.1080/03634520500356394.

Rydland, V., Grøver, V. and Lawrence, J. (2014) The potentials and challenges of learning words from peers in preschool: A longitudinal study of second language learners in Norway. In A. Cekaite, S. Blum-Kulka, V. Grøver and E. Teubal (eds) *Children's Peer Talk: Learning from Each Other* (pp. 214–234). Cambridge: Cambridge University Press.

Rymes, B. (2010) Classroom discourse analysis: A focus on communicative repertoires. In N. Hornberger and S. McKay (eds) *Sociolinguistics and Language Education* (pp. 528–548). Bristol: Multilingual Matters.

Rymes, B. (2014) *Communicating Beyond Language: Everyday Encounters with Diversity.* New York, NY: Routledge.

Rymes, B. and Pash, D. (2001) Questioning identity: The case of one second-language learner. *Anthropology & Education Quarterly* 32 (3), 276–300.

Sanders-Smith, S.C. and Dávila, L.T. (2019) Progressive practice and translanguaging: Supporting multilingualism in a Hong Kong preschool. *Bilingual Research Journal* 42 (3), 275–290. https://doi.org/10.1080/15235882.2019.1624281.

Sato, M. and Ballinger, S. (2016) *Peer Interaction and Second Language Learning: Pedagogical Potential and Research Agenda.* Amsterdam & Philadelphia: John Benjamins Publishing.

Saville-Troike, M. (1988) Private speech: Evidence for second language learning strategies during the 'silent' period. *Journal of Child Language* 15 (3), 567–590.

Sayer, P. (2011) Translanguaging. TexMex, and bilingual pedagogy: Emergent bilinguals learning through the vernacular. *TESOL Quarterly* 47 (1), 63–88. doi:10.1002/tesq.53.

Schieffelin, B.B. and Ochs, E. (1986) Language socialization. *Annual Review of Anthropology* 15 (1), 163–191. https://doi.org/10.1146/annurev.an.15.100186.001115.

Schultz, K. (2009) *Rethinking Classroom Participation: Listening to Silent Voices.* New York, NY: Teachers College Press.

Scovel, T. (2000) A critical review of the critical period research. *Annual Review of Applied Linguistics* 20, 213–223. https://doi.org/10.1017/S0267190500200135.

Searle, J.R. (1969) *Speech Acts: An Essay in the Philosophy of Language.* Cambridge: Cambridge University Press.

Sheng, Li., Bedore, L.M., Peña, E.D. and Fiestas, C. (2013) Semantic development in Spanish- English bilingual children: Effects of age and language experience. *Child Development* 84 (3), 1034–1045.

Shrestha, D.D. (2015) Resettlement of Bhutanese refugees surpasses 100,000 mark. *United Nations High Commissioner for Refugees*. Retrieved from http://www.unhcr.org/news/latest/2015/11/564dded46/resettlement-bhutanese-refugees-surpasses-100000-mark.html.

Silverstein, M. (1979) Language structure and linguistic ideology. In P. Clyne, W.F. Hanks and C.L. Hofbauer (eds) *The Elements: A Parasession on Linguistic Units and Levels* (pp. 193–247). Chicago, IL: Chicago Linguistic Society.

Singer, A. (2010) Immigration. In A. Berube, W.H. Frey, A. Friedhoff, E. Garr, E. Istrate, E. Kneebone, R. Puentes, A. Singer, A. Tomer and H. Wial *State of Metropolitan America: On the Front Lines of Demographic Transformation* (pp. 64–75). Washington, DC: Brookings Institution Metropolitan Policy Program.

Singleton, D. and Ryan, L. (2004) *Language Acquisition: The Age Factor*. Clevedon: Multilingual Matters.

Slavkov, N. (2017) Family language policy and school language choice: Pathways to bilingualism and multilingualism in a Canadian context. *International Journal of Multilingualism* 14 (4), 378–400. https://doi.org/10.1080/14790718.2016.1229319.

Snow, C.E., Burns, M.S. and Griffin, P. (eds) (1998) *Preventing Reading Difficulties in Young Children*. Washington, DC: National Academies Press.

Souto-Manning, M. (2013) *Multicultural Teaching in the Early Childhood Classroom: Approaches, Strategies, and Tools, Preschool-2nd Grade*. New York, NY: Teachers College Press.

Spolsky, B. (2004) *Language Policy*. Cambridge & New York: Cambridge University Press.

Spolsky, B. (2012) Family language policy – the critical domain. *Journal of Multilingual and Multicultural Development* 33 (1), 3–11. https://doi.org/10.1080/01434632.2011.638072.

Steele, J.L., Slater, R.O., Zamarro, G., Miller, T., Li, J., Burkhauser, S. and Bacon, M. (2017) Effects of dual-language immersion programs on student achievement: Evidence from lottery data. *American Educational Research Journal* 54 (1_suppl), 282S–306S. https://doi.org/10.3102/0002831216634463.

Storch, N. (2002) Patterns of interaction in ESL pair work. *Language Learning* 52 (1), 119–158. https://doi.org/10.1111/1467-9922.00179.

Story of the Bhutanese Community (n.d.) *Shangri-Lost*. Retrieved 21 August 2017 from http://www.shangri-lost.org/about-us/pittsburgh-bhutanese-community/.

Swain, M. (1997) Collaborative dialogue: Its contribution to second language learning. *Canaria de Estudios Ingleses* 34, 115–132.

Swain, M. and Lapkin, S. (2001) Focus on form through collaborative dialogue: Exploring task effects. In M. Bygate, P. Skehan and M. Swain (eds) *Researching Pedagogic Tasks: Second Language Learning, Teaching and Testing* (pp. 99–118). London: Routledge.

Swain, M., Brooks, L. and Tocalli-Beller, A. (2002) Peer–peer dialogue as a means of second language learning. *Annual Review of Applied Linguistics* 22, 171–185. https://doi.org/10.1017/S0267190502000090.

Swerdlow, S. (2006) Understanding post-Soviet ethnic discrimination and the effective use of US refugee resettlement: The case of the Meskhetian Turks of Krasnodar Krai. *California Law Review* 94 (6), 1827–1878.

Tabors, P.O. (2008) *One Child, Two Languages: A Guide for Early Childhood Educators of Children Learning English as a Second Language* (2nd edn). Baltimore, MD: Paul H. Brookes Publishing.

Tabors, P.O. and Snow, C. (1994) English as a second language in preschool classrooms. In F. Genesee (ed.) *Educating Second Language Children: The Whole Child, the Whole Curriculum, the Whole Community*. Cambridge: Cambridge University Press.

Tabors, P.O. and Snow, C.E. (2003) Home and community influences. In S.B. Neuman and D.K. Dickinson (eds) *Handbook of Early Literacy Research*. New York, NY: Guilford Press.

Tholander, M. and Aronsson, K. (2003) Doing subteaching in school group work: Positionings, resistance and participation frameworks. *Language and Education* 17 (3), 208–234. https://doi.org/10.1080/09500780308666849.

Tiwari, H. and Rai, D. (2013) *The Story of a Pumpkin: A Traditional Tale from Bhutan*. Trans. N. Adhikari and T. Farish (Bilingual Nepali-English edn). Concord, NH: New Hampshire Humanities Council.

Toohey, K. (2000) *Learning English at School: Identity, Social Relations, and Classroom Practice*. Clevedon: Multilingual Matters.

Toohey, K. (2018) *Learning English at School: Identity, Socio-material Relations and Classroom Practice* (2nd edn). Bristol: Multilingual Matters.

Tuominen, A. (1999) Who decides the home language? A look at multilingual families. *International Journal of the Sociology of Language* 140 (1), 59–76. https://doi.org/10.1515/ijsl.1999.140.59.

Twitchin, J. with J.J. Gumperz (1996/1979) *Crosstalk*. BBC Enterprises and BBC Education & Training. London: BBC Active.

United Nations General Assembly (1951) UN Convention Relating to the Status of Refugees, Resolution 429(V) § (1951). Retrieved from http://www.refworld.org/docid/3b00f08a27.html.

United Nations High Commissioner for Refugees (2005) *UNHCR Statistical Yearbook Country Data Sheet; Bhutan*. Retrieved 30 September 2017, from http://www.unhcr.org/464183650.html.

United Nations High Commissioner for Refugees (2011) *UNHCR Resettlement Handbook*. Geneva, Switzerland: UNHCR.

United Nations High Commissioner for Refugees (2017) *Frequently Asked Questions about Resettlement*. Geneva, Switzerland: UNHCR.

Unsworth, S. (2016) Early child L2 acquisition: Age or input effects? Neither, or both? *Journal of Child Language* 43 (3), 608–634. https://doi.org/10.1017/S030500091500080X.

Unsworth, S., Argyri, F., Cornips, L., Hulk, A., Sorace, A. and Tsimpli, I. (2014) The role of age of onset and input in early child bilingualism in Greek and Dutch. *Applied Psycholinguistics* 35 (4), 765–805. https://doi.org/10.1017/S0142716412000574.

Valdés, G. (1999) *Learning and Not Learning English: Latino Students in American Schools*. New York, NY: Teachers College Press.

Van Lier, L. (2004) *The Ecology and Semiotics of Language Learning: A Sociocultural Perspective*. New York: Kluwer Academic Publishers.

Velasco, P. and Fialais, V. (2018) Moments of metalinguistic awareness in a Kindergarten class: Translanguaging for simultaneous biliterate development. *International Journal of Bilingual Education and Bilingualism* 21 (6), 760–774. https://doi.org/10.1080/13670050.2016.1214104.

Volk, D. and Angelova, M. (2007) Language ideology and the mediation of language choice in peer interactions in a dual-language first grade. *Journal of Language, Identity, and Education* 6 (3), 177–199.

Vygotsky, L.S. (1978) *Mind in Society: The Development of Higher Psychological Processes*. Cambridge, MA: Harvard University Press.

Warriner, D. and Bigelow, M. (eds) (2019) *Critical Reflections on Research Methods: Power and Equity in Complex Multilingual Contexts*. Bristol: Multilingual Matters.

Willett, J. (1995) Becoming first graders in an L2: An ethnographic study of L2 socialization. *TESOL Quarterly* 29 (3), 473–503. https://doi.org/10.2307/3588072.

Wong Fillmore, L. (1976) The second time around: Cognitive and social strategies in second language acquisition. Unpublished PhD thesis, Stanford University.

Wong Fillmore, L. (1979) Individual differences in second language acquisition. In C.J. Fillmore, D. Kempler and W.S.-Y. Wang (eds) *Individual Differences in Language Ability and Language Behavior* (pp. 203–228). New York, NY: Academic Press.

Wong Fillmore, L. (1991a) Second-language learning in children: A model of language learning in context. In E. Bialystok (ed.) *Language Processing in Bilingual Children* (pp. 49–69). Cambridge: Cambridge University Press.

Wong Fillmore, L. (1991b) When learning a second language means losing the first. *Early Childhood Research Quarterly* 6 (3), 323–346.
Wong Fillmore, L. (1996) What happens when languages are lost? An essay on language assimilation and cultural identity. In D.I. Slobin and S.M. Ervin-Tripp (eds) *Social Interaction, Social Context, and Language: Essays in Honor of Susan Ervin-Tripp* (pp. 435–446). Mahwah, NJ: Lawrence Erlbaum.
Wong Fillmore, L. (2000) Loss of family languages: Should educators be concerned? *Theory Into Practice* 39 (4), 203–210.
Wortham, S.E.F. (2006) *Learning Identity: The Joint Emergence of Social Identification and Academic Learning*. Cambridge: Cambridge University Press.
Wray, A. (2002) *Formulaic Language and the Lexicon*. Cambridge: Cambridge University Press.
Wright, W. (2010) *Foundations for Teaching English Language Learners: Research, Theory, Policy, and Practice*. Philadelphia, PA: Caslon Publishing.
Zappa-Hollman, S. and Duff, P. (2015) Academic English socialization through individual networks of practice. *TESOL Quarterly* 49 (2), 333–368. DOI: 10.1002/tesq.188.

Index

Afford(ance) 8, 14, 19, 110, 129–135, 144
Age (and language learning) 3–6, 11, 62, 66, 144
Amplifier (of another person's speech) 15, 119, 123
Amy 14, 15, 16
Animator (of a speech act) 31, 115, 119, 123
Anton 15, 145, 146
Artifacts (cultural) 23
Ascription (of competence/incompetence) 116
Assimilation 63, 73, 156
Austin, John L. 30–31, 38, 118, 120
Author (of a speech act) 31, 123

Bhutan (Bhutanese) 1, 42–43, 47–48, 54, 63, 74, 155–157
Bilingual classrooms (*see also* Dual language classrooms) 150–151
Bloome, David 146, 161
Blum-Kulka, Shoshana 5, 13, 17, 58, 145
Bodily practices (*see also* Embodied) 24, 26, 29, 32, 35–37, 60, 96–97, 123, 127, 167–168
Bourdieu, Pierre 22, 23–31, 35, 37, 73, 110, 118, 119, 134–135, 151
Bronfenbrenner, Uri 20–21

Capital (social, symbolic) 27, 119, 123
Cekaite, Asta 13, 14, 117, 146
Centrality 86, 92, 95, 105, 108, 132–135, 141, 164–166
Circle Time 47, 51, 53, 75, 81, 87, 88, 96, 97, 115, 122, 150
Cole, Michael 21–23, 27
Comembership 37
Communicative Repertoire (*see also* Repertoire) 12, 34, 35–37, 121–123, 127–131, 132–133, 147–148

Competence 13–16, 20, 37, 65, 85, 86–87, 92, 94, 98, 106, 110, 116, 119, 121–123, 130–137, 141, 144–147, 153, 162
Context (definition of) 20–22, 148
Contextualization cues 35–36, 127
Cross purposes 8, 145, 148
Culturally responsive teaching 151, 152

Density (of social networks) 134–135, 163, 165–166
Doing school (*see also* Procedural displays) 16, 146, 150
Donato, Richard 22–23, 141
Double bind 17, 122, 144
Double opportunity space (of peer interaction) 13, 144–145, 148
Doxa 73
Dual language classrooms (*see also* Bilingual classrooms) 150–151

Ecological Systems Theory 20–21
Ecology (language) 16, 21, 130, 132, 144
Effect (perlocutionary effect) 30–31, 32, 38, 111–117, 120, 127, 131, 140, 146–147, 167–168
Effectiveness ratio 114
Embodied (*see also* Bodily practices) 24, 26, 29, 32, 35–37, 60, 96–97, 123, 127, 167–168
ESL (English as a Second Language) 16, 37, 43
Ethics (ethical research) 54–56
Ethnographic 2, 51

Felicitous/felicity conditions 30, 32, 118, 120
Field (*see also* Social Field) 24–29, 32–33, 37, 60, 75, 104, 105, 111, 121–123, 129–131, 132–135, 141, 143, 148, 151, 167–168

Index

Force (illocutionary force) 30–32, 38, 111–115, 119, 168
Form (locutionary form) 30–32, 38, 111–115, 119, 168

Gal, Susan 33, 57, 134
García, Ofelia 33–34, 58, 60, 123, 150
Gaze 32, 36, 123, 127, 129, 167
Gesture 23, 32, 36, 121, 123, 127, 129, 131, 167
Gibson, J.J. 130
Goffman, Erving 31, 34, 123, 138
Goodwin, Charles 32, 115
Goodwin, Marjorie Harness 32, 84
Gumperz, John 35–36

Habitus 24–27, 29, 33, 35, 37, 60, 66, 68, 70, 73, 76, 121, 134–135, 148, 151, 153
Harvey 15, 16
Hatch, Evelyn 10
Hawkins, Margaret 15, 145
Head Start 1, 7, 12, 27, 43, 44–45, 47, 50, 55, 64, 68, 71, 72, 75, 106, 119, 148
Hearer (role) 31–32, 111, 115, 118, 119, 127, 167
Heath, Shirly Brice 29

Improvisation 44, 135
Incompetence (ascription of) 116
Input 4–5, 10–14, 23, 33, 67, 86, 107, 133
Institutions/institutional 30–31, 34, 75, 121, 132, 144, 146
Interaction (and language learning) *see also* Participation (and language learning) 2–6, 10–19, 21–23, 37, 65, 103, 105, 108, 131, 136, 138, 139–146, 160, 162
Interaction Hypothesis 10
Intersemiotic complementarity 127
Irvine, Judith 57

Kindergarten readiness 64–65, 68–69, 82, 133
King, Kendall 18, 59, 152
Kramsch, Claire xi, 29, 119
Krashen, Stephen 4, 10
Kroskrity, Paul 57–58

Langauge policy 57–60, 81–83, 154
Language ideologies (beliefs about language) 57–59, 60–74
Lantolf, James 22–23, 141
Layering (in research) 18, 38, 147–149
Legitimate language 29–30, 37

Linguistic suffocation 62–63, 130
Long, Michael 10
Long, Susi 12

Mackey, Alison 11, 18, 152
Market 28–29
Michaels, Sarah 29
Misrecognition 26, 30
Moral order 117, 118
Multilingual(ism) 6, 29, 33–35, 44, 55, 57, 59, 74, 121–123, 131, 144, 150–154
Multimodal(ity) 35, 121, 123–131

Nora 4, 147
Norton, Bonny 13

Parents 43–44, 47–50, 53–55, 58–65, 67–70, 73–74, 77–80
Participation (and language learning) *see also* Interaction (and language learning) 2–6, 10–19, 21–23, 37, 65, 103, 105, 108, 131, 136, 138, 139–146, 160
Participation frameworks 31–32, 115–119, 127, 140, 167
Peer interaction (and language learning) 5, 11–17, 86, 102, 107, 139–148, 151, 162
Peripherality 15, 16, 86, 104, 108, 110, 132–135, 138
Piker, Ruth 12, 13–14, 15
Play/peer play (and language learning) 11–13
Positionality (*see also* Researcher positionality) 50–56
Positioning, position (social) 13–19, 28–29, 30, 31, 48, 49, 52, 53, 55, 85, 86–104, 105, 107–108, 110, 117–119, 127, 130–131, 132–140, 141, 145–148, 161–162, 165
Power 13, 17, 24, 27, 30, 34, 55, 110, 134
Practical sense 26
Practice theory (*see also* Social practice) 23–37, 58, 60, 73, 83–85, 88, 104, 111, 118–120, 121–122, 129–131, 134–135, 140, 153–154
    Language as social practice 29–38, 110–120
Principal (of a speech act) 31, 123
Procedural displays (*see also* Doing school) 16, 146, 150
Production format 31, 123

Ratified (speaker, participant, hearer) 14, 15, 17, 115

Refugee (Refugee resettlement) 1–2, 20, 40–44, 54–56, 61, 73–74, 155–159
Repertoire (*see also* Communicative Repertoire) 12, 34, 35–37, 121–123, 127–131, 132–133, 147–148
Researcher positionality (*see also* Positionality) 50–56
River City 1, 3, 7, 39–46, 51, 54, 56, 59, 63, 73, 74, 156–159, 160–161
Rydland, Vibeke 11, 12, 14, 17
Rymes, Betsy 36–37, 137, 146

Sanne 2, 3, 10, 15
Silence 29, 103, 141–143
Silverstein, Michael 57
Social Field (*see also* Field) 24–29, 32–33, 37, 60, 75, 104, 105, 111, 121–123, 129–131, 132–135, 141, 143, 148, 151, 167–168
Social network analysis 86, 133–134, 162–166
Social practice (*see also* Practice Theory) 23–37, 58, 60, 73, 83–85, 88, 104, 111, 118–120, 121–122, 129–131, 134–135, 140, 153–154
    Language as social practice 29–38, 110–120
Socialization 17, 49, 59, 81, 83–84, 149–151
Socio-emotional learning 2, 60, 68–69, 83, 130
Sociocultural theory 22–23, 27, 141–142
Sofia 2, 3, 10, 15
Speaker (role) 31–32
Speech acts 29–32, 110–120, 127, 167–168

Speech events 31–32, 118–120
Spolsky, Bernard 58–59
Submersion language learning ('sink or swim') 6, 143–145, 150, 153
Subteaching 84–85, 87–88, 145–146, 153
Swain, Merill 11, 22–23, 141, 143
Symbolic competence 119
Syntax (grammatical complexity) 36–37, 109–110, 111, 113, 132–133, 144, 153–154, 167

Tabors, Patton O. 5, 6, 17, 122, 152
Tattling (tattle) 88, 113, 116–119, 122, 149, 167
Thorne, Steven 22–23, 139, 141
Toohey, Kelleen 14–15, 16, 147
Translanguaging (translingual) 32–35, 121, 123, 150

Underlife 34, 150
Uzbekistan 50, 61, 158–159

van Lier, Leo 21
Vocabulary 11–12, 14, 36–37, 107–113, 131, 132–133, 140, 143–144, 153–154, 167
Vulnerability (of research participants) 55
Vygotsky, Lev 22–23

Willett, Jerri 15–16, 147
William 15, 145–146
Wong Fillmore, Lilly 4–5, 147, 152

Yessara 145, 146

For Product Safety Concerns and Information please contact our EU Authorised Representative:

Easy Access System Europe

Mustamäe tee 50

10621 Tallinn

Estonia

gpsr.requests@easproject.com

www.ingramcontent.com/pod-product-compliance
Lightning Source LLC
Chambersburg PA
CBHW070611300426
44113CB00010B/1493